THE RETURN OF
SACRED
ARCHITECTURE

"This brave and perceptive work explores the debacle of modern architecture and points the way to a healthier new architecture, based on proportion and sacred principles, which reveres ecology and the cosmos."

A. T. MANN,
AUTHOR OF *SACRED ARCHITECTURE*

". . . captures truths that we intuitively know, but haven't the training and background to articulate and illustrate as fully as is done in this fine work."

MITCH HOROWITZ,
EXECUTIVE EDITOR AT TARCHER/PENGUIN

"This is a significant and important book that expresses the perennial wisdom that has been the basis of covert mystery school teachings throughout the ages. It is most pertinent for society at large as well as all students of the Arts and Architecture who are searching for the knowledge, understanding, and meaning of Plato's concepts of Goodness, Beauty, and Truth."

THOMAS SAUNDERS, FELLOW OF THE ROYAL INSTITUTE OF
BRITISH ARCHITECTS AND AUTHOR OF
*THE BROILED FROG SYNDROME:
YOUR HEALTH AND THE BUILT ENVIRONMENT*

"The talk is of 'sustainability' these days. Here is a book by an author who has realized that social, cultural, and spiritual sustainability are even more necessary. The return to timelessness is our only hope. Highly recommended."

KEITH CRITCHLOW,
AUTHOR OF *ISLAMIC PATTERNS* AND *ORDER IN SPACE*

ABOUT THE COVER

In 1988 the famous Chinese-American architect Ieoh Ming Pei received the most extraordinary and prestigious commission of his career. The exhibition space at the Paris museum the Louvre was to be doubled by the creation of a vast, underground gallery and Pei, a Modern architect, was to design the entrance to the new space. He chose not to house the entrance in a typical Modern box, nor to make a Post-Modern comment on the existing museum; instead, he visualized a pyramid of steel and glass in the courtyard.

In what he described as an intuitive search for the right form, Pei and his staff of designers, without conscious intent, settled on a shape that closely follows that of the Great Pyramid of Giza, a marvel of sacred geometrical principles. Pei's glass pyramid wasn't the most logical or efficient way to enclose the functional space, nor was it consistent with Modern architectural theory. It was chosen for the sheer archetypal power of the form, which in this case has triumphed over the scientific-materialistic bias of his previous work.

Pei is not the only leading exponent of modern design who has returned in one way or another to the ancient tradition of sacred geometry. Le Corbusier experimented with the "golden ratio" and even wrote a book, *Modular,* advocating its use. R. Buckminster Fuller, the inventor of the geodesic dome and the epitome of the scientific architect, based the design of his domes on the Platonic solids.

The forms and images of sacred geometry are archetypal and thus return again and again, even in the work of those who, for ideological reasons, refuse to consciously recognize them.

THE RETURN OF
SACRED
ARCHITECTURE

The Golden Ratio and the
End of Modernism

Herbert Bangs, M.Arch.

Inner Traditions
Rochester, Vermont

Inner Traditions
One Park Street
Rochester, Vermont 05767
www.InnerTraditions.com

Library of Congress Cataloging-in-Publication Data
Bangs, Herbert, 1927–
  The return of sacred architecture : the golden ratio and the end of modernism / Herbert Bangs.
       p. cm.
  Summary: "An inspirational call for a return to the tenets of traditional architecture as a remedy for the dehumanizing standards of modern architecture"—Provided by publisher.
  Includes bibliographical references and index.
  ISBN-13: 978-1-59477-132-3
  ISBN-10: 1-59477-132-4
  1. Architecture, Modern—20th century—Philosophy. I. Title.
  NA680.B24 2007
  720.1—dc22
                                                                2006027438

Printed and bound in Canada by Transcontinental Printing

10 9 8 7 6 5 4 3 2 1

Text design and layout by Jon Desautels
This book was typeset in Sabon with Trajan used as a display typeface

To send correspondence to the author of this book, mail a first-class letter to the author c/o Inner Traditions • Bear & Company, One Park Street, Rochester, VT 05767, and we will forward the communication.

This book is dedicated to those architects and architectural students who are as confused and misled as I once was. I hope that my experience may shorten their path to a proper measure of understanding.

CONTENTS

The Cathedral of Chartres.

FOREWORD

The golden arches of
McDonald's.

After you read this quietly impassioned and deceptively significant book, the chances are you will never look at, or think about, architecture in quite the same way again.

Most of us know there is something grievously wrong with modern architecture. A lot of it is just ugly; much more of it is dead, empty, and boring. And when vast sums of money are spent on some national, civic, corporate, or personal monument, more often than not the result is garish disharmony and/or a pompous, self-conscious "originality."

But just what is it specifically that distinguishes among the good, the bad, the ugly . . . and the dysfunctional? Once you've read this book, you will know. You will understand what "works" and what does not, and *why* it does or doesn't. This is not a simple matter of opinion, with some opinions perhaps more informed than others. However politically correct it may be to think so, however deeply ingrained in our collective psyche the cliché may be, "beauty" most emphatically is *not* "altogether in the eye of the beholder."

Everyone knows that Marilyn Monroe was a beautiful woman, and everyone knows that Eleanor Roosevelt was not (". . . altogether in the eye of the beholder," indeed! How does such nonsense ever take root, much less get uttered in the first place?). Beethoven's Ninth Symphony is a more beautiful piece of music than "The Star-Spangled Banner." The Cathedral of Chartres is a more beautiful building than your local Wal-Mart or McDonald's. If you don't know that—in your gut, in your heart, in your soul—God help you, because no one else will.

It is obvious. Few will argue the point. When all the beholders behold in unison, it is no longer a matter of opinion. But discerning the objective criteria upon which such universal judgments are made is not so easy, especially in a cultural milieu that places little value upon the arts in general and, in fact, distrusts emotion. The revealing and clear exposition of these criteria and their application to architecture past and present is but one of many factors distinguishing *The Return of Sacred Architecture* from the relatively few other solid books on the subject.

The next question then imposes itself: If objective criteria exist, if they are known, why is so much contemporary architecture ugly, dead, or pompous? That is ultimately a social/philosophical question rather than a scientific one.

Not so long ago, architecture was typically the highest and most complete artistic expression of a sophisticated civilization. It provided the framework within which the other art forms manifested. It was where the lion's share of any given society's creativity was directed; the architecture expressed and enshrined its soul. In fact, if we had no written history at all, we would be able to get a very good idea of the living essence of any given civilization simply by looking closely at where its creative energy is expended: Ancient Egypt's creative energy went into its temples, pyramids, and tombs; Rome's went into its roads, massive civic projects, and coliseums; ours today goes into elaborate missile defense systems and disposable products designed to feed our materialistic, consumer-driven culture.

In an age of unprecedented technological progress, architecture has lost its once preeminent position. Millions of people make pilgrimages to experience the Gothic cathedrals of Europe, the Taj Mahal and temples of India, and the pyramids, temples, and tombs of Egypt. But no one comes to America just to see Wal-Mart or, for that matter, Wall Street (Disneyland maybe, poor saps! But that's another story). No one goes to France to experience the suburbs of Paris, or to England to witness the latest in council flats. In our age of high-tech marvels and triumphs of design—space shuttles, computers, and Ferraris—the harmonious modern structure is a rarity (usually it's a private building or home, more often than not following or based upon some familiar traditional style: in other words, a technologically gussied-up version of something rooted in the past). The emotionally moving, strictly contemporary public building is rarer still. And even the few that qualify for that honor come hedged about with conditionals. The surface sheen often disguises a dysfunctional inner anatomy; a building may look good, but it doesn't do the job it was designed for.

In other words, all beholders behold "beauty" all right, but the beauty is only skin deep. Herbert Bangs does not hesitate to take on even the sacred cows of the new architecture—Le Corbusier, Philip Johnson, Mies van der Rohe, and to a lesser extent Frank Lloyd Wright—and his careful analyses provoke a series of eureka! moments. (Ah! I *knew* there was something phony there! Just couldn't put my finger on it.)

What is it, then, that's gone wrong? Part of the answer is formal: The Cathedral of Chartres (in fact, all of the sacred architecture of the past) is built upon certain demonstrable mathematical, harmonic, and geometrical principles. And even the secular architecture of the past, a Renaissance villa or palazzo, for example, makes use of those same principles, whereas Wal-Mart and McDonald's do not. Meanwhile, the vast majority of contemporary architects have never been taught the principles, do not know about them, and don't care. Bangs's description of the typical architect's training is particularly illuminating.

The other part of the answer seems obvious but isn't. The architecture of the past that endures is overtly religious (or sacred), while virtually all major contemporary architecture is secular. This, to champions of the modern, is seen as proof of the Advancement of Learning, since *sacred* has become little more than a polite synonym for *superstitious*. Contemporary architecture—no matter how ugly, dead, boring, or dysfunctional—is "scientific" and therefore represents a giant step forward in human evolution.

But the distinction is illusory; the conflict is not between superstition and reason, nor between today's enlightened science and primitive, discredited credulity, but rather between warring belief systems. The pseudo-conflict was summed up and inadvertently resolved by that much underrated, largely forgotten all-American philosopher President Calvin ("Silent Cal") Coolidge, who declared, "The man who builds a factory builds a temple; the man who works there worships there, and to each is due, not scorn and blame, but reverence and praise." And in a similar vein, "Civilization and profits go hand in hand."

A couple of lines of comic dialogue may be worth three hundred pages of trenchant sociological/philosophical analysis. In the 1983 comedy *Trading Places,* Dan Ackroyd plays a snobbish, uptight, insufferable young executive. He is riding to work in a chauffeur-driven limo with his rapacious, multimillionaire father and uncle, and at one point in the dialogue, he asserts with some heat: "Money isn't everything!"

"Grow up!" snaps the uncle.

The old gods have been overthrown, and it is no longer the job of the architect (or, for that matter, the artist, poet, dancer, musician) to summon them through ceremony and ritual. The architect no longer need resort to complex, three-dimensional geometry to produce the desired emotional effect. His task has been simplified, reduced to two dimensions, and just a single straight line at that: the Holy Bottom Line, for the Church of Progress is the One True Church.

Herbert Bangs is hardly the first person to notice and deplore architecture's precipitous artistic decline and diminished social significance, nor even the first to cut through the verbiage of standard architectural jargon to get to the root of the problem. There is no shortage of critics, some of them eloquent, informed, and vociferous (e.g., Prince Charles, the late Lewis Mumford). Unlike Herbert Bangs, only a very few speak from a lifetime of professional architectural experience. Fewer still are capable of providing a convincing diagnosis . . . or a prognosis for a possible, eventual healing.

It is self-evident that a new era of architectural (or any other kind of) enlightenment will not be initiated by Wal-Mart, Wall Street, or Washington, D.C. But the principles upon which the sacred architecture of the past was built are eternal, and there is nothing to prevent individuals from accessing them again, in a manner appropriate to our very different, technologically oriented age. Technological progress should be civilization's ally, not its antithesis.

Once you've absorbed *The Return of Sacred Architecture,* you will understand why the great architecture of the past still beckons and entrances, and why little that's modern does. Bangs is particularly good at analyzing, describing, and illustrating in detail the specific elements that make good architecture "work," and without which it will not and cannot work.

Art matters. Architecture matters—though it is no longer fashionable to say so. (The *New York Times* section devoted to the arts is called Arts and Leisure; imagine the ruckus there'd be if the science section were called Science and Tinkering.) As G. I. Gurdjieff taught, impressions are "food"; everything we take in through our senses is food. We pay lip service to that when we say reading is "food for thought," but that is to be taken literally. Feed ourselves nothing but junk literature and we will have junk thoughts; immerse ourselves in TV and Hollywood violence, stupidity, and degraded sex and our emotional centers will be insensibly affected by them. Live and work day in and day out in places that are ugly, dead, boring, and dysfunctional and our psyches, sooner or later, will suffer, though the malaise might be so subtle it never becomes a conscious realization . . . especially since virtually everyone else in the modern world is subject to the same sensory onslaught. But once we understand what is at stake, we can take both defensive and constructive measures.

The Return of Sacred Architecture provides invaluable information and rare and original insights into the reality of the situation, but it also provides practical lessons. These can be put into action—at no matter how modest a level—initially individually, perhaps eventually collectively. Meanwhile, until we are able to take positive steps, at the very least we can remember (every time we are subjected to ubiquitous Church of Progress architectural propaganda) that inscribed in deep but invisible letters above the entrance to every building there is this message:

"Government Warning: This Building May Be Injurious to Your Health. Enter at Your Own Risk."

JOHN ANTHONY WEST

John Anthony West is a writer, scholar, and Pythagorean who has studied and written about ancient Egypt and Egyptian sacred science since 1986. He maintains that the heart of Egyptian sacred science reveals a dynamic understanding of harmony and proportion, the expression of which—through art and architecture—appeals to and enhances man's highest nature. West is the author of many books, including *Serpent in the Sky: The High Wisdom of Ancient Egypt* and *The Traveler's Key to Ancient Egypt: A Guide to the Sacred Places of Ancient Egypt*.

ACKNOWLEDGMENTS

The rose has five petals and five sepals, and five—the marriage of the first female and male numbers, two and three—is the number of love. The rose was thus the flower of Isis, Aphrodite, and Venus, and in Christian thought it has been associated with Saint Mary Magdalene. Superimposed upon a circle, the symmetry of the rose defines the pentagon and the five-pointed star, each of which, in its internal proportions, exemplifies the golden ratio.

I wish to acknowledge the unfailing support of my wife, Christine, who not only read and reread the text and encouraged me to go on, but also provided an emotional and intellectual environment within which creation could proceed.

I am indebted to David Durack, Susan Arfuso, Lois Alsop, and the late Judy Van Hook, who read the manuscript in its early stages, found that it spoke to them, and urged me to seek a wider audience. I deeply appreciate the invaluable assistance of the author and Egyptologist John Anthony West, who carefully and critically read the manuscript and assisted me with the necessary changes, and who has consistently been positive, helpful, and supportive. Finally, I want to thank those who at my request took photographs of buildings that illustrate the text: Robert Kuller; my wife, Christine; and my granddaughter, Farin Van Teagarden.

I regret the unfortunate dominance of the logical, rational, "masculine" way of thinking that is expressed in the sexism of our language, and in some of the languange in this book, as opposed to "feminine" intuitive comprehension. I have commonly used Man as a synonym for humankind, and because there is no short, simple pronoun that applies to both sexes, I have retained the familiar usage of the male pronoun *he* in the interest of brevity and rhythm.

While I have written from the Eurocentric and Christian sociohistorical perspective, the ideas expressed here are applicable to contemporary societies across the globe. The Modern architecture of the West is only a small part of world architecture, but the scientific and materialistic way of comprehending reality developed as an expression of peculiarly Western institutions. Under the onslaught of Western military, economic, and political power, every modern culture has succumbed to the philosophical assumptions upon which scientific materialism rests. The institutions of the East, no matter what their ultimate worth, have crumbled, and the architecture of the West has become, to an unprecedented extent, the architecture of the world.

Chartres Cathedral: The south transept and nave wall.

1
INTRODUCTION:
A RADICAL
REVELATION

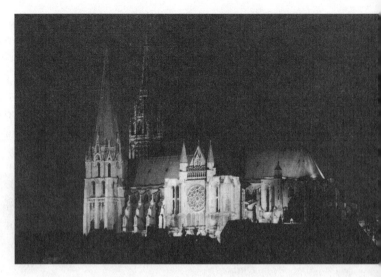

Chartres Cathedral at night.
(Photograph courtesy of Chartres
Cathedral.)

Ten years ago my wife and I traveled to Chartres, a small town sixty miles southwest of Paris, to visit the famous cathedral built there at the beginning of the thirteenth century. We arrived after the cathedral had closed for the night, but as we sat at the window of a little café across the street, floodlights were suddenly turned on the south facade. The effect was stunning. Until then, I had believed that the rational, scientific architecture of the twentieth century represented the peak of architectural achievement. Yet no Modern or Post-Modern building I had ever seen or studied could be compared to this wonderful creation. When I entered the cathedral the following day and walked through an interior bathed in light from the stained-glass windows, I understood with certainty that in school and practice I had learned nothing of the deeper, esoteric meaning of space and form that is the essence of architecture.

As a student I had been taught that the design of a building was an "architectural problem" that could be solved through a process of rational analysis. The result would be an efficient and economical shelter, enlivened by the aesthetic sensitivity of the individual architect so that the building would be pleasing as well as useful.

Chartres Cathedral proved that all of this was nonsense. It made no attempt to be an economical shelter; it skirted the edge of the possible; it cared nothing about being pleasing, but it seized the imagination and opened the door to a new way of thinking, not merely about architecture, but about the purpose and meaning of life.

1

In the light of this insight, I looked at other buildings of the past—even those of the recent past—and saw that the "scientific" architecture I had been taught to venerate as a "brave new world" of architectural design was but the last, perhaps the final, stage of a long decline. Even the buildings of the so-called old masters of the Modern movement were now seen to be inferior to the best work of their predecessors, and I usually found the work of most contemporary architects to be ill conceived, while the vernacular buildings, the simple utilitarian structures of our time, were uniformly ugly.

I now realize that the creation of a building such as Chartres Cathedral was possible only in an age that possessed a set of assumptions, concerning the nature of existence, that were far different from ours. The assumptions that govern societies are not usually expressed as such: indeed, why should they be, since they are assumed to be beyond question. They are the commonly held, unspoken beliefs that lie behind the formal philosophical expression of the ideas they represent. They are the background, as it were, of the characteristic quality of the art, religion, and technology of the time. To question their validity is to question the essential values of the society within which one was reared and the "truths" by which one exists. An extraordinary and fearful leap of the imagination is required to defy them.

Our science is lopsided and distorted in its refusal to deal with anything other than those elements of existence that are quantifiable or perceptible to the five senses. It is therefore only as a pseudo-science that it is applied to the formulations of philosophy and the practice of architecture.

The dominant assumptions of today are given formal expression through what is called philosophical or "scientific" materialism. To a philosophical materialist, only that which can be weighed and measured is real, and this reality is thought to be accessible to the rational mind. The materialist "paradigm," or model, of the universe thus denies the existence of any reality other than a material reality. All that has traditionally been of the highest consequence to the individual—meaning and purpose in life, the continuity of existence after death, disinterested love and the visions of the great mystics—are regarded as unreal. The idea held by the ancients and transmitted to us through Plato—that there exists that which, for want of a better definition, we call a "spiritual" reality—is dismissed.

This philosophical position is directly relevant to the practice of architecture. The denial of a spiritual reality and the continuing effort to understand the world as a purely material phenomenon is profoundly destructive of the idea that building involves more than the construction of utilitarian shelter. The ancient function of the architect or artist was to express, in material form, insights into a higher spiritual reality, thus making those insights available to others. In the absence of a belief in a spiritual reality, it has been suggested by Modern theorists that the proper function of the architect is to ornament or decorate simple utilitarian shelters and make them more aesthetically pleasing. The cool, distant term *aesthetics* is broadly applied in lieu of "beauty" or "truth," and serves to paper over a fatal split between architecture as art and the architecture of the mundane, material world.

Although the origins of the present materialist philosophies are found in the eighteenth-century "Enlightenment," until the early twentieth century there remained a continuous, however eclectic, architectural tradition. At that time there occurred so radical a break with the past that it deserves to be called a revolution. It represented nothing less than a determined attempt to totally discard tradition and apply the principles of scientific materialism to the design of buildings.

The initial impact was electrifying. Those of us who were students in the forties and fifties were true believers, enthusiasts, and, at least while still at school, were able to convince ourselves that we would somehow, through good design, make the world a better, more beautiful place than we had found it. Now, fifty years later, our dreams seem to have been pathetically naive; the promise of Modernism has proved illusory, and many of us have learned to venerate the work of the past, even that of the Beaux Arts architects that we once rejected with scorn.

It is now apparent that the architectural revolution was foredoomed to failure, since within our science, and the scientific-materialist culture that it has fostered, there can be no philosophical recognition of the vital importance of the arts, and of the architect as artist and magician. Indeed, if the materialist paradigm was fully supported by the evidence, if there was neither spiritual reality nor transcendental purpose to existence, beauty would be irrelevant and our architecture would rightly be concerned only with questions of utilitarian efficiency.

Those who intuitively reject this dismal vision must recognize that no improvement can be anticipated as long as architects, and the larger society, remain wedded to the premises of the materialist paradigm. For over 300 years the paradigm has maintained its hegemony over Western thought, but now, as a result of a convergence between what I call the "other tradition" and advanced scientific investigation, we may predict its destruction. The first effects will be felt in our lifetimes: they are in fact being felt even now, and the next few centuries, the beginning of the Aquarian Age, will inevitably see a major reconstruction of society, science, and religion. Such a reconstruction will result in a revival of the pre-Enlightenment and ancient way of perceiving reality. The effect of such a "return of the spirit" on architecture and the other arts will be profound. We may confidently expect that the new architecture will be ecologically aware; it will relate man to his instinctual roots; and it will express the order and harmony of the cosmos in the form of building and space.

Architecture as art. Chartres: The Crossing.

The materialists have decided that metaphysics, the branch of philosophy that seeks to explain the nature of being and the origin of the world, is irrelevant to the pursuit of scientific fact. Yet the decision to ignore metaphysics is not based on any fact, and is itself a negative metaphysics.

2
THE SCIENTIFIC ARCHITECTURE OF THE TWENTIETH CENTURY

The Architectural Revolution

The Federal Center Building, Chicago, Illinois, designed by Mies van der Rohe. The facade is a sealed Cartesian cage of glass and steel.

From the Italian Renaissance until the beginning years of the twentieth century, architectural design was dominated by images that had their origin in the distant past. First ancient Rome, and later Greece, were the models from which architects drew their inspiration, but as time passed, every culture and period from Egypt to the Renaissance was used as the basis of a mélange of eclectic styles that were consistent only in that they retained a remnant of the canon of proportion and measure handed down from antiquity.

Many of those eclectic buildings were beautiful in their own right, many were careful adaptations of beautiful prototypes, and many displayed the outstanding talent of dedicated artists, but in the absence of an accepted philosophical or religious tradition it was not possible to express the materials and techniques of the time in a valid, contemporary architectural style. As architectural practice drew further away from the ancient canon of order and proportion, the beautiful building became the exception rather than the rule, and the growing ugliness of the eclectic buildings erected in the recent past continues to debase the environmental fabric within which we live.

World War I made a radical reassessment possible, not only of the society that many considered responsible for the catastrophe, but of this eclectic architecture as well. Before then, eclecticism had been too strong to succumb to a direct challenge. In light of the postwar disillusionment, it was seen that the various historical styles had little to do with the thrust of the twentieth-century, scientific-industrial culture. In response, a number of architects and designers were inspired to develop a new and revolutionary approach to both architecture and the related arts.

Particularly influential were a group of teachers and students from the Bauhaus, a school of architecture and design established in Dessau, Germany, after World War I. Among these were the founder, Walter Gropius; the subsequent director Ludwig Mies van der Rohe; and Marcel Breuer, an instructor. The French architect Charles Edouard Jenneret, known as Le Corbusier, independently evolved a similar approach to that of the Bauhaus. The American architect Frank Lloyd Wright is also considered a Modernist, but differed significantly in his work and writings from the Europeans.

The basis of the Bauhaus approach, the need to recognize and design for new materials and technology, was entirely reasonable. The Bauhaus teachers and pupils were, moreover, driven by a sincere humanism, a desire to improve the living environment of twentieth-century man. In an age dominated by mass-produced, machine-made products, the Bauhaus did not attempt to revive the traditional craftsmanship of the previous centuries as the Arts and Crafts movement had done in England. Rather, the artists and architects of the Bauhaus wished to accept the technology of machine production as the source of a potential cornucopia of material wealth and well-being. They intended to produce high-quality designs for the machine, and thus ensure that the artifacts of their contemporary civilization would be not only useful, but also beautiful. The enthusiasm with which they regarded the possibilities of mechanical mass production even led some Bauhaus architects to imitate, with handicraft methods, the effects achieved by machines. Le Corbusier went so far as to describe a house as "a machine for living."

The modern architecture that evolved from this program was dubbed the "International Style," and was applied to every type of structure. We are all familiar with the office towers, apartment blocks, schools, warehouses, and factories erected under its influence. It was, however, not accepted without a struggle.

Tom Wolfe, who wrote *From Bauhaus to Our House*, a clever and insightful book about the advent of the International Style in America, was amazed at both the arrogant confidence of those who became followers of the movement and the docility of those clients who were persuaded to accept buildings designed in a style that he says they didn't

The work and ideas of the three so-called Modern masters—Ludwig Mies van der Rohe, Le Corbusier, and Frank Lloyd Wright—still serve as models and examples for their successors. Their fame extends far beyond the world of architecture.

5

The Bauhaus building in Dessau, Germany, designed by Walter Gropius. All the elements of the new architecture that was soon to sweep the world are seen here. Gropius, the founder and director, was a Jew and was forced to flee when the Nazis took power. He was replaced by Mies van der Rohe, who struggled to keep the school open despite continuing Nazi hostility. Eventually Mies (as he is usually called) followed Gropius to America and the school was closed. (Photograph courtesy of Wikimedia Commons.)

The term "Modern" was applied to the scientific architecture that emerged after World War I; the term "Post-Modern" was applied to the later modifications that occurred after the 1960s. The widely accepted terms are confusing in that they refer to styles rather than time. Time has passed and Modern is no longer modern. The term "International Style" refers to the architecture that emerged principally from the Bauhaus and the work of Le Corbusier.

really want and didn't really like.[1] Wolfe is probably right about both the arrogance of the converts and the reaction of the clients, but he does not adequately explain why the style went from triumph to triumph to become truly international, dominating the practice of architecture.

Implicit in the theories of Le Corbusier and the Bauhaus founders and underlying their obvious innovations was the application of scientific rationalism to the design process. In the new architecture, only that which could be justified by what was considered "scientific" logic could become part of a design. The Bauhaus architects and their associates thus expressed in their designs the worldview of twentieth-century scientific materialism. Since the new architecture was in accord with the spirit of the time, those who became followers had the confident belief that the future was theirs. Their certitude was communicated to clients and critics, who understood that to oppose the new style was tantamount to a declaration of cultural inferiority, and the commissions and publicity poured forth. Rather than being a product of academia, as Tom Wolfe would have us believe, the Bauhaus approach was seized upon by the students and demanded from the faculties. Those schools that did not offer to teach the new way of design were simply overlooked by the best potential students and, to survive, were forced to conform. By the latter part of the twentieth century, the International Style had become the style of all major architectural design.

The innovative designers who founded Modern architecture and the International Style sought a clean break with the entire Western tradition that had preceded them. They emphasized the use of industrial materials such as steel, glass, and reinforced concrete. They maintained that all materials should be used without apology or concealment, in a manner consistent with their "nature." They sought to base the plans and elevations of a proposed building upon a logical analysis of the program. They strove to eliminate everything considered unnecessary to utilitarian function; thus they excised ornament, trim, decorative moldings, and the pitched roof. They sought the visual expression of the structural system and the expression of the interior spaces in the exterior facade. They worked with large planes of simple surfaces. They used sheets of glass to break down the barrier between the interior and the exterior, and they designed spaces that flowed one into another. All of this seems familiar and even commonplace today, but at that time it was revolutionary. The founders of the International Style were confident that society could be reconstituted through the scientific design of buildings and well-made, mass-produced artifacts. Today, their confidence seems naive, but at the time it inspired its adherents with a passionate faith in their mission. As that faith and evangelical fervor faded, the whole Modern movement came under critical scrutiny. The personal styles of the master architects who had founded the movement in the 1920s and 1930s had evolved within a milieu that, to some degree, had preserved the ancient canon of proportion and harmony. Proportion and harmony were reflected in their buildings, but those who followed were further removed from the old "unscientific" tradition and lost the key to the intuitive knowledge that the masters possessed. In its absence, work in the International Style was seen to tend toward sterility and an idiosyncratic search for originality, or for novelty itself. This was rightly criticized, as was the lack of accent or detail that might ornament or explain the structural system and the intended use. The first serious attack was mounted in 1966 by Robert Venturi, a Philadelphia architect, in a book entitled *Complexity and Contradiction in Architecture*.[2]

In his book, Venturi subjected the work of previous architects, particularly those of the later Italian Renaissance, to a logical, linguistic analysis. In the sense that an analysis could provide formulae for the process of contemporary design, and in the use of the analytical, scientific method of study, the book was entirely consistent with the theoretical approach of Le Corbusier and the Bauhaus. The impact on the profession, however,

Le Corbusier was the single most important architect of the twentieth century. His influence was pervasive, and the ideas expressed in his work and writings continue to dominate contemporary architectural practice. Corbusier may or may not have been a great architect, but everyone would agree that he was a great polemist. (Photograph courtesy of the Fondation Le Corbusier. © 2006 Artists Rights Society [ARS], New York /ADAGP, Paris/FLC.)

Le Corbusier completed Ville Savoy, a private house near Paris, in 1931. Note how the mass of the building, supported by the thin steel columns, is aloof from the site; note also the white, industrial-looking finish of the walls, the flat roof crowned by sculptural forms, and the band of inoperable glass. All the elements of the International Style are already present. And like many other buildings in the style, this one turned into a technical and environmental nightmare. It was abandoned as unlivable by its owners and during the Second World War was used as a cow barn. Only later, when Le Corbusier achieved fame, was it restored.

An architectural "program" describes the purpose of the building, the way it is to be used, the site, the budget, and any other constraints that might be imposed by either a client, the building code, or the building's relation to nearby structures. It is, in effect, the task that the architect is charged to complete.

came not from the analysis of historical design decisions, but from the somewhat unrelated assertion that the direction taken by contemporary architecture was wrong. The simplicity of the Modern styles was repeatedly and unfavorably contrasted with the perceived richness and complexity of those of the past. Indirectly, Venturi was advocating the eclectic use of various classical motifs to create interest and personal expression.

Venturi, who has a flair for witty comments, turned Mies van der Rohe's famous aphorism "Less is more" on its head and proclaimed "Less is a bore," as indeed it often was in the hands of later designers who treated the International Style as a formula. He referred to Modern architecture as "puritanical," and at the same time condemned it as banal and pretty, falsely complex, and falsely simple. After the original icon-smashing shock had been absorbed, the main effect of the book, perhaps unintended, was to paper over the break with the past that had occurred at the beginning of the Modern movement and justify the reintroduction of traditional, eclectic forms into the spare planes and spaces of the International Style.

The Sainsbury Wing (at left) is an addition to the National Art Gallery in London, designed by Venturi, Scott Brown & Associates in 1991. Note the odd location of the blind windows and the way the classical pilasters are spaced to create a false perspective. At right, the masonry wall abruptly terminates at a steel and glass curtain wall that seems to continue behind the rectangular openings punched in the masonry at the left. The effect is that of a thin masonry false front imposed upon a contemporary facade. This superficially clever design mocks the Prince of Wales's wish that the addition recognize and harmonize with the earlier building at the right.

Venturi followed the first book with a second, equally influential, with the catchy title *Learning from Las Vegas,* in which he and his associates proclaimed that Levittown, the Las Vegas commercial strip, and the "A&P parking lot" are "almost all right."[3] In other words, the patterns and directions that could be identified within the chaos of a competitive commercial culture were somehow to become the basis of a new Post-Modern architecture.

Venturi and his followers denied the validity of the scientific, or biotechnical, basis of modern architecture: the idea that the logical analysis of a program, together with the scientific-cultural knowledge available in the society, could in itself determine the form of a building. Other leading Post-Modernists denied the ability of intuition to guide the architect in achieving a synthesis of information that would result in an integrated form. Finally, they all denied the power of forms—in themselves and apart from the cultural context—to communicate meaning. "Meaning," according to Post-Modern theory, could only be expressed and communicated through the "symbols," discursive as well as nondiscursive, that had been established in society.

The task of the architect, then, was to be reduced to the manipulation

The illustrations in Venturi's first book drew attention to Mannerism, an Italian style of the late Renaissance, in which the ancient standards of order and proportion were deliberately distorted to achieve a form of personal and theatrical expression.

This Best Products Company catalog store in Towson, Maryland, was made to look as if the facade were pried up at one corner like the side of a cardboard box. It is immoral to use a building as an advertising gimmick, and this one is certainly ugly, if not ordinary. (Photograph courtesy of John McGrain, Baltimore County Official Historian.)

The application of Post-Modern theory would logically result in buildings designed like cornflakes boxes, where the bright colors and gay logos disguise the tasteless product inside.

of symbols to adorn sheds constructed by engineers. Symbols, to Venturi and his followers, are understood to communicate only immediate or mundane knowledge, as do logos and signs; they do not have the power to illuminate a higher reality.

The effect of Post-Modern theory on the profession has been not only to shatter the certainties underlying the theoretical basis of Modern architecture, but also to shatter that remnant of confidence in the value of their work that many architects had managed to retain. Ultimately, this may be found to be desirable and necessary; some of the acid criticism of egocentric architectural ventures, such as those noted by Venturi, was and is, much needed. The immediate effect, however, has been disastrous.

Modern architecture arose from an ethical decision to use science and technology to improve the constructed environment. While the Post-Modernists write of their concern for social issues and the common good, the architecture that has developed in response to their theories is essentially amoral in that it recognizes no ethical directive and is reduced to the pursuit of novelty, amusement, and excitement. Venturi, himself, has compared the facade of Amiens Cathedral to a billboard, and would probably find a picture of a Campbell soup can to be the equivalent of a stained-glass window. The amorality involved in such comparisons is consistent with the reigning philosophy of scientific materialism, which cannot logically recognize a transcendent ethic whereby the value of a work of art might be judged. Post-Modernism is thus in the mainstream of contemporary architectural thought: the theories are persuasive because they represent the extension of the current concepts of science as applied to architecture.

If we examine the actual work produced as an expression of those theories, the fallacy is exposed. Guild House, in Philadelphia, designed by Venturi and his associates, has been widely publicized and defended by skillful argument. To an unprejudiced eye, however, the building is not only ugly and ordinary, but—an anathema to the egocentric modern architect—boring as well.

Modern was succeeded by Post-Modern, which was followed by Pop, Minimalism, and other "isms," but the rational-scientific basis is common to all. If any trend or evolution of form and style can be discerned, it is an ever greater thrust toward technological innovation and what is approvingly called "personal expression." Both are logical developments within the context of scientific architecture. In an age in

In *Learning from Las Vegas*, Venturi defends the intentional design of buildings that are "ugly and ordinary." Guild House in Philadelphia, a Quaker-sponsored home for the aged (Venturi and Rauch), is not ordinary—it is loaded with architectural tricks—but it *is* ugly, just how ugly can be seen here. Critics have praised the hideous entrance, with the doorway hiding behind the monstrous pillar and the out-of-scale name.

The Guggenheim Museum in Bilbao, Spain, designed by Frank Gehry, is a recent example of architecture conceived as technologically innovative sculpture. Denied ornament, the building itself has become ornament; it is a gigantic, hard, sharp stainless-steel sculpture, incompatible with both its surroundings and the ostensible purpose for which it was constructed. Such buildings are "hidiotic," a combination of hideous and idiotic, with direct antecedents not only to the New York Guggenheim Museum and the Sydney Opera House, but to Disneyland, the ultimate triumph of crude popular culture, as well. (Photograph courtesy of Wikimedia Commons, GNUFDL license.)

which technological progress is regarded with fascination by both the media and the public, any building or structure that is technically novel or daring is an instant success. And in an age that regards the triumph of the ego as the supreme expression of a human destiny that ends only in the grave, the most fanciful and unusual buildings are the most highly regarded.

Are there any alternatives to the scientific architecture of our time? Even during the heyday of the style of the 1950s and 1960s, a few architects struggled to produce buildings that neither imitated obsolete styles nor marched in step with the architectural mainstream. Of these, only Frank Lloyd Wright managed to secure a popular following, but his style was highly personal, difficult to imitate, and the underlying principles that made Wright's buildings successful were not understood. Architects and students admired, but did not follow, Wright's example and in the architectural schools, as well as in the work commissioned by business, industry, and public agencies, Modern architecture swept all before it.

The Wasteland

It has been eighty years since the founding of the Bauhaus and seventy years since it was closed by the Nazis, and its teachers and students dispersed across the world. The innovative architects who seized the moment and established the "scientific" principles and the technological bias that still dominate the imagination of almost every practitioner of the art are gone. Their immediate followers and their Post-Modern successors have grown old. The influence of this small group of creative individuals nevertheless remains: The forms and styles they introduced have become the accepted norm within which architectural design still proceeds. But when we look at the buildings, landscapes, and cityscapes that have been constructed in response to their work and theories, it is apparent that something has gone terribly wrong.

We live our lives in an architectural wasteland. We enjoy our material success in a monotonous landscape of tract housing, commercial strips, faceless high-rise office districts surrounded by belts of slums, and industrial "parks," where huge, windowless buildings sit in acres of blacktop parking and grass. Architects who are sensitive to the environmental ruin that they contemplate around them are powerless, and can feel only a helpless fury.

The famous French architect Le Corbusier published *The Radiant City (La Ville Radieuse)* in 1933.[4] The illustration above is of a model of his Voisin plan for Paris. (Reproduced from *The Radiant City* courtesy of Fondation Le Corbusier. © 2006 Artists Rights Society [ARS], New York/ ADAGP, Paris/FLC.)

*Le Corbusier proposed
a massive reconstruction
of central Paris at the
incredible density of almost
8,000 individuals per acre
in enormous blocks of tall,
elevator flats.[5] While this
appalling scheme, the epitome
of the "wasteland," was
rejected, it was not greeted with
the horror that it deserved, but
instead had worldwide influence
on the design of large-scale
public and private housing.*

*The actual construction of
the Voisin plan would have
been inconceivable without
the massive intervention of
the state. The dedication
of Le Corbusier's book to
"AUTHORITY" is therefore
entirely appropriate and reveals
the fascistic bias of his early,
most influential work.*

Most of us have grown so accustomed to the ugliness that surrounds us that we no longer see it. We have learned to shut our eyes and we unconsciously assume that the world has always been as it is now. Clearly this is not so. A remnant of a more beautiful world is visible in the buildings, both humble and great, that have escaped the environmental destruction wrought by the onslaught of our contemporary culture.

The destruction of that remnant proceeds side by side with the continuing construction of a scientific environment. In Europe the devastation is even more poignant than in the United States for there is much more to lose. Corbusier's grandiose plan to demolish the Right Bank of Paris and replace it with gigantic tenements was rejected, but piecemeal and higgledy-piggledy, all over the world, demolition and rebuilding continue, at a lesser scale but much as he had proposed.

Across the English Channel, Prince Charles has protested the wanton destruction of beautiful buildings and an environment that had been constructed over centuries. In his fine book, *A Vision of Britain,* he retains some measure of optimism as he looks to the future.[6] Yet even he confesses

I walked on this road north of Towson, Maryland, when I was a boy. There were white-board fences on either side, and in the distance were meadows and grazing cows. The church crowned the hill, the only large building visible on the skyline. A mindless ugliness has replaced what was once beautiful.

This high-rise, reinforced concrete public housing development stands in a rural area of Egypt between the desert and the Nile River. At first sight our tour group mistook it for a prison. There is no rational reason for this kind of construction in such a location. It is rather a matter of housing authority prestige: the desire to appear scientific and modern. According to the guide, the buildings are detested, here as elsewhere, by those forced by circumstances to live within them.

to depression and dismay as he encounters an endless series of senselessly ugly buildings and dreadful development schemes. It would seem so easy to do it right—he lays down a few simple rules that architects could follow—but there is a stubborn determination to do it wrong.

It is not, of course, only the architects who are responsible for the wasteland. They respond to powerful social and economic forces set in motion by the underlying assumptions that govern our lives. These forces are the ultimate cause of the debacle.

Yet we who are architects have much to answer for. We accepted with unquestioning enthusiasm the supposed virtues of scientific design and led the way to its acceptance. We glorified the automobile and designed buildings not to the scale of human beings, but to the scale of speeding machines. We discarded the ancient standards of the craft and were happy to see fine buildings demolished in order to erect Modern and Post-Modern monstrosities. We accepted a philosophy that denied, among other things, the ability of form to convey meaning, and we ignored the esoteric essentials of our own tradition.

Architects may not be responsible for the endless acres of ticky-tacky housing, the chaos of commercial and industrial development, the frenzy of high-speed traffic, and the wanton destruction of the natural environment. Commercial forces drove these as they drove the urban-renewal programs that ravaged the central areas of our cities. But architects lent their skills and support, and found ways to justify their participation.

A Vision of Britain *contains a two-page spread of London painted in the eighteenth century by the artist Giovanni Antonio Canal, known as Canaletto. Over it has been placed a pair of transparent leaves upon which is imprinted a photograph of the same scene as it appeared in the late twentieth century. The contrast is shocking and depressing.*

15

At the beginning of the twentieth century, a stone eighteenth-century house was demolished in order to build this "up-to-date" house on the site. Today the old house would have been restored and, if necessary, enlarged. The change in attitude is quite recent.

Moreover, the new architecture was imposed, not welcomed. The theoreticians of the Bauhaus, as early as the 1920s and 1930s, lamented that "the public is not with us."[7] When given the opportunity for choice, informed and sensitive laymen clearly prefer buildings of the past, even the relatively recent past, to the architecture of our own time. We no longer realize how unusual this is. Although styles have come and gone, until now architects and their clients have always been confident that the structures they built represented an advance on all that had gone before.

The situation is not recognized by architects or their critics, who, ostrichlike, continue to assume that since the work of our time is "scientific," it must be superior. Only now has it begun to be reluctantly acknowledged by some that the vast majority of our buildings, including those designed by architects, are constructed cheaply and efficiently, but conceived without concern for the psychic or spiritual needs of those who will inhabit them. Buildings so conceived are dead before the first line has been put on paper and the first spadeful of earth is turned on the site.

The problem is not that of a specific style like International, Pop, or Modern, nor is it confined to architecture. The decline in the quality of architecture is paralleled by confusion and disorientation in the other arts, and is without historical precedent. While other movements and styles have tested the limits of our intuitive understanding of harmony and balance, none has ever embraced the nihilism that is characteristic of the present time.

Much of the art of the later twentieth century is, in fact, anti-art. It is the deliberate expression of a social alienation so great that it cannot be expressed except through an attack upon the idea of art itself. At some deeply buried level of comprehension, this alienation must be widely shared, for such anti-art atrocities are hailed by the critics and the public as self-expression, as marks of genius, and are housed in museums.

Architects are not often permitted the luxury of this kind of "self-expression." The nature of their art, including the resources that must be devoted to the construction of the buildings they design and the utilitarian requirements of shelter, makes it unlikely that they can build unless they are willing to work within the limits established by their respective societies. They are thus faced with a moral dilemma: to build badly or not to build. In order to build, they must prostitute their art to social forces that are inimical to the practice of their art, and that in their hearts they despise. At some deeper level of their awareness they know this, and it accounts for the repressed anger that many architects feel.

The scientific architecture of the twentieth century was created by men and women who were themselves alienated from the intuitive levels of their being. The most deadly and pervasive characteristic of this architecture is the systematic rejection of the individual in all the infinite complexity that an individual represents. Architects and their masters talk of housing units, not homes. The blank, repetitive facades of their buildings are modeled on a Cartesian grid and exhibit the empty

This bland and empty painting of Campbell soup cans by the famous Pop artist Andy Warhol celebrates the banal as the creative and is thus an attack on any art that seeks to explicate a deeper meaning. Be this as it may, Warhol is considered an important artist. He speaks for a generation and represents an artistic movement. There is a museum in Pittsburgh dedicated to his work. The destructive impulse that lies behind this image is evidently shared by many. (Picture courtesy of Wikimedia Commons, GNUFDL license.)

Most of the major buildings of our time are, in a sense, fascistic. They glorify the state or the corporation and express a callous disregard for the people who will live and work in them. Many of the architects who led the way into Modernism, moreover, were involved with political fascism. Le Corbusier, who dedicated The Radiant City *to "AUTHORITY," sought commissions in Soviet Russia and paid little heed to Stalinist repression. He later appealed to Mussolini for patronage, and after the defeat of France accepted a position as chief of the state housing organization in the Vichy government.[8] Mies van der Rohe, who believed that art and politics need not mix, tried desperately to work with the Nazi regime in the forlorn hope that the Bauhaus would survive and some of his designs would be accepted.[9] Philip Johnson, who cofounded the Museum of Modern Art in New York and brought Mies van der Rohe to America, tried and failed in the 1930s to start an American fascist party. In 1939 he watched the burning of Warsaw with his Nazi friends and called it a "stirring spectacle."[10]*

---

anonymity of a honeycomb. The unfortunate men and women who must inhabit these dreadful structures are deliberately isolated from the earth and air, from the interplay of personalities that once took place on the street, in shops, or in the square. The need for buildings or spaces in which the ancient rituals of religious and civic life might take place is ignored, or is so debased in the name of efficiency that they are meaningless.

It is the image of the machine that is triumphant in the contemporary wasteland. Le Corbusier not only wrote of the home as "a machine for living"; he also visualized the city as a gigantic machine.[11] This vision was extraordinarily persuasive, for it represented an image of science and technology in the service of material wealth, a characteristic ideal of our era. Accepted by our leaders and imposed upon an all-too-willing populace, it has led to an architecture of alienation that has shaped our cities and will inescapably affect the lives of our people. The sheer volume of twentieth-century construction ensures that the emotional and psychological affects of this environmental disaster will remain for generations.

To grasp the extent of the disaster, we must ignore the slick coffee-table books and magazines and go behind the carefully staged photographs and the ad agency hype with which new buildings are introduced to the public. It is necessary to look for ourselves not only at buildings that are publicly recognized, but also at average buildings designed by average architects, and the way in which the theories, ideas, and forms of the leaders of the profession filter through the media and are expressed in the environment in which we, as a people, live, work, and play.

The Architecture of Alienation

The alienated architects of the twentieth century refused to recognize the instinctive roots of man in his relation to the earth, to the sky, to the elements of his material existence. They sought to deny the unconscious mind, the intuition, and the supernatural awareness. In the name of science they accepted a narrow, mechanistic vision of human life, without purpose and without God. Our architecture reflects their vision.

The apostle of alienation was undoubtedly Le Corbusier. In his groundbreaking book *The Radiant City (La Ville Radieuse)*, published in 1933, he acknowledged that the individual home was the basic unit of urban life, but the "homes" in the enormous apartment towers with which he proposed to replace the Right Bank of Paris were conceived as "machines for living" and were based on a limited group of typical floor plans that could be substituted for one another like the parts of a

The Farnsworth house in Plano, Illinois, designed by Mies van der Rohe, was one of the most influential structures of the twentieth century. It inspired a generation of Minimalist architects and set a pattern for the steel-and-glass structures that continue to be erected today. As Dr. Farnsworth soon discovered, it was uninhabitable.

"Mock-up" of Le Corbusier's cell. (Photograph from *The Radiant City*, courtesy of Fondation Le Corbusier. © 2006 Artists Rights Society [ARS], New York/ADAGP, Paris/FLC.)

The demolition of Murphy Homes in Baltimore took place one night only thirty-six years after the grand opening. The "high-rise" public housing in St. Louis designed by the world-famous architect I. M. Pei met the same fate. (Photograph reprinted courtesy of the *Baltimore Sun*, © 1999.)

machine. These, in turn, were based on a "minimum living unit" that Le Corbusier appropriately called the "cell."

Le Corbusier describes his creation as follows:

> Before undertaking my researches into *The Radiant City*, I had already satisfied myself to the point of certainty that a human cell of 14 m² per inhabitant could provide a basis for calculations which would lead to the expansion and flowering of men's lives in a machine age.[12]

I cannot contemplate the mock-up of such a cell without dismay. In this mean little space we are to see the expansion and flowering of men's lives indeed! The arrogance and ignorance expressed in his statement are appalling, and the implications for the dignity of human life are fearful. It is, nevertheless, typical of the men and women of twentieth-century science. As a representative of that science, Le Corbusier was a hero to architects of my generation, and his ideas were accepted without question by his followers. Huge, publicly funded elevator apartment houses were built all over the world in imitation of Le Corbusier and acclaimed by the regular media and the architectural press. These same buildings have been thoroughly hated by those forced by circumstances to live within their walls. In covert rebellion, their inhabitants have often allowed them to slide into a disgusting squalor, worse than that of the slums they were intended to replace. In some of the buildings, social disorganization became so great, and crime and violence so endemic, that the only solution, finally, was total demolition.

The enormous structures proposed by Le Corbusier were to be hermetically sealed. He wrote at length about the advantages of sunlight and "pure, fresh air," but the sunlight was to be filtered through glass and the air recirculated mechanically. Le Corbusier's proposal was nevertheless enthusiastically accepted by twentieth-century scientific architects and has become the normal way in which a large building is designed and constructed.

But there is no logical or scientific reason why buildings should be so constructed. I am convinced that the real reason for sealing the buildings is an unconscious desire to break the link between man and the natural environment, the sunlight and the air.

Architecture was once regarded as shelter that opened to the world beyond the window or door. It was the openings—the windows and doors—that were detailed and emphasized. When we look at contempo-

The doorway of the eighteenth-century Hammond-Harwood house in Annapolis, Maryland.

Doorway of a contemporary glass-walled office building in Timonium, Maryland. You can't find the door, and there is no sense of human scale.

rary buildings we see hard, sheer walls without openings and with only a minimum of flat detailing. Through the use of large sheets of glass, these building "envelopes," as they are called, enable those who possess sufficient clout and status to seize a location near a perimeter wall with a "view," or a panoramic picture of the world outside. A view from the upper floors can be spectacular and provide enormous satisfaction to the egos of the few who can control the allocation of space in the structure. Most of the others are condemned to spend their lives at a desk, juggling papers under fluorescent lights and an air diffuser.

Anyone who has designed the floor plans of one of these buildings is aware of the battles waged by mid-level employees to secure an office with a window. While prestige and status are certainly involved, the struggle is concerned more with access to the space and light of the world beyond the polished glass skin of the curtain wall. The desperation of those who dwell in these spaces for much of their waking life is a measure of their dissatisfaction with the typical environment of a corporate office building.

View through the glass window of a Baltimore office building.

Some corporate leaders are aware of this dissatisfaction, and in recent years have tried to relocate their staff to suburban buildings surrounded by lawns and trees. In these huge new buildings, however, the struggle for a window—for light and air—continues, intensified because of the more desirable environment outside the walls. And even in suburbia where noise and pollution are not a problem, the windows do not open, but only present a picture, as it were, of the grass and trees.

With single-minded intensity, architects of the twentieth century have pursued a vision of the sealed environment to its ultimate conclusion, which is not an office at all, but rather the Farnsworth house by Mies van der Rohe.

The Farnsworth house is essentially a unit of one of the large corporate glass-and-steel structures designed by Mies van der Rohe, in this case set down in a meadow near a river. The clear, pure geometry of this translucent, rectangular prism—floating over the meadow and linked to the ground only by eight steel, wide-flanged sections acting as columns—is beautiful, but the beauty is that of a highly polished and finished sculptural artifact rather than a dwelling. The entire exterior wall is glass. While the interior is visually open to the natural landscape,

One of a complex of U. S. F. & G. office buildings in a suburb of Baltimore.

East side of the Farnsworth house in Plano, Illinois. The front, facing the river, is shown on page 19. Note the two hopper windows. These and a double door are the only openings into the building.

it is relatively inaccessible, for there are only two small low operable windows and one unobtrusive double door. The visual openness is belied by the impermeability of the glass barrier, while the functional distinction between the interior and exterior space is clear-cut.

One could plead efficiency or necessity when designing a sealed office building. Here, the motivation is certainly ideological. Nature is to be enjoyed, but only by an observer, not a participant. To stand upon the earth, it is necessary to pass through the door to the porch, descend a flight of steps to a transitional platform, and then descend another flight of steps to the pristine and apparently unused meadow. The twentieth-century conception of the scientist as a detached, objective observer of the natural world has been carried over into the design of a home. Here the inhabitant is isolated and alienated from the earth in a beautiful glass cage that seems to float suspended in space.

The concept of the sealed environment has been carried out in other major structures of the corporate economy. These include factories where enormous, complex machines are housed and things are actually made, as well as ancillary warehouses and shipping and loading facilities. These vast structures reflect the equally vast and impersonal systems of

Sweetheart Cup Company, Hampstead, Maryland.

Ludwig Mies van der Rohe (1886–1969), with Frank Lloyd Wright and Le Corbusier, was one of the three "old masters" of Modern architecture. He emphasized the use of beautifully detailed steel-and-glass in buildings defined by simple geometrical plane surfaces, swept clean of any ornament or extraneous detail. Through his (designed) buildings in Germany and the United States, then as director of the Bauhaus and later of the I.I.T. School of Architecture, he had a profound impact on the development of contemporary design. (Photograph courtesy of the Library of Congress.)

production and distribution for which they were built. They dwarf the workers within them. They are usually designed not by architects but by engineers who do not pretend to have a knowledge of beauty but seek only to satisfy functional demands at the lowest possible cost. Occasionally, the design of such buildings falls into the hands of a sensitive and concerned designer, whether architect or engineer. The buildings may then possess a somber beauty of their own, but it is a beauty related to the scale of the machines they are designed to house—and not to the scale of the human beings they are supposed to serve.

This same lack of human scale is dramatically visible in the photograph below. The buildings in the foreground of this Philadelphia street are shabby but comforting. The structures behind them are repetitive grids into which people are somehow to be fitted.

Philadelphia street. The dignified, once comely buildings in the foreground are a world away from the rigid "beehives" behind them.

THE SCIENTIFIC ARCHITECTURE
OF THE TWENTIETH CENTURY

The photograph above, at right, was taken from the balcony of an obsolete powerhouse, now an innovative bookstore in Baltimore City. From the balcony one looks west across the plaza to the National Aquarium, the Trade Center, and the corporate office buildings constructed along the waterfront. The open water, the flags, the crowds of people, and the way the space is enclosed by the sheer walls of the buildings that rise around it make this one of the more exciting and attractive of our contemporary urban spaces. Nevertheless, something is lacking.

A mile to the north, the city fathers in the early nineteenth century laid out a group of four rectangular squares around a monument to our first president. Standing in this space, surrounded by the buildings of an earlier time, one immediately perceives what is lacking in the Harbor Place space. It is again the sense of human scale, the relation of the individual to the space. The older squares were constructed so that a person standing within any particular section of the space would relate to the whole design. The monument, for instance, is brought down to the level of a pedestrian by the little building upon which it rests and by an iron fence and stone balustrades. The buildings and sculpture relate to the monument. The square belongs to the people who move within it; its beauty will influence their lives.

Buildings constructed by public and semipublic corporate authorities include those meant to house schools, courtrooms, theaters, and museums. The schools are critical, for our children spend many of their

Left: Mount Vernon Place, in Baltimore, Maryland, was once described by Lewis Mumford as "the finest urban space in America."

Right: Harbor Place, Baltimore.

27

waking hours in them. A hundred years ago our public schools were expected to be beautiful; care and attention were lavished upon them. Now they are expected only to be efficient. The Modernists condemned the application of historical styles to the design of schools, but they have chosen the image of the factory to take its place. It is now often difficult to distinguish, at first glance, a contemporary public school building from a factory. A factory for people? What will be the effect upon the generation that spends its formative years enclosed within its walls? Does anyone care? Even fifty years ago windows could be opened, and children studied by natural light. Now schoolrooms are artificially lighted and ventilated, the windows reduced to a token, free play structured and confined to a gym. Those who lack the broader vision that would

Loch Raven Senior High School, Baltimore. Note the tiny classroom windows in the otherwise blank facade.

lovingly respect the individuality of the children entrusted to their care are unlikely to assign any importance to the beauty of the buildings in which they are housed.

In the new building of the Maryland Institute, an art school in Baltimore, there is nothing that relates the structure to human scale or to any human function. It is a technologically bold, arrogant sculptural shape that encloses a "building" that is unrelated to the cold, polished glass skin. I cannot imagine what it must be like to live and work in this structure. I can only say that the sight of it fills me with sadness and regret.

As might be expected, in a time of atheistic materialism, the most depressing failure of contemporary architecture is to be found in the design of churches or temples. These buildings, once constructed to link the earth and the heavens, the flesh and the spirit, and to incorporate into their fabric eternal truths, are now little more than meeting halls, given a high-pitched roof or a tower in dim reflection of an art of the past when men were closer to God.

The church at Ronchamps, one of the later buildings designed by Le Corbusier, is an exception, for here he chose to reject the pseudo-scientific rationalism of his earlier work. The dark interior and the heavy, sloping roof recall the mystery of the cave, the opening into the body of the earth. The building is a place of meditation and may reflect a long-repressed, luminous insight of the architect.

Maryland Institute College of Art, Baltimore. Abstract sculpture on an inhuman scale. This ghastly building has been praised by critics and was voted the best local building of the year.

The Chapel of Notre-Dame-du-Haut in Ronchamps, France; Le Corbusier, architect. This building, so unlike Le Corbusier's main body of work, caused consternation among his followers but in due course found its inept imitators. Le Corbusier, a professed atheist, was subsequently chosen to build a monastery for the Dominicans, the initiators of the Inquisition and the persecutors of his Cathar ancestors.

The entrance facade of the Chapel of Notre-Dame-du-Haut in Ronchamps.

Photographs of the building are almost always those taken of the dramatic view from the southeast, as shown (on page 30, at top). On page 30, at bottom, we see the entrance facade from the north, perhaps even more interesting in its plastic complexity. The entrance itself is somewhat strangely wedged between the twin towers. The mysterious interior space is shown in the photograph on page 93.

The Unitarian temple built by Frank Lloyd Wright in Madison, Wisconsin, is a good example of how a bad idea is quickly picked up by other architects. It features a high-pitched roof tilted steeply upward over the meeting room. The congregation thus confronts a huge window of Wright's design at the end of the chancel. An uncomfortable blaze of Apollonian light pours through a tracery of mullions designed in his geometrical manner, representing God, I suppose, as interpreted by Frank Lloyd Wright.

The search for the spectacular at the expense of the simple, the functional, and the harmonious results in "gimmicks." Gimmicks are superficial and flashy effects that are unrelated to either the utilitarian

Unitarian temple, Madison, Wisconsin, designed by Frank Lloyd Wright. (Photograph courtesy of Robert Kuller.)

function or any deeper spiritual purpose. The gimmick employed in the Wright building is particularly easy to imitate. A new church near my home is a typical example. Here the roof of the square nave has been pried up at one corner. The altar has been placed there and the congregation faces a glare of light through the clear glass of the industrial-type windows behind the organ.

Driving along Interstate 83 in Maryland, I passed another church built as an expression of the same gimmick. This more closely follows the example of the Unitarian church in Madison, Wisconsin, but here the window at the end of the chancel faces an expressway! I was told the foundation is shaken by the heavy trucks. What can be the effect on ritual and prayer?

It is, however, the individual house, not the apartment, the workplace, or the larger communal environment that emotionally and psychologically represents shelter from what, in many ways, is perceived as a cold and alien world. Our scientific architects, however, even the most

Left: Interior of Presbyterian church, Baltimore. The altar, once the functional center of a temple or church, has shrunk to insignificance.

Right: Church on Interstate 83, Timonium, Maryland. The similarity to the Frank Lloyd Wright church on page 31 is obvious.

renowned among them, have failed to design a house that is acceptable to the vast majority of potential patrons. Although the media and the architectural periodicals continue to feature houses designed in the spare, white tradition of the International Style, houses in which structural tricks and gimmicks favor novelty over livability, houses "enlivened" with traditional motifs, and houses dominated by purposeless, "exciting" spaces, very few houses, even costly ones, have been designed by professional architects in accordance with Modern or Post-Modern ideas. Modern architecture has effectively been shut out of participation in the home-building industry.

I find it hopeful that, in the face of all the media hype, most people, at least for their own homes, reject the architecture of alienation and cling to an eclectic semblance of the architecture of the previous age.

Unfortunately, almost all of these eclectic houses are also ugly, particularly those produced by builders for the speculative market. We now have styles such as "Neo-Victorian" and "Neo-Georgian," in which

When I was a student, then later a young architect, I ascribed the continuing rejection of Modern houses by the public as arising from ignorance, or coming from a "Philistine" habit of mind. Only toward the end of my career did I understand that it was a well-founded reaction to an architecture that was arid, perhaps even cruel, and that failed to respond to emotional and psychic human needs.

This contemporary Neo-Georgian house is located in suburban Baltimore, just across the hill from the much superior 1904 house shown on page 16. It shows a lack of scale in the columns and portico, disorganized massing of the elements, and an ignorance of the basics of proportion. It is, sadly enough, one of the best of its type.

roofs take odd and dysfunctional turns, bay windows and peculiar projections bulge out from the walls, and the interior spaces feature "cathedral" ceilings and "Tuscan" columns. There is a lack of organization that results from a lack of an ethical direction, a lack of accepted prototypes, and a lack of any purpose, other than that of satisfying the uninformed taste of those who buy.

They are, nevertheless, a sign of some remaining vitality and discrimination in a public that has been brainwashed into accepting the other structures of our commercial culture. Those buildings are not only equally ugly but also uniformly inhumane. And if architecture does return the truest image of a culture, what image does it return of ours? It is an image of the power of the state and the corporation, an image of our technological achievements and our standard of living. It is an image of a society in which the psychic and emotional needs of individual men and women are ignored or denied by the alienated architects of the scientific revolution.

But how does all this happen? After all, architects who dedicate themselves to a profession from which they can expect only a modest material reward do so from motives that are idealistic and admirable. How does it happen that they spend their lives producing the ghastly buildings of our commercial culture? How is their idealism gradually suborned and lost to both the individual architect and his or her society?

The answer, of course, is to be found in the way their hopes and expectations are shaped by the dominant institutions of our society. The underlying problems are philosophical, perhaps metaphysical, and are rooted in assumptions that we accept unthinkingly. These problems are rarely addressed by architects, historians, or critics, who do not realize their relevance. They are certainly not understood by students, whose attitudes to the practice of their craft are still unformed when they begin their architectural education.

The immediate and most telling indoctrination of our contemporary architects therefore takes place in the architectural schools.

"Standard of living" should be called "commodities per person," since only the quantity of material goods and services available per person is included, and neither the quality of the natural and constructed environment nor the quality of the goods and services that are offered is considered.

3
MAKING THE MODERN ARCHITECT

The Failure of the Schools

The young, aspiring architect comes to the profession already grounded in the ideology of scientific materialism. He is where he is because of talent and inclination. By a secret, indefensible intuition he wishes to create that which is beautiful, and yet logically, within the philosophy that he has come to accept, there is no convincing explanation of beauty itself. This dilemma is tacitly ignored in the architectural schools of our large universities, where the architect is trained to design buildings for "builders" to erect.

The schools recruit prominent architects as instructors, particularly those who represent the cutting edge of theory and practice. The direction given the students tends, therefore, to be timely and fashionable. Modern, International, Post-Modern, Minimalist, and Pop stylistic movements have succeeded one another, or have been reflected in the emphasis given at various institutions. Common to all these "isms" are the assumptions of the contemporary scientific-materialist culture that are, briefly restated, that the material reality perceived through the senses is the only reality and that it may be comprehended through logical thought.

These assumptions are neither expressed nor discussed, but they underlie both the curriculum and the attitudes of the instructors. The curriculum follows something of the old apprenticeship system that the architectural schools replaced. It is organized around "studio" courses,

An architectural student presents his work to a jury of faculty and visiting critics at the University of Pennsylvania, 2003.

each allotted six or eight weeks of semester time, in which groups of students design buildings under the tutelage of a studio master, generally a faculty architect or engineer. In the studio, working separately or in teams, students complete the preliminary design of a building, and prepare drawings by hand or computer to be presented to a jury of faculty and visiting critics. Architectural students here learn to analyze an assigned program, sketch their conceptions, and translate them into plans, elevations, sections, and perspectives. Finally, they make drawings of the proposed building—similar to those that would be presented to a client—to show to the jury.

The strength of the process is the opportunity to design a wide variety of buildings without the usual constraints of money, the mechanical and electrical systems, the need for structural stability, or the vagaries of a difficult client. A principal weakness is that these are not actual buildings, but imaginary paper creations, and in this unreal laboratory, paper plans take precedence over actual construction. This leads students to fantasy, egocentrism, and conceit, and these are too often identified with creativity. Students, therefore, are not prepared to face the technical and economic realities encountered in a working architectural office and many, after graduation, become bitterly disappointed. They blame themselves for what they assume to be *their* failure, and some leave the profession.

Since the time allotted to a "design problem" is so short, the famous epigram of Mies van der Rohe, "God is in the details," is not applicable, for there is no time to study and contrive details. Neither would there be time to study and contrive systems of ornament, if they were to become an accepted part of a modern architectural style. In fact, the absence of ornament in Modern architecture is reinforced by the studio system of the schools.

Another weakness of the studio system is the way the various projects are received and graded by a jury of faculty and visiting architects, much as juries rate architectural drawings in professional competitions. A principal disadvantage of the jury system, the lack of time to adequately study the various entries, is exaggerated in the schools, where only fifteen or twenty minutes are allotted each student's work. What is generally the most successful is that which is novel or different, and the skill with which the drawings are executed usually takes precedence over whatever merit the building would have if it were actually constructed.

The jury system of grading thus reinforces a general tendency on the part of the students to seek a striking, even bizarre, solution that is attractive on paper. Jurors tend to overlook questions of practicality,

When I was a student, in accordance with Modern theory and despite thousands of years of architectural history, the use of ornament was simply and totally ignored. Faculty and students alike seemed unconscious of any loss, but my best friend, Alonzo Tartt, once felt impelled to draw a bright red fireplug in front of the facade of my studio problem. I liked it, but this impudence was, as I should have expected, singled out and criticized by the jury.

MAKING THE MODERN
ARCHITECT

again partly because of time constraints. Their apparent lack of interest is noted by the students and contributes to a further divide between the design conception and the problems of actual construction.

Architects are nevertheless expected to be conversant with a wide range of practical skills, including knowledge of the materials and methods of construction, patterns of circulation, structural and mechanical design, and the requirements of building codes. A series of courses are therefore offered that teach the fundamentals of these subjects, but they are only partially integrated into the design work that takes place in the studios. Similar but much more complex courses in the same subjects are offered to engineers, who are required to study them in much greater depth, and are therefore better prepared to engage in actual construction.

Students, therefore, come to see the function of an architect, as opposed to that of an engineer, to be one of providing beauty and delight. Since these concepts of beauty and delight are fundamentally irreconcilable with the materialistic assumptions upon which engineering is firmly based, the perceptive student becomes aware of a conflict between architecture as engineering and architecture as art that is never really resolved.

This conflict emerges clearly during the four or five years spent in studying studio problems. On the one hand, the rational, scientific analysis of structure and space is what is taught, while on the other the work is evaluated and graded on the basis of its so-called aesthetic appeal. When I studied architecture at the University of Pennsylvania in the 1950s, this factor of aesthetic appeal tended to dominate the process of design, even though its existence could not be logically or scientifically justified. The studio courses were, in fact, directed largely to refining what was considered to be a subjective and individual aesthetic intuition. To the critics, a design either looked good or it looked bad, and students were supposed to learn to recognize the difference by a trial-and-error referral to their own aesthetic sensitivity.

There was, however, no theoretical discussion of "aesthetics" itself, and what it might be, or, oddly enough, of beauty either, although that was presumably what architecture was about. Neither was there any unifying vision on the part of the various critics or masters that could relate the material, utilitarian-functional aspect of our work to the mysterious aesthetic sensitivity, or even provide some simple understanding of what the aesthetic sense might be. This was not the result of negligence on the part of the instructors; I do not think they ever considered the matter, or thought it necessary to do so. They simply assumed that the direction

Jury grading student work at the University of Pennsylvania.

The term aesthetics *had, by my time, almost completely replaced "beauty and delight." There might be some value in beauty and delight, but aesthetics could be readily discarded as unnecessary in the "real" world that we would soon enter. Years later I remember a client saying as he studied a proposed design, "Yeah, this has got aesthetics to beat Hell, but you can't sell aesthetics!"*

Kahn, even then, had completed a number of famous buildings. Modest and unassuming, he was completely devoted to architecture as art and was venerated by many of his students. When I worked on a studio project under his direction, I was disappointed to find that he encouraged a slavish imitation of his own buildings, not so much from simple egotism as from an absolute conviction that his way was the only right way. There is a Zen saying: "When you meet the Buddha on the road, kill him!" (Photograph circa 1977, courtesy of the Louis I. Kahn Collection, the University of Pennsylvania and the Pennsylvania Historical and Museum Collection.)

initially established by the Bauhaus and the "Modern masters" was the right way to go and were content to swim with the flow. We students were also remarkably incurious and did not raise the question either, although in retrospect it is apparent that the issue is vitally important, even essential, to an understanding of architecture.

The idea that the practice of architecture was primarily a scientific and technical discipline seemed, without exception, to be accepted by all of our regular faculty members. Louis Kahn, for instance, who was just beginning to acquire a name for himself at that time, took his responsibilities as a teacher seriously, and met with groups of students in the evening to talk about architecture and what it meant to him. It appeared, from what Kahn said, that even the powerful geometric forms that he intuitively sought, and that made much of his work of lasting significance, were not valid in themselves, but were accepted only if they could be logically justified in terms of some utilitarian requirement.

This analytical, rational aspect of Kahn's thinking sometimes led to dreadful results when carried to conclusion. On one occasion the majority of Kahn's studio group designed high-rise offices similar to a theoretical project of his that used the octet truss, recently invented by Buckminster Fuller. In imitation of Kahn, his students dutifully made beautiful drawings of multistoried, completely sealed structures that zigzagged from side to side to conform to the structural configuration of the truss. These strange and impractical shapes were justified as an expression of resistance to the pressure of the wind!

When the grades were assigned, one of the jurors was Lucio Costa, a famous Latin-American architect. He had been brought in as a visiting critic by the humanist author Lewis Mumford, then a faculty member, to serve as a studio master. Costa told Kahn that what he had been asked to review was not architecture, but something deadly, and destructive of the human spirit. Two attitudes were thus seen to be opposed: the logical, scientific attitude responsible for new and daring technological forms and the older humanism that was primarily concerned with enhancing the lives of those who would inhabit the buildings. Costa's remarks were not well received by the dean and the other jurors and he did not return.

The spirit of the school was better represented by R. Buckminster Fuller, well-known inventor of the geodesic dome and the octet truss. When Fuller came to lecture at the school, he spoke as a dedicated materialist to whom "beauty" did not seem to be a concern. He based his architecture, he said, on the logical and scientific analysis of the

Test erection of the all-aluminum Spitz Planetarium Dome by Geodesics, Inc., Raleigh, North Carolina. The dome was designed and constructed by Jerry Batey, who worked for Geodesics, Inc., in 1956–57. In the foreground are the large steel tubes used in the Union Tank Car Company dome built in Baton Rouge.

most efficient way to enclose space. Fuller referred to a house as an "energy valve." He seemed to be the epitome of the scientific architect. He showed us slides and we were dazzled by the beauty of the domical structures that had supposedly evolved in accordance with his theories.

The delicately articulated geodesic frames, covered in clear Mylar, seemed to belong to another world. They seemed to foreshadow a future wherein the beauty apparent to our aesthetic sense would be the expected result of the logical application of modern, scientific technology to the problem of spatial enclosure. There appeared to be no need to invoke an aesthetic sense to account for the effect, since the aesthetic pleasure supposedly flowed from the perfect expression of scientific logic in the form of these structures.

No one questioned Fuller at the time regarding the supposed utilitarian basis of his work. His lecture was couched in an impressive technical-scientific jargon that awed his audience, but his presentation was so muddled that no one understood what he was trying to say. If we reevaluate his achievement in creating the geodesic dome, we find that despite Fuller's claims to the contrary, the domes were efficient only for roofing

R. Buckminster Fuller was an architect, engineer, and inventor, but above all a free and creative spirit. Fuller was a little man with short legs. I remember him with affection, sitting on the edge of a drafting table at Geodesics, Inc. with those little legs dangling in the air. (Photograph courtesy of the National Archives: Photograph No. 79-2072.)

Octet truss, Columbia, Maryland.

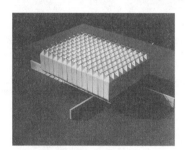

I was so intrigued by Fuller that I took a leave of absence from the university in order to work at Geodesics, Inc., for several months. Some years later, still enamored of the scientific approach, I designed this model of a space-frame structure, based on Fuller's invention of the octet truss, to submit in an informal competition for the design of a pavilion for the 1964 New York World's Fair.

large industrial or public spaces. There was too much wasted space in the sloping ceilings, and the difficulties of fitting rooms, furniture, doors, and windows into the circular form were prohibitive. Moreover, there seemed to be no evident structural advantage in a domed structure based on a geodesic, great-circle configuration, as opposed to one based on lesser-circle geometry, such as we see if we examine the lines of latitude and longitude on a modern globe.

Fuller's structures were based upon the geometry of the Platonic solids: the domes were projections of the dodecahedron and the icosahedron, while the famous octet truss was a combination of the octahedron and the tetrahedron. I doubt if Fuller cared that his work was organized around ancient, archetypal forms, but I believe that he sought them instinctively, and they made his buildings beautiful. Fuller was not a charlatan but rather a dedicated and sensitive man. After having worked for him in 1957, I afterward concluded that he intuitively knew that the geodesic configuration was right, but he could not admit that it was right for reasons that had little to do with logical, scientific analysis.

Although it was possible at the time to recognize that the ideas of such icons as Kahn and Fuller were inconsistent, if not fundamentally flawed, neither students nor faculty (other than Lucio Costa that one time) questioned the theoretical basis of the Modern architecture that was taught in the schools and practiced by the masters. Students, with rare exception, lack the background to criticize the assumptions transmitted by faculty. Moreover, as was the case with Lucio Costa, criticism was not welcomed by those who had based their lives and work on the scientific, technological approach to design.

Nevertheless, in spite of the problems and weaknesses of the formal architectural education that we received, my years at Penn were among the happiest and most exciting of my life, and I believe this to be true of my fellow students as well. Our morale was extraordinarily high, particularly at first, when we were willing to trust our instructors and accept the tacit assurance that they understood what they were doing and where we were going. The challenge to innate creativity and the freedom to dream that was part of the studio system were extraordinarily exhilarating.

We were further supported by the idea that we had a mission to improve the conditions of life, not just for the few, but for all. We had accepted the idea of the architect as a romantic hero—the "Truth Against the World" expressed by Frank Lloyd Wright—and did not think to ask that other question, "What is Truth?" *The Fountainhead*, a famous novel of the 1940s, later made into a movie starring Gary Cooper as the architect Howard Roark, reinforced this image. Ayn Rand's picture of the architect as creative genius, carrying mankind forward on his shoulders and only incidentally getting the incredibly beautiful girl, was irresistible to a band of adolescent, would-be architects like ourselves.

Yet in my last year at Penn there was a sense of the unease and lack of confidence that was beginning to pervade the profession. The certainties that had fired the imaginations of those who had created the International Style had become less certain, and the abrupt break with the past was dimly understood to have cost us our historical heritage. It was not easy to see ourselves as part of a great tradition extending back millennia into the past; instead, contemporary architects appeared to be technicians, producing buildings to programs within specified budgets. As students we were free to indulge our creative fancy, and to consider ourselves to be romantic heroes in the manner of Howard Roark, but we were not unaware of what went on outside, in the "real" world. Not only did we see architecture as an art increasingly circumscribed by budgets,

Why was Ayn Rand's book important to students in the 1960s—and perhaps even now? The writing was very clever and the caricatures, particularly of architects, gave us a feeling of superiority. We were young and naive and could project ourselves into the roles of hero and heroine. Now, Howard Roark and Dominique Francon seem like waxen puppets, curious two-dimensional figures in an n dimensional world. Nevertheless, the book did a great deal of harm to those of us who were most impressionable.

mechanical systems, utilitarian functions, and the dictates of uninformed clients, but we saw more and more actual construction slip from the hands of architects into those of builders and engineers as well.

After all, what was the special expertise of an architect? What was the essential difference between our skills and those of the engineers? In the end we were distinguished from the other building professions only by our reliance on the mysterious aesthetic sense that caused our critics and professors to consider a design good or bad. But if the aesthetic sense was considered to be a purely subjective phenomenon, there was no objective standard by which it could be evaluated. It was thought to be a matter of "taste," and in a democratically oriented society one person's taste was presumably as good as another's. There seemed to be no basis for an architect's claim to possess a superior insight into that which was beautiful, and if that claim was invalid, what was an architect for?

The idea that proportion, harmony, and beauty follow laws that could be studied as a discipline was never voiced, much less taught. Yet every past culture that we had studied in our architectural history courses was aware of these laws, and its buildings were designed in accordance with them. The famous front elevation of the Parthenon was shown, in our architectural history course, to demonstrate the application of the golden rectangle to the facade, but no explanation of the mathematical significance of the form, much less the esoteric or spiritual significance, was ever given. The same may be said of all the other shapes and forms upon which architects had based their designs from remote antiquity until the twentieth century. The popular wisdom is that architects are supposed to be good at mathematics, but the only mathematics that we seemed to need was the mundane arithmetic required for the simplified engineering design thought suitable for architects. The kind of mathematics that had produced the Parthenon was ignored.

The problem was not endemic to Penn; it applied to all the architectural schools at that time, and to the best of my knowledge still persists. A. T. Mann, in his book *Sacred Architecture*, writes of his experience as a student at Cornell: "Year after year, in the presence of some of the greatest architectural minds in American practice and academia, I waited for one of them to approach the subject that I yearned to understand—the sacred basis of architecture—but no one ever did."[1] Mann's experience was similar to mine, but unlike him, I had no idea that there *could* be a sacred basis to architecture. I only knew instinctively that something was wrong, and in my confusion supposed that it was the lack of rigor in the logical and scientific analysis of a problem.

The situation remains the same to the best of my knowledge. In a recent visit to the Graduate School of Fine Arts at the University of Pennsylvania, I found that the changes that have occurred in the intervening forty years are superficial.

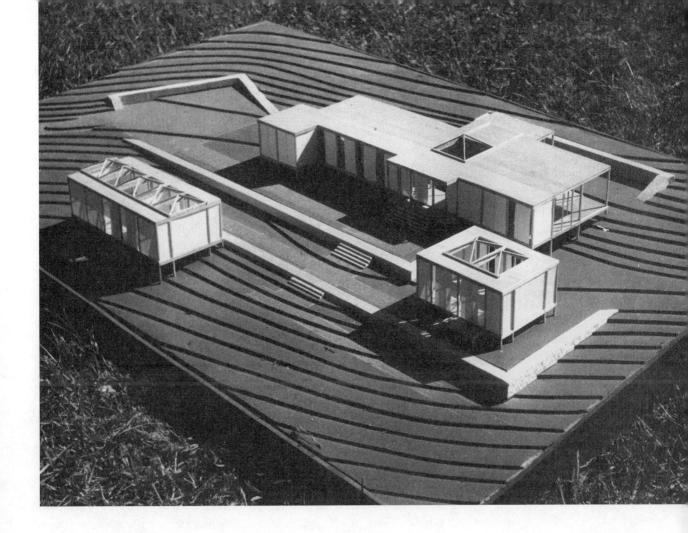

Why are the laws of proportion, harmony, and form so neglected, even ignored, in the schools? First, the accepted wisdom sees a linear progression of culture from remote prehistory to our own era. The great buildings of the past can, therefore, be briefly admired and the ancient, archetypal geometry on which their design was based dismissed as superstition. Second, contemporary buildings, no matter how empty and barren in contrast to the monuments of the past, are automatically considered superior because they are consistent with, and grew out of, the scientific-materialistic assumptions of the eighteenth, nineteenth, and twentieth centuries. The judgment of their mentors is accepted by the students, who, unless forced by some thunderclap of revelation to finally know the truth, retain this myopic view and transmit it to others to the end of their professional lives.

Significantly, the university was the first institution to be captured by the advocates of the materialistic philosophy that has come to dominate our age. The university is, along with business, government, and

I was deeply hooked on scientific rigor. The model above was designed for my master's thesis as a prefabricated, mass-produced prototype, made of aluminum tubes and preformed panels. Every part was light enough to be carried by one man. It was great fun, but one day I had a vision of a world covered with millions of these structures and was horrified.

My experience at Chartres, described in the introduction, was such "a thunderclap of revelation." With that revelation began the search for understanding that has culminated in this book.

the media, an essential link in the structure of modern society, which is increasingly a reflection of that same philosophy. Those who taught, or seemed to advocate the study and adoption of design principles that were related to an ancient, occult science, could not but be suspect as heretics against the new religion of science. We have seen how even the mild humanism of a man like Lucio Costa was rejected. How much more dangerous would be the idea that beauty itself was based not upon a subjective aesthetic sense, but upon objective laws that reflect a spiritual reality! To assert such a position would be to indirectly challenge the tacit acceptance of the assumptions upon which our society and our schools are based. These assumptions, however, and the aesthetic approach to the meaning of beauty that is a logical and inescapable development from them, are fundamentally inimical to the practice of architecture.

The university is in an unenviable position. It continues to be the locus of much of the scientific effort that has established the reigning materialist philosophy. At the same time, it usually contains a "School of Fine Arts," or its equivalent, dedicated to preparing students for an occupation that, within that philosophy, can logically be regarded as only peripheral to the larger needs of society.

As is typical of all large public institutions caught in this kind of a bind, the university continues to hedge. As a bulwark of orthodox scientific belief, it cannot advocate the practice of the arts as a way of approaching a deeper reality than that which can be uncovered through the analysis of material causality. At the same time, a school of fine arts must justify its presence on the campus. The loosely defined concept of aesthetics provides a way out of the dilemma. The school can proceed to teach the search for the beautiful while denying its true significance.

The Plight of the Practicing Architect

Upon graduation, the aspiring architect faces the real world that he learned to fear as a student. In this world, "real" only in that it more closely reflects the prevailing assumptions and organization of the society in which he must function, the architect must seek to express the idealism and creativity that he has brought to the profession. He quickly learns that his worst fears are to be realized and that within the structure of his society there is scant hope of fulfilling his dreams.

The duty of an architect had once been to build the temple of man, and that temple was not just a building specifically devoted to the worship of God. It was the human environment. Every structure that rose upon the face of the earth was designed to reflect the order, the mystery, and the magical powers inherent in the cosmos. Architecture was then the art of incorporating spiritual insight into the fabric of the environment that we create for ouselves in which to work, play, and worship. It was the expression of that spiritual insight which has long been thought to constitute beauty in a building.

Architectural "workstations" in a contemporary office. The architects are isolated in cubicles with their computers and files. The drawing tables have disappeared and the plans are generated by machines. (Photograph courtesy of Gregory Arfuso.)

The Temple of Seti I, Abydos, Egypt, exemplifies order, mystery, and magic.

Architects are still motivated to spend long and materially profitless hours in the hope that they may achieve something that they and the world find beautiful, but those who accept the premises of rational materialism cannot logically admit either the existence of God or the divinity of man. Such an attitude can find only a debased architectural expression. Without a belief that there is a value and a purpose in their work that transcends their material existence, and in the absence of an awareness of the cosmos and the earth that perceives both as living realities, their best efforts will inevitably fail.

Today, after the revolution, architects see themselves as technicians, and are so seen by those who hire them. They derive some satisfaction from regarding themselves as the coordinators and, in a way, the masters of the various engineering disciplines engaged in building projects, but the sense of their ancient, sacred role is so completely gone that few architects are even aware of what has been lost. The best of them possess a vague, humanistic desire to somehow "make things better," but even they have little confidence in the value of adding aesthetics to a utilitarian structure. They begin to negotiate with their clients, therefore, from a position of weakness, and are usually unable to convince them that a concern for aesthetics has any value at all.

Most young architects accept the situation, suppress their hostility and resentment, blame themselves for the failure of their dreams, and strive to achieve the social and financial success that our society considers a worthy goal. Others, more painfully disillusioned, find another vocation, and we thus winnow out of the profession many of those who are best suited to serve it.

The experience of A. T. Mann is again typical. He writes that after five years at Cornell University, and after working for leading firms in New York and Rome, "I had to leave the world of architecture in order to discover the first seeds of meaning in the field I love."[2] Mann left his work, traveled and studied, and was able to find a new way to express what he regards as significant in architecture. Most are less fortunate; they seek to open their own practice, are unable to find clients, and spend their professional lives working for others, producing buildings that are a poor compromise with those they once imagined they would create.

Inevitably, the profession has come to be controlled by large, corporate architectural firms that can guarantee the production of a reliable product, on schedule and at an accurate price. Architecture has, in other words, become a business like any other, and the leaders of the profession, with few exceptions, are seen not as creative artists but as successful businessmen. The advent of computer-assisted design can only accelerate the process. The architect, as artist, is further removed from the actual construction of buildings, and the quantitative productivity made possible by the computer is drastically reducing both the quality of the work and the number of practitioners.

It was once considered a privilege to be a member of the American Institute of Architecture. Now the need for such an organization is questioned, and practitioners complain that the institute does not do enough to promote federal legislation favorable to them. *Architecture,* the magazine once published by the institute, has become another slick coffee-table publication extolling the virtues of the ghastly buildings produced by the corporate architects of our time.

Jonathan Hale, architect and author writes:

> I spoke to a group of architects about intuition one morning. I talked about vision and about how buildings connect people to the world. I talked about how the magic and the sense of place comes from ourselves. I had worried that they might say all this talk about vision and intuition was "soft." I hadn't expected the reaction I got: they looked sad. They were way beyond worrying about softness. They were wondering whether there was any reason for architecture at all. "Maybe what we do just isn't that important," one said. How glum they looked.[3]

A. T. Mann still practices architecture for selected clients but is now primarily an astrologer. He has written some fifteen books on astrology, architecture, and related subjects, and has developed a unique, visual and "architectural" approach to understanding the horoscope.

Architects are aware of the persisting decline in the value society places upon their work. The early visions of the architect as a romantic hero, typified by Frank Lloyd Wright's "Truth Against the World" or by Howard Roark, the hero of Ayn Rand's novel, are reluctantly relinquished, or seen to be puerile in the context of the actual situation. And, in that situation, they find themselves unarmed as they confront the destruction of their dreams. As social beings, they have never questioned the basic assumptions that lie beneath those values that are so inimical to the practice of the profession they once embraced with idealism and love. They are unarmed because they do not realize that it is those assumptions that deny their intuitive knowledge of purpose, meaning, and the existence of God.

It is paradoxical that as the real power and influence of the profession declined, architects were urged by their critics to fill a still more significant social role. Siegfried Giedion, for instance, in *Space, Time and Architecture,* a book that spoke for the aspirations of the Modern architects of the 1940s and '50s, said that the main task of the contemporary

The International Style did depict a way of life appropriate to our period. Why did Giedion, an enthusiastic supporter of Modern architecture, refuse to recognize this fact? It can only be that at some intuitive level he was aware of the aridity and inhumanity of the work that he praised.

architect was the interpretation of a "way of life valid for our period."[4] Architects read this impressive pronouncement without the faintest idea of what they were supposed to do, or how to do it.

Karsten Harries wrote in a recent book:

> To make their home in the world, that is, to build, human beings must gain more than physical control, they must establish spiritual control. To do so they must wrest order from what at first seems contingent, fleeting, and confusing, transforming chaos into cosmos. That is to say, to really build is to accomplish something very like what God is thought to have done when creating the world. Small wonder that the architect has been so often thought of in the image of the Creator, the Creator in the image of the architect.[5]

Harries has succinctly stated a noble vision of the role of the architect, but one unrelated to the actual position of the architect in our society. He has, however, inadvertently indicated the religious nature of the problem. How can an architect be called upon to establish *spiritual* control in an age in which the dominant philosophy of scientific materialism denies the existence of a spiritual reality altogether?

Harries concludes that we must take leave of God and find our inspiration in the human order. He has titled his book *The Ethical Function of Architecture,* but if the individual human life is ephemeral and without a transcendental meaning, the ethic of which he writes is logically dependent upon social conditioning, a far weaker imperative. In the pursuit of pleasure, amusement, diversion, or novelty, or under the influence of a charismatic leader, social conditioning is all too often overthrown. We are then left in an amoral position such as that found in the writings of the Marquis de Sade, where the most frightening thing is not the lecheries, but the boredom, frustration, and futility that lies behind them.

Jonathan Hale, in his book *The Old Way of Seeing,* describes the failure of intuitive vision, which he considers responsible for the degradation of the architectural environment.[6] He writes of the "magic" in old buildings, streets, and cities. But for the making of magic, it is necessary that there be a magician who understands magic as a way of shaping reality. A belief in this kind of magic is obviously incompatible with the materialist paradigm.

Colin Wilson, when young and poor, in the traditional "outsider" position, wrote a book actually called *The Outsider,* about poets, artists, and philosophers of the Modern era who have been unable to accept either the materialist assumptions or the formulations of conventional

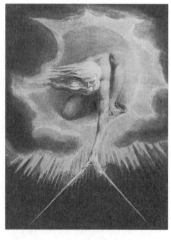

God the Creator, with the compasses in his hand, depicted by the poet William Blake.

religious belief.[7] For Wilson, such people are outsiders, and it is interesting to note that architects are not listed among those he has studied. Architecture is a social art and must operate within the confines of the existing social order. The architect who cannot do so must either develop a personal following or leave the profession. This does not mean that architects do not experience the alienation of which Wilson writes; it means that it is rarely expressed in their work. All young architects who want to spend their lives in the creation of beauty are, by the nature of their dream, outsiders.

One after another, classes of eager and enthusiastic young students pass through the universities to receive their architectural degree and enter the world of the practitioner. Over the door to that world should be inscribed "Abandon Hope, All Ye Who Enter Here." But the saddest part of the matter is that given the rare and occasional opportunity to produce a work of power and imagination, the architects of our time lack the ability to do so. They are unprepared, of course, by their training and education, but in a deeper sense they are unprepared by their social background and the assumptions on which that background is based. They are not magicians and cannot become such until they are able to step beyond the parameters of their social conditioning. At some level of awareness they must know this. Perhaps the knowledge accounts for the sadness Jonathan Hale encountered when he spoke about vision and intuition to a group of architects.

4
THE
MATERIALIST
PARADIGM

A New Model of the Cosmos

The clock was an obvious model for those "savants" who developed the materialist conception of the cosmos. The photograph is of the working parts of a coil-spring clock.

The ancient function of the architect as artist was to express in material form insights into a higher spiritual reality and thus make those insights available to other men. In the absence of a belief in such a reality, some modern theorists maintain that the function of an architect is to ornament or decorate simple utilitarian shelters and make them more pleasing aesthetically. The term *aesthetics* implies a fatal split between art and life, and an attitude that regards beauty as an unessential addition, separate from the structure and function of the whole.

This modern attitude has been shaped by the materialist philosophies that have developed over the last three centuries. It is visible in the form of the buildings we now construct, and it has led to the loss of confidence in the value of contemporary architectural design, which I have identified above. The materialist model of the cosmos is ultimately responsible for the architectural debacle of our time.

The essential tenets of the material philosophies are here summarized as the "materialist paradigm." The materialist paradigm is a model of the cosmos that recognizes as real only those phenomena that can be apprehended and measured through the five senses, or through an instrument such as a microscope or telescope that enhances the perception of the senses. Within the paradigm, that which is real is only that which has weight and measure and occupies space. Time is related to

50

space by the measured movement of objects in space. Every observed "real" phenomenon is considered to have a material cause. It is believed that the world, or cosmos, can be ultimately explained by the application of the rational intellect to the objective, mathematical analysis of the relevant sense data. The method whereby quantifiable phenomena are to be studied is analytical and reductive. The whole is to be understood by reducing it into its parts, studying these in detail and in isolation, and re-combining them according to the principles of mechanical causality—in other words, as if they were parts of a machine.

The problem posed by the existence of life and consciousness as real but nonmaterial phenomena was supposedly resolved by Darwin's theory of evolution. Darwinians believe life began through the accidental transformation of chemical compounds into simple life-forms as a result of the chance concurrence of certain chemicals in the presence of suitable temperatures and pressures. These simple forms were then said to be gradually transformed, by natural selection and the survival of the fittest, into complex ones, a process that continued until it reached higher animals. After Darwin, it was possible to believe that all of existence, including life itself, was no more than a vast and impersonal mechanism. Materialism was thus elevated to the status of a comprehensive theory of the principles and laws that regulate the universe and underlie all knowledge and reality.

There is no logical place in the materialist paradigm for a belief in the existence of a Supreme Being, or in any transcendental purpose for existence, or in any form of life after death. The persistence of such beliefs is regarded as the result of human weakness in the face of a terrible truth. Awareness itself, including that of the materialist philosophers, is considered to be only the result of a survival adaptation to the exigencies of existence. The mystic vision, the experience of love, the intuitive awareness of a deeper reality within the soul, and the affirmative response to beauty are dismissed as unreal subjective phenomena.

In the Christian West, materialism was elevated to its present status as a coherent philosophy at the beginning of the Modern era. At that time a European philosophical movement called the Enlightenment established the way in which we still attempt to understand the world. It is characterized by rationalism, an impetus toward learning from observed data, and a spirit of skepticism and empiricism in political, social, and religious thought.

The enlightenment experienced by seventeenth- and eighteenth-century savants was not the attainment of mystical insight, as the word would suggest. It was, above all, a denial of the stifling religious and spiritual dominance claimed by the Christian Church. This is not to

> *Art mirrors the spirit of its age. Of all the arts, it is architecture that returns the truest image.*
>
> —JOHN ANTHONY WEST
> IN LECTURE

say the Church was completely rejected: each individual made his own compromise with the institution. Nevertheless, important members of the new philosophical movement felt an underlying hostility to the Church and to the Christianity taught by the Church. This hostile attitude was critical to the formation of the current scientific worldview that denies the validity of *any* religious belief.

The Church, particularly the Roman Catholic Church (as that institution was termed after the Reformation), has throughout its existence persecuted "heresy," which came to include anything and anyone that ran counter to its teachings. The discoveries resulting from the new scientific enterprise were therefore rejected, and the persecution of scientists—as well as Jews and dissident Christians—continued until the growing secular power of the nation-state afforded some protection. Hostility to the Church felt by those later anointed as the new priesthood of science was, therefore, at least in part, the result of a well-founded fear of the cruelty and brutality that might be imposed by that institution.

The foolish insistence on the literal truth of the Christian Bible led to its rejection by an ever-growing number of the most influential thinkers of the past three centuries. Yet while the rejection of the Bible as the "Word of God" did not imply a rejection of the religious impulse, or even of Christianity, it was difficult to separate one from the other. The great historical fiction, successfully promulgated by persuasion and force, was that salvation was to be found only through adherence and submission to the dogmas and authority of the Church. When that authority was shaken, not only the Church was discredited, but the transcendental, spiritual insight as well.

While individual men might continue to govern their lives in accordance with the ancient belief in a nonmaterial reality, the theoretical conception of the cosmos that governed their society was increasingly mechanistic, atheistic, and materialistic, and science continued to resist any attempt to introduce a more holistic vision of existence. The materialist system was simple and easily understood: a mechanical model of the universe at a time when machine technology was emerging as a major social force was immensely appealing. The vast body of contradictory and confusing evidence was therefore ignored or suppressed. Characteristically, we prefer what is safe and familiar, and when confronted with the complex and strange, we take refuge in a simple, if inadequate, paradigm, and desperately resist any evidence that might threaten to overthrow it. The history of science is replete with examples of such behavior, as is the history of humanity, and as the acceptable patterns of scientific belief continued to harden in the nineteenth and twentieth centuries, it became increasingly difficult to consider an intellectually persuasive alternative to the materialistic metaphysical position.

It is not suggested, however, that a philosophy that consigned to oblivion all that was long considered to be of the deepest human significance was universally or even widely accepted by the population as a whole. It is, rather, that over the last three centuries, the paradigm has captured the imagination of most of the keenest minds, and has thus come to dominate the institutions that lead and direct the change and development of society. These institutions include not only the schools and universities, but also the communications media, the administrative bureaucracies, and the centers of business, military, and financial power.

Today, the Western Christian nations dominate the world, and the most powerful of these are the ones that have most completely accepted the paradigm. The material abundance that their people possess is the greatest that has ever been achieved. The astonishing advance that has resulted from the intensive study of the material realm has brought power and prestige to leading scientists, and the bonding of science to the technology of the emerging industrial revolution has reinforced their authority, and that of the paradigm they embrace.

Although the immersion of mind in the material world has been denied as a worthy objective of human existence by every major religion including Christianity, in a remarkable reversal, religion itself has come to be increasingly irrelevant to the intellectual elite. Uniquely in the history of human experience, a wholly material philosophy has come to dominate the conceptual framework of our lives. No new religion or reinterpretation of existing faiths has challenged the materialist conception of the cosmos, and the morality that was once sustained by an almost universal religious belief has waned and decayed. For the great majority of people in the West, "religion" has become the province of the Roman Church on one side and the Fundamentalists on the other. A similar situation exists in Islam, while in the East the great philosophical systems of Hinduism, Buddhism, and Taoism are in retreat before the advances of Western materialism. "Science" has become the new religion of modern man, complete with priesthood and dogma, and the fervency of the believers is attested by the militancy of those who support atheistic doctrines for which, as we shall see, there is no rational justification whatsoever.

Today, the paradigm has never before seemed as strong and pervasive in its original home in the Christian West and continues to extend its sway over the rest of the world. The result can be seen in the developing global environmental disaster and in the growing social disorganization that confronts humanity two thousand years after the birth of Christ and the beginning of the Piscean Age.

Nihilism, Despair, and the Decline of the Arts

This huge, polished aluminum statue was bought by a Baltimore public arts commission and erected at great expense in front of an eclectic railroad station designed by Daniel Burnham. It resembles, and was intended to resemble, a joined pair of gigantic male and female paper dolls. It achieves its effect by means of the grotesque size of the metal replica. It is deliberately out of scale with the fine old building it was supposed to adorn, and it thus attacks not only the building, but also the artistic and cultural tradition the building represents. It can be seen as an expression of protest, but is empty of further content. It is, therefore, an image of nihilistic despair.

The age of the rational mind, an age that denies intuition, denies transcendental purpose, and denies beauty, is an age characterized by nihilism and despair. Nihilism and despair are experienced by not only the poet, artist, or architect who can no longer believe in the significance of his own work or take pride in its integrity, but also all of those who accept the paradigm. These individuals, unlike medieval men and women, can no longer think of themselves as semidivine beings who are possessed of a soul or spiritual entity that does not die but is indissolubly linked to the ultimate mystery that we call "God."

I remember my own experience as a child in the 1930s, when I first became aware of the scientific vision of existence. I remember feeling the terror of the void, and I found no relief from that vision in the bland and empty teachings of the local Methodist church. I still recall the pastor with anger and resentment, and yet he was a worthy man who was simply unable, in the context of his time, to convey the assurance of a living faith.

So it was for a child. And yet even the men of science, when contem-

plating the futility of an existence that is accidental and without transcendent purpose, and hence without God, experience despair. The great
Victorian mathematician and philosopher Bertrand Russell, who as a
young man himself had what could be considered a mystical experience,
summarized the materialist perception as follows:[1]

> That man is the product of causes which had no prevision of the
> end they were achieving; that his origin, his growth, his hopes and
> fears, his loves and beliefs, are but the outcome of accidental col-
> lisions of atoms; that no fire, or heroism, no intensity of thought
> and feeling, can preserve an individual life beyond the grave; that
> all the labors of the ages, all the devotion, all the inspiration, all
> the noonday brightness of human genius, are destined to extinction
> in the vast death of the solar system; and that the whole temple of
> man's achievement must inevitably be buried beneath the debris of
> a universe in ruins—all these things, if not quite beyond dispute,
> are yet so nearly certain, that no philosophy which rejects them can
> hope to stand. Only within the scaffolding of these truths, only on
> the firm foundation of unyielding despair, can the soul's habitation
> henceforth be built.[2]

Bertrand Russell: 1872–1970.
(Photograph courtesy of the Pratt
Library, Baltimore.)

Mr. Russell, a dedicated scientist, has conveyed more clearly than
could anyone of this generation the pain, the fear of the void, and the
hopelessness of those who feel they are compelled by the convictions
of their intelligence to accept the materialist assumptions. At the same
time, and quite typically, there is hidden in the splendid rhetoric of this
"bearer of bad tidings" a certain smug and perverse egotistical satisfaction in his own stoic acceptance of the dreadful prospect, while the
confident use of the terms "beyond dispute" and "nearly certain," as we
shall see, is belied by the facts.

But if Mr. Russell, a scientist and a leader of humanity, no matter
how misguided, succumbs to "unyielding despair," what of those architects, poets, and artists who find their work trivialized by the doctrine
of aesthetics?

As we have said, the theory of aesthetics is a necessary development
of materialist philosophy. Since, within the philosophy, phenomena that
have other than a material basis cannot logically be recognized as "real,"
it is difficult for materialists to rationalize the importance of beauty to
the individual. The usual solution has been to propose the existence of a
peculiar "aesthetic sense," a special faculty that responds to beauty with
an experience of physical or mental pleasure. Some believe this pleasure

to be connected to ego satisfaction, the ability to absorb the intricacies of the work, thus triumphing over a complex, highly organized whole. Others adopt the Freudian interpretation, and see art as an attempt to escape into the ideal world that was once glimpsed as a child. Since neither these nor any other materialist explanations are convincing, the whole subject of beauty, its relation to truth, and its place in our lives is largely ignored by materialist philosophy.

The counter-proposition, that the creative artist or architect can achieve intuitive insights into the nature of a higher reality that are inaccessible to logical analysis, and that the role of the artist in society is to make those insights a part of the common heritage of humanity, is not taken seriously and is dismissed by those who support the materialist paradigm.

This loss of what had been the traditional function of the artist and the denigration of the human soul, which follows acceptance of the paradigm, have resulted in the alienation and despair felt by many of the most prominent poets and artists of the past two centuries. Examples in literature are William Blake, Wordsworth, Matthew Arnold, Dostoyevsky, Camus, T. S. Eliot, and the "Beat" poets of my generation, a few among many. In the case of the visual arts, the image of the disaffected painter or sculptor starving in a garret became an accepted part of nineteenth- and twentieth-century folklore, so much so that it came to be considered the normal condition of artistic creativity. In a curious inversion, some artists and poets turned on themselves and proclaimed their insight a sickness. In the novel *Doctor Faustus*, Thomas Mann's hero Adrian Leverkuhn deliberately contracts syphilis in order to heighten his creative powers. Nietzsche, who in the latter part of the nineteenth century proclaimed the death of God, *did* contract syphilis and went mad. Most only sought to withdraw from a vision of reality that they intuitively felt to be a perversion of the truth, or to formulate some compromise that would enable them to continue to participate in a social reality that they detested. Others continued to denounce the prevailing trend of their societies. In architecture, Frank Lloyd Wright designed a hypothetical utopian community, Broadacre City, as an expression of his Emersonian democratic ideals.[3]

It might be supposed that such widespread opposition by so many sensitive individuals would have sounded some sort of an alarm, perhaps on the principle of the canary in the coal mine, but it did not, and despair has become fused with anger. Artists, writers, and musicians, and, of late, even architects, have with a force born of hatred proclaimed that in the absence of anything but their own ego, that ego was supreme. They

When I was a teenager I was caught up in the mystique of science and fascinated with the forms of crystals that I collected at every mine, quarry, or rock cut within my reach. I studied geology but in desperation fled to the arts, focusing on sculpture and dance, and finally became an architect. Eventually, here, too, I encountered the wasteland.

have therefore sought to destroy the basis of order in the arts, along with whatever transcendental ethic might be applied in the evaluation of their own work. The process has been facilitated by the media and the restlessness of our society, ever seeking some new sensation that may serve to obscure the pointlessness of an existence that does not acknowledge the immediate presence of the great mystery that we call God.

If the most noble function of an artist is to express in material form his or her insight into the great mystery, then the denial of the significance, even the existence, of that insight made a decline in the arts and in the art of architecture inevitable. The decline, at first, was imperceptible, but as the new assessment of man and the cosmos became ever more persuasive, there was a progressive loss of inspiration. Jonathan Hale places the beginning of the present steepening decline in the 1840s, when architects in the United States began to base the form of their new buildings on those of ancient Greece. This was the time when the ideological impact of the materialist paradigm was beginning to be felt in the larger

The Second Bank of the United States served as a model for the Grecian Revival buildings of the nineteenth century. This little building in Baltimore was constructed of granite and marble in the same style, not as a bank, but as a public school.

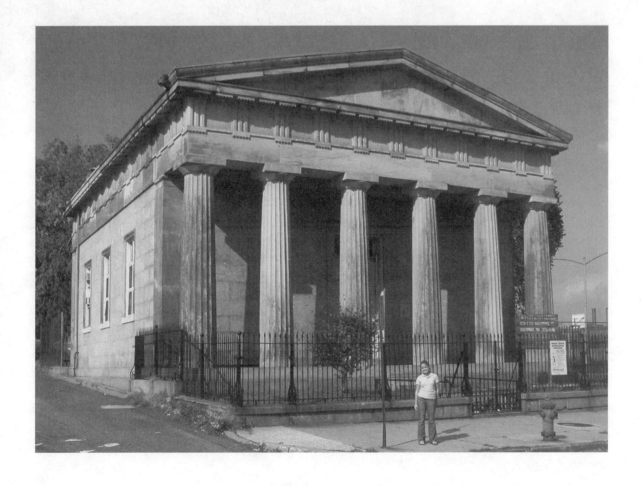

The main reading room in the
Fine Arts Library at the University
of Pennsylvania, designed by
Frank Furness at the height of the
Victorian Gothic revival.

society, and the effect, then as now, was to dry up the sources of genuine
creativity. Once the connection to the intuitive and instinctual sources of
inspiration was broken, architects retreated to the use of the forms and
motifs of an earlier culture.

This is not to say that fine buildings were not constructed, and that
brilliant architects did not achieve magnificent solutions to the new architectural problems that were emerging with the rise of machine-age civilization. In every age there are artists who, through their peculiar genius,
are able to transcend the social and intellectual conditions in which they
grow and develop. It is the province of such gifted individuals to initiate a
reformulation of the art of their time so as to express ancient truths in new
ways. However, when the assumptions upon which a culture is founded
are hostile to their vision, they are able to exert only a minor influence
upon the larger society. The art and architecture of that society is then
dominated by those of lesser vision, and the environment that we construct becomes, through succeeding generations, progressively debased.

In the nineteenth century, the troubled state of the then contemporary design was not recognized. It was not recognized until recent years,

when the failure of the Modern and Post-Modern styles at last linked the decline of architecture to the scientific-materialistic philosophy that still maintains its sway over the institutions of our society. We now see that in their rush to be considered scientific, and thus to acquire legitimacy in the new age of logic, reason, and efficiency that was dawning, the Modern architects of the twentieth century abandoned the ancient canon of proportion and the equally ancient reliance on a developed intuitive understanding. These no longer served to guide the emergence of architectural form. Logic, reason, and efficiency, while important in their own right, did not translate into architecture. The founders of the Modern movement stood at the end of a great tradition, and despite their infatuation with science and technology, they could still rely on the intuitive knowledge honed by that tradition. We, their successors, gradually lost our way.

The materialist paradigm continues to dominate our artistic vision, and the art of architecture has continued to decline. Modernism has been largely replaced by Post-Modernism, wherein the scientific rationalism of the former has had a pastiche of eclectic forms grafted upon it, stunts are performed in construction, and the idiosyncrasies of individuals are hailed as evidence of great talent. Faced with the inability to be other than banal, the banal is celebrated as the creative.

Ironically, by the time the principles of reductive and mechanistic science had become widely disseminated and accepted with enthusiasm by the old masters of the Modern movement, they had already been compromised by the discoveries of twentieth-century physics. As the further findings of theoretical physics have shattered the validity of the materialist paradigm, the implications of these discoveries for architects, and for the society within which they must work, are at last becoming widely known. The impact on the paradigm, and on what I call the "Other Tradition," will be profound.

5

THE RETURN OF THE SPIRIT

Napoleon's expedition to Egypt in 1798 first awakened the Western world to the existence of a vast pre-biblical civilization. Napoleon was a Mason and must have been motivated by an intense curiosity regarding the source of so much traditional Masonic lore. The drawings and descriptions of his scholars, the "savants" whom he brought with him, burst upon Europe like a thunderclap and were a major factor in the revival of the "Other Tradition." (Photograph from *Description d'Egypt* commissioned by Napoleon.)

The "Other Tradition"

The Other Tradition is founded upon the recurrent esoteric insight granted individual men and women into the meaning of existence and the nature of the world. It is characterized by a belief in the symbolic interpretation of reality, in the existence of Divinity, and in the transcendental purpose of life. It is, in fact, the ancient tradition. It was old when Jesus walked by the Sea of Galilee and when the Buddha sat beneath the Bodhi Tree. It was before Plato and before Pythagoras. It is older than the Pyramids and the Sphinx. It is apparent in the magic of the hunt on the cave walls of Cro-Magnon man, and in the ritual burial of their dead. It has survived in the West in the remains of the original esoteric insight in contemporary religion, and in societies such as those of the Masons, the Rosicrucians, and the Theosophists. It lives on, essentially unchanged, in those few primitive societies that survive in the world today.

In the West, however, it has been subject to continuous and unrelenting attack, first by the Church, which could not tolerate a rival, and then by science, which, despite clear evidence to the contrary, continues to deny the existence of the spiritual phenomena that are an integral part of the tradition. The Church, from the time of its alliance with the Roman Empire to the seventeenth century, when it was restrained by the growing power of the secular state, has attempted to extirpate, with unrelenting ferocity, any spiritual insight, esoteric teaching, or magical practice that threatened its monopoly of spiritual and occult knowledge.

The weapons of science are milder but still effective. They include ridicule, derision, and in some cases imprisonment, particularly when the powerful medical establishment sees its prerogatives infringed upon. And as science consolidated its hold on the imagination, and it became possible to speak of a scientific community, orthodox scientific belief was tacitly required of all those who wished to enter, and to have their work or theories granted a hearing. Information regarding those phenomena that could not be explained by the prevailing scientific wisdom either did not emerge or did so in the negative context of a refutation.

The Other Tradition has, nevertheless, survived. In the post-Enlightenment West, it included those who understood the scientific basis of the materialistic philosophy, with its claim to hold the keys to the comprehension of all phenomena, but in their several ways stubbornly continued to assert the existence of a spiritual reality above and beyond the material world accessible to our senses. They established contact with one another, they produced books and periodicals, and they maintained a continuous interest in what came to be called the occult. Most espoused no specific faith but possessed a conviction, derived sometimes from introspection and sometimes from direct experience of the "supernatural," that their lives had purpose and meaning. They often turned to Eastern religions, or succeeded in redefining the faith within which they were raised to recognize the mystical and metaphysical elements that lay within it.

They would have been condemned as heretics in the Middle Ages, but the Church has lost the political power to compel its adherents to accept all aspects of its teachings. Even militant fundamentalism, which continues to threaten and intimidate, is unable to use the machinery of the state to physically destroy those who dare to reject the primitive cosmology that fundamentalism represents. Paradoxically, therefore, as materialism tightened its grip on the imaginations of men in the late nineteenth and early twentieth centuries, the collapse of the Church as the preeminent, pervasive institution of Western Christian society and the loss of its coercive power liberated individual men and women to seek the deeper truth that lies at the heart of all religious experience.

In the latter part of the nineteenth century, even as the assumptions upon which materialism is based became more firmly embedded in the structures and institutions of society, and architecture, as art, began to slide at increasing speed down an ever steeper slope toward decoration and triviality, there was a revival of public interest in experience and evidence that was not readily subject to scientific investigation. Manifestations of

The last widespread outbreak of witch burning occurred as recently as the seventeenth century, when the hysteria and fear initiated by the Church exploded in a frenzy of torture and execution, and thousands of women were killed. The mystical insight was regarded as particularly dangerous: even when the mystic was a part of the ecclesiastical structure, he or she was often persecuted by the "holy mother" Church. Saint John of the Cross was imprisoned; Saint Francis of Assisi narrowly escaped being charged with heresy; and the books of Meister Eckhart were destroyed. As late as 1600, the hermetic mystic Giordano Bruno was condemned as a heretic and burned to death at the stake in Rome.

There is sacred science and secular science. Our own secular science is obviously very sophisticated, and marvelous things have been accomplished through it, but it is not effective in bringing us any closer to the gods. Sacred science is based, in part, on devotion, but also on a profound knowledge of cosmic principles.

—JOHN ANTHONY WEST
IN LECTURE

what are today referred to as "paranormal phenomena" were seized upon by the press toward the end of the nineteenth century and became the subject of books and of newspaper and magazine articles. More recently, there has been a veritable explosion of interest in what is still referred to somewhat derisively as the "occult."

All this material was initially lumped together as "spiritualism," a term derived from the spiritualists, or spirit mediums, who were associated with much of the early phenomena. In the sixteenth century, if the spiritualists had been so unwise as to reveal their practices, they would have been killed or even burned alive. In the nineteenth century it was possible for rational persons of good standing in their communities to investigate the phenomena. As a result, the evidence for the continuation of some form of existence after death continued to accumulate, until in any other milieu it would have been considered overwhelming. The work of Ian Stevenson is particularly convincing. One of his books, *Twenty Cases Suggestive of Reincarnation,* is listed in the bibliography.

The so-called extrasensory powers were also widely reported, and in the twentieth century were carefully studied as "parapsychological" phenomena. While the reality of incidents of paranormal phenomena was eagerly accepted by those hungry for a meaning to life other than the bleak nihilism proposed by the philosophical materialists, "science" dogmatically continued to deride or deny their existence.

A major break in the wall of scientific opposition came at the close of the nineteenth century, when Sigmund Freud not only recognized the existence of what he termed "the subconscious," but was also able to couch the concept in terms acceptable to at least some scientific minds. It remained for his follower Carl Gustav Jung to go further and incorporate psychic or spiritual elements into his own system of psychoanalysis. Although the work of Freud is beginning to slip into obscurity, that of Jung remains a key influence among the prophets of the "New Age." Jung's interests were many and varied; he was involved in such esoteric concerns as astrology, alchemy, gnosticism, mythology, and shamanism. He conferred respectability on these subjects by asserting their importance as aspects of personality, or archetypes, that were clinically significant.

At the same time, there was a new interest in the theological systems of the East, long contemptuously regarded as "heathen," and in native traditions, such as those of the American Indians. The great monuments of Eastern religious and philosophical insight and speculation, such as the Upanishads, the Bhagavad-Gita, and the Vedas, became available in translation, while the work of anthropologists began to demonstrate

The traditional skepticism of which scientists are so proud is, in fact, directed largely to whatever may challenge the reigning theories. The view of the scientist as one engaged in a dispassionate search for truth is tenable only for a select few.

the beauty and complexity of religious and social systems that had been labeled "primitive" and summarily dismissed.

These various threads were united with the valid achievements of material science and woven into a religious system called Theosophy, complete with its own cosmology, by an extraordinary woman, Helena Petrovna Blavatsky. Theosophy has grown into a worldwide society that continues to have a great influence within the Other Tradition. It provides a way of understanding reality and relating human life to divine purpose that is intellectually acceptable in the context of scientific knowledge. Blavatsky herself saw no conflict between science and religion. She wrote in her book *The Secret Doctrine:*

> There can be no possible conflict between the teachings of occult and so-called exact science where the conclusions of the latter are grounded on a substratum of unassailable fact. It is only when its more ardent exponents, overstepping the limits of observed phenomena in order to penetrate into the arcana of Being, attempt to wrench the formation of Kosmos and its living Forces from Spirit, and attribute all to blind matter, that the Occultists claim the right to dispute and call in question their theories.[1]

Helena Petrovna Blavatsky: 1831–1891. (Photograph courtesy of the Archives, the Theosophical Society, Pasadena, California.)

Rudolf Steiner (1861–1925), the founder of Anthroposophism, expressed the same thought. Theosophy, he said, is not "antagonistic or contradictory to the facts advanced by natural science: only with the materialistic interpretation of these facts it can have nothing to do."[2] Steiner first became known as an editor of Goethe's scientific writings. He reintroduced into twentieth-century thought Goethe's rejection of the mechanical, quantitative approach characteristic of modern science, and his emphasis on the importance of the human observer. The Anthroposophical Society, founded by Steiner in 1912, reflected an intense preoccupation with the arts as a way of approaching what Steiner visualized as the spiritual worlds. Steiner did not see the arts as a luxury or as entertainment: he saw them as vital paths leading to the higher development of the self. He created radically new forms of drama and dance, and used color and form in new ways in painting, stained glass, sculpture, and architecture.[3]

Steiner's work should have been of particular significance to architects. Untrained and inexperienced, but relying on his psychic intuition, he designed and constructed two daringly original buildings, the Goetheanums in Dornach, Switzerland. Those of Steiner's followers who are involved in the design and construction of buildings are virtually alone

Rudolf Steiner: 1861–1925.
(Photograph courtesy
of the Rudolf Steiner
Nachlassverwaltung, Dornach,
Switzerland.)

in their emphasis on intuition, on the importance of spiritual insight, and on the significance of the ancient, sacred geometry that they attempt to introduce into their work.

Yet despite the advances in esoteric understanding, the edifice of science in the post-Enlightenment world remained unshaken until the latter part of the twentieth century, when the intellectual tools of modern science were turned against science itself. The same kind of skepticism that had once been so devastating to the claims of the Church was found equally devastating to the claims of the scientists who saw themselves as interpreters of the one true mechanistic reality. A close examination of the basis of their claims yielded remarkable results. It was seen—and once seen was obvious—that mechanistic science had *by definition* excluded anything that lacked weight and measure from the truncated philosophies that had developed alongside it. In other words, those elements of existence so vital to the happiness and spiritual development of humanity were no less real because they had been omitted from the materialist paradigm. The fault lay in the way in which the original assumptions had been framed. The claim of material science to have the ability to encompass all reality is valid only if scientific reality

The second Goetheanum in Dornach, Switzerland.

is defined, in a circular way, as that which can be explained by material science.

In recent years, new academic disciplines have arisen that have undertaken studies in the history and sociology of science. They have demonstrated the way in which acceptable scientific truth is grounded in the peculiar social, economic, and political milieu in which it is placed. At the same time, candid memoirs dispelled much of the *mythos* that clung to the figure of the scientist as a priest of the "Church of Progress."[4] The fundamental conceptual flaws implicit in the paradigm that had been glossed over or ignored have been revealed, and while those who constitute the scientific establishment continue to stonewall the critics, they are aware that the comfortable certainties on which it once rested have been shaken.

The devastating blow that has ensured the eventual destruction of mechanistic science has, however, been struck by the theoretical physicists, precisely those who were instrumental in introducing the mechanistic concepts on which the materialist paradigm is based. A handful of creative individuals in the twentieth century advanced a new vision of the nature of matter and the structure of the cosmos, and this vision has been accepted by their peers. It is of such importance that a fundamental revision of the methodology, the immediate objectives, and the ultimate purpose of all the sciences must be the result. While the far-reaching cultural implications of the new physics are not widely understood or accepted, it is already evident that its advent has ensured the ultimate triumph of the Other Tradition.

The first Goetheanum, beautifully handcrafted of wood, was considered the finer of the two by many of Steiner's followers, but was burned to the ground by arsonists in 1922. The second Goetheanum was built of sprayed concrete reinforced with wire mesh, then a radically new technique and one that gave free play to Steiner's plastic imagination. It was finished in 1928, three years after Steiner's death, and remains today the center of the anthroposophical movement.

The New Physics

Photograph of a spiral galaxy taken by the Hubble space telescope. (Photograph courtesy of NASA.)

Beginning in the early part of the twentieth century, a series of experimental discoveries, and the theoretical models that were advanced to explain them, forever destroyed the certainties of Newtonian physics. The first of these was *The Theory of Special Relativity,* written by Albert Einstein and published in 1905. It provided a common basis for both the mechanics of Isaac Newton and the later electrodynamics of James Clerk Maxwell and Michael Faraday. Einstein's theory proposed a world in which the concepts of time and space derived from the direct perceptions of the senses were no longer valid. The philosophical implications of this aspect of the theory were enormously significant, although not immediately recognized. Classical physics had been founded on the assumption that the world of our common, daily, sensorial experience was consistent at all levels with the world that was being explored through the new scientific technology. Einstein revealed that this might not be so: The reality explored by science could be so configured that it might be incomprehensible in terms of human experience.

Einstein's special theory was followed in 1915 by *The General Theory of Relativity,* in which he stated that space and time are warped by the gravitational fields of matter, and matter itself, the irreducible basis of classical physics, is seen as a form of energy. The Newtonian concept of solid, material objects moving in empty Euclidian space was further shattered by the discoveries of atomic physicists. To the astonishment of these savants, atoms seemed to be not rigid spheres, but planetary organizations of minutely charged particles moving in proportionately vast spaces around incomprehensibly small nuclei. Further investigation revealed that these particles possessed strange properties—sometimes they appeared as waves and sometimes as particles—properties also found to be characteristic of light. Energy, whether from light or heat, was found to be emitted in small packets called quanta, hence the name "quantum theory."

Quantum theory describes a reality in which the material objects of classical physics have dissolved into wavelike patterns of probabilities that can be described mathematically but cannot be visualized in terms of analogies drawn from our daily experience. Matter and energy are seen to be interchangeable aspects of a complicated web of relationships that include the intervention of the observer as part of an interrelated whole. An objective description of nature, the goal of classical physics, is thus not possible.

We now understand that space and time in both classical physics and our daily experience may be only useful abstractions, valid within a limited range of observed phenomena. The universe has once again become a vast, mysterious, and ultimately unknowable matrix in which we live as in a dream. It is no longer possible to believe that the persistent application of the reductive methods of scientific investigation to a world conceived as a machine will enable us to comprehend in any way the ultimate nature of reality.

Today, however, one hundred years after the publication of Einstein's first paper, the philosophical impact of the new physics has barely begun to be felt in the larger society. Even scientists, apart from the leading astronomical and atomic physicists, have continued to follow the same reductive methods of investigation and description of what is still regarded as a mechanical universe that were laid down in the seventeenth century by René Descartes.

We can, however, confidently expect this situation to change. Physics, particularly that part of physics that deals with the structure of the universe and the nature of material substance, is the key to the legitimacy of the metaphysical position adopted by the scientific-materialist establishment. The defection of the physicists, and their rejection of the certainties of Newtonian mechanics, has rendered the application of a mechanistic model to the structure of the other sciences invalid, and has created a climate in which the assumptions on which they rest must be questioned.

In this new climate, the other main support of the paradigm, the Darwinian theory of evolution, has already been questioned, not by those who reject the theory because they believe it contradicts biblical truth, but by those who simply find it inadequate to explain the observed facts. These critics believe there must be some purposive element of which we are as yet unaware that has shaped the evolution of species from what are recognized as lower to higher forms. They maintain that it is impossible, even considering the vastness of geological time, for natural selection to account for the numbers and complexity of the present array of species.

Although the reductive approach has enabled us to make astonishing progress in our knowledge of the so-called hard sciences such as chemistry and geology, it has proved less effective in dealing with life sciences such as biology, medicine, and sociology. It has often been ludicrously inept at dealing with human psychology, and with the creative arts. Even in the domain of the hard sciences, serious problems have arisen that indicate that the exclusive use of the reductive approach is coming to an end.

There is now a growing pressure in many disciplines to adopt a holistic, or systems, approach to further scientific investigation. In the manner of modern physics, such an approach would emphasize dynamic and simultaneous interconnections rather than chains of mechanical causality. It would include the human mind as an essential part of the system studied, and would at the same time abandon the hubris of the materialists and accept that there are limits to the scope of rational understanding. Should this occur, it might once again be possible to acknowledge the significance of mystical insight as a way, perhaps the *only* way, for us to comprehend something of the structure of the cosmos and the meaning of existence.

The convergence of the Other Tradition with the new physics, and the restructuring of the sciences, will result in serious scientific study of the occult phenomena that have been long denied by our lopsided science and labeled "unreal." Since such phenomena cannot be readily quantified or considered as parts of mechanisms, the methodology of science

In paleoanthropology, the neat Darwinian progression of hominid figures depicting the evolutionary ascent of man over the past 100,000 years has been challenged. Long ignored or suppressed information has been uncovered that indicates that the human species has been on this planet far longer than the Darwinians have as yet been willing to admit.[5]

While the situation is still unclear, it seems evident that not only will Darwinian evolution solely through the mechanism of natural selection be modified or even discarded, but our understanding of the origins of man will be substantially revised as well.

must be revised to encompass the qualitative evaluation of these phenomena by the observer, using a holistic approach to the study. The new sciences will accept, rather than ignore or seek to destroy, our awareness of these nonmaterial phenomena, and will recognize the deeper levels of human experience as valid subjects of study.

The religious systems that have failed to provide for the spiritual needs of the post–Enlightenment generations, particularly the form of Christianity that became the religion of the West, will be revised or replaced. Many of the physicists who have explored the new scientific vision of reality have written of their growing awareness of the presence of a transcendental Deity—not the anthropomorphic Deity of ecclesiastical Christianity—but one of an all-pervading cosmic mind. The convergence of this new vision and that of the ancient Eastern religious philosophies has been discussed by both scientists and spiritual leaders. The work of H. P. Blavatsky, although seldom acknowledged as a source, continues to be influential. It is said that Einstein always kept a copy of *The Secret Doctrine* on his desk, an indication of the link between the occult science of the theosophists and that of Post-Modern physics. It has been suggested by some of the men and women on the cutting edge of the new physics that the universe they now explore is beginning to resemble a great thought rather than a great machine.

The Mystical Vision

The mandala is an archetypal image that has been used across time and in many cultures to concentrate the mind in order to enter a higher state of awareness. The picture above is of a great mandala, a medieval rose window at Chartres Cathedral.

The belief that it is possible to achieve communion with the all-pervading cosmic mind while in a state of contemplation and love and without the intercession of a church or formal religious system is an ancient one that still persists in many areas of the world. In the Christian West, however, it has always been considered dangerous, since it affronts both the Church and, more recently, our contemporary, mechanistic science. It affronts the Church because it denies the claim of the Church to be the only path to salvation. This was the essential sin of the Gnostics, for which they were forcibly suppressed and destroyed. And it affronts science because it recognizes the existence of a higher spiritual reality that lies beyond the boundaries of scientific comprehension.

The great mystics of the Christian faith have proclaimed their insight to a hostile and uncomprehending clergy, and their vision has been ignored or derided by science. Yet the mystical understanding has always been present and accessible to the human mind. When I write of the emergence of the mystical insight, therefore, I refer to a changing social and intellectual climate in which mysticism is accepted as a way, perhaps the only way, that we can experience a direct awareness of the cosmos, or, in the traditional phrase, come to a knowledge of God.

This changing climate may be seen, curiously, in the separate careers of the Huxleys, grandfather and grandson. Thomas Henry Huxley (1825–1895) was recognized by H. P. Blavatsky in her first book, *Isis Unveiled,* as one of the arch representatives of the obdurate rationalist refusal to recognize anything other than that which possessed a material, quantifiable basis. His grandson Aldous Leonard Huxley (1887–1963) wrote *The Perennial Philosophy,* an anthology of mystical writings linked by an explanatory commentary that is the finest introduction to the principles and essence of the mystical insight available in the West.[6] Huxley titled his book *The Perennial Philosophy* because the mystical insight appears in every known society and throughout all recorded history, and doubtless even to the dim beginnings of human life. It is the basis of all religions and philosophies that seek to relate man to the cosmos and to the Supreme Intelligence. The existence of this insight is an incontrovertible fact, and unless we are to regard the greatest saints and seers, our most notable philosophers, and the founders of the great religions as charlatans, we must accept the truth of their experience.

It is possible to say *the* experience because the uniformity with which the mystic experience is described is remarkable, particularly when considering the difficulty of communicating the essence of that which is said to be impossible to communicate at all. That mystics born into different cultures, times, and stations in life should all experience, and attempt to describe what we recognize as essentially the same vision, is breathtaking in its implications. It is an incontrovertible indication that the insight is valid, and assures us that we can rely on the mystical experience of others as a guide in forming our own paradigm of the world.

An essential aspect of the experience has been described as knowing the oneness and unity of all things in God. Such knowledge cannot be communicated discursively or even understood intellectually: it can be grasped only in a state of actual identity with the Supreme Principle. Those who have attained this state of identity have assured us that it is the end and purpose of life, and that the destiny of all sentient beings is to return to the Divine Ground from which they have sprung. This Divine Ground is the Kingdom of Heaven, which Jesus calls upon us to enter and become the Sons of God; it is the Nirvana of the Buddhists, and the State of Bliss of the Moslems. We are taught that this "Heaven"

Aldous Huxley: 1894–1963.
(Photograph courtesy of Erowid.)

must be sought in material existence, in this or in a series of further incarnations, which will continue until we have achieved identity with the Ultimate Reality.

Although any one of us, at some time in our various lives, may be given insight into the nature of the ultimate reality, the full revelation is said to be granted only to those who are willing to undertake the transformation of the self that is a required precondition. Aldous Huxley describes the nature of that change as becoming loving, pure in heart, and poor in spirit. An involvement in the rational, scientific world of our time must be recognized as an almost insuperable barrier to achieving such a transformation. Architects, therefore, who by the nature of their art must rely upon the commitment of wealth and social forces to erect the buildings they design, may be too involved in the world to obtain the ultimate degree of understanding, or to reach the ultimate height of awareness said to be characteristic of the mystic state.

Why, then, should the recognition of the mystic vision be of vital and particular importance to architects, who are engaged in the gritty process of creating form from matter, that which many mystics regard as the lowest expression of the Divine? It is precisely because the mystic insight is the assurance of things unseen, of a higher, nonmaterial reality, and of the existence of purpose, meaning, and significance in our experience of the world. It is the assurance that there exists another deeper level of understanding of ourselves, of the cosmos, and of our relation to the cosmos, to which we can aspire and express in our work. It is, in brief, our assurance of the existence of God and of the presence of God in our lives. And for those who are granted some measure of mystical insight, it remains their responsibility to their fellow men to bring back into the world of material form the understanding they have gained.

The mystical vision led Meister Eckhart and Saint John of the Cross to attempt to communicate in writing that which writing cannot communicate. It lies behind the music of Saint Hildegard of Bingen and the late quartets of Beethoven. It is present in the vaults of Chartres Cathedral, in the Parthenon, in the pyramids and temples of Egypt, and in other monuments of antiquity. It is also present in innumerable small and humble buildings where, through their rhythm and proportion, we may perceive something of the higher vision once glimpsed by the builder or architect.

It is not expected that architects become mystics, dedicating their lives to the pursuit of the ultimate vision. They would then, obviously, no longer be architects. We possess different talents and capacities, and while the mystical experience is said to be open to all, few, in any incarnation, will achieve it. Even so, we can recognize something of that vision in the lives and in the work of architects who have gone before us. It is impossible, for instance, to stand with an open heart in the nave of Chartres Cathedral and not be aware that the unknown authors of that mighty structure had been granted a vision of eternity that transcends our mortal lives. Once aware of such a vision, we are led to a deeper comprehension of the great truths embodied in the mystic tradition. We then must seek to incorporate those truths into the architectural expression of space and shape, bringing into material form such measure of understanding as we can achieve.

Architecture is both symbol and shelter: symbol of the Divine Reality and shelter for our physical bodies. Today, we have forgotten or lost our knowledge of the esoteric function of symbols, and of an architecture that was intended to communicate an eternal truth. Symbol and shelter are unbalanced in the world of the materialist paradigm. Building is held to be only the production of shelter, or at best an aesthetically decorated shelter, as Venturi puts it, a decorated shed. We are held to a standard of practicality that has come to mean accommodating the needs of shelter at the least possible cost. That kind of practicality is the curse of the modern world.

The mystic has everywhere and in every age insisted that the purpose of life is to return to the source of all things; to achieve a unity with the cosmos; to develop an understanding of who we are; and to grow in an awareness of the totality of our being. This state of awareness is the goal of our existence. We are here, incarnate on the earth, to pursue the higher state of consciousness that is our birthright. Therefore, when we accept the validity of the mystic vision, we accept that the truly practical is that which moves us closer to God. It is, then, art that is useful, and our much vaunted technological advance, the very idea of progress, is ultimately frivolous. Beauty, however, is eminently practical.

Architecture, as symbol and shelter, must respond to the physical, material needs of our bodies upon this earth, as well as to the deeper, nonutilitarian artistic and instinctual needs of our souls. To neglect the function of shelter would again create an imbalance in the two aspects of the art. We may, however, confidently assert the greater importance of building as art over that of building as utility. In other words, although it is necessary that a building be satisfactory as shelter, it is of greater importance that it be beautiful.

6
INTUITION AND THE CREATIVE MIND

The Mind and the Unconscious Mind

The individual mind is like a mountain of ice floating in a cosmic sea. Only the part above the surface is visible; the vast bulk lies under the water. (Photograph courtesy of the National Archives, College Park, Maryland.)

No scientist has proposed an acceptable theory of mind, nor do we understand the relation of the mind to the brain, or to the material existence itself. But we all experience the phenomena of mind directly, and can reflect and marvel at the way words, forms, and emotions flow into awareness, apparently without conscious volition. It is this flow that constitutes the individual. It responds to our will, and is conditioned by experience, by attitude, by instinct, and by intuition. The part of the "stream of consciousness" involved with the direct interaction between the mind and the environment is normally in the forefront of our awareness. It is this conscious mind that responds to stimuli, that converses with our friends, that adds up the grocery bill, that engages in the manifold actions of daily life. This is the arena of logical analysis, of rational thought. It is active, continually formulating symbolic representations of aspects of the interaction of the self with the environment.

In our post-Enlightenment, modern world, the conscious mind was once believed to compose the whole of mental phenomena and completely define the individual personality, or the self. The theories of Freud and Jung postulating the existence of a part of the mind labeled "unconscious" or "subconscious" were originally greeted with derision. Indeed, the intellectual climate of the time was such that even the founders of psychoanalysis reveal a *sub*conscious bias in the terms chosen to describe the mental phenomena they identified.

The evidence for the existence of the unconscious, however, is so overwhelming that our material science has been forced to accept the presence of this underlying matrix from which our active consciousness arises, and the terms used to identify this matrix have even passed into popular culture. The matrix itself, however, is little studied and little understood.

The mind has often been compared to an iceberg, in which only a relatively small portion, representing the consciousness, or individual awareness, is visible and the vast bulk of the matrix lies beneath the surface of the sea in which it floats. Unlike an iceberg, the depths of the unconscious mind are unfathomable, and while we have terms such as *introspection, intuition,* and *insight* that refer to the process by which we gain conscious access to the deeper layers of the mind, neither the process nor these areas of "knowing," at least in the Christian West, have ever been systematically explored.

A beginning was made by Carl Gustav Jung, who tried to structure the original insight into the existence of the unconscious by breaking it down into categories he termed the "personal unconscious" and the "collective unconscious," categories that are useful for discussion but may have little basis in fact. The personal unconscious, as the term suggests, has its origin in the experience and hereditary predispositions of the individual. Because it can be understood as resulting from the action of material causality, it is acceptable to the contemporary scientific mind and has become a part of our culture. Because the idea of the collective unconscious cannot be so understood, it was not as well received, and stands apart from the common knowledge of educated men and women.

According to Jung, the concept of the collective unconscious arose as a necessary conclusion drawn from his clinical experience. He found in dreams, in the free associations of patients, in the myths and symbols of societies widely scattered across time and space the same repeated, spontaneously arising images. He held that these images represented formulations of instinctual material that had come into being as a result of the collective experience of the human race. He therefore postulated the existence of a part of the mind that transcends the individual and reflects the historical experience of the species.

Jung defended his theory by pointing out that even the most dedicated materialist had to recognize the existence of the instincts as an obvious fact governing complex behavior in the animal world. The existence of a higher, even more complex organization of instinctual

There are indications from many sources that the medieval alchemists were engaged in an exploration of the deeper layers of the mind, then a dangerous and heretical practice.

Carl Gustav Jung, 1875–1961, physician, psychologist, and seer. (Photograph courtesy of Wikimedia Commons.)

material was a reasonable expectation, given the greater complexity of the human mind. Jung, however, was a man of early-twentieth-century science. He did not, at least in the beginning, take the next step and affirm that the existence of the mystic insight revealed infinite depths within the unconscious mind through which it was possible to approach the ultimate mystery of God. Nor was he able to transcend the analytical bias of his milieu and accept that all the materials thrown up by the unconscious mind are parts of a total continuum that can be made available to our conscious awareness.

Within this continuum the instincts are concerned more directly with survival, both the survival of the individual and the survival of the species. The deeper levels of the continuum are the realm of the higher spiritual knowledge, that which has been called the wisdom of the heart, and is related to the pure, disinterested intellect and the exercise of creativity. It is when we enter this realm that we may perceive transcendental truth or experience mystical ecstasy.

The power of the unconscious mind can be recognized on the most mundane and personal level, for even there it can modify our behavior in opposition to our conscious intent. Sigmund Freud relates an anecdote concerning a set of keys, lost by a patient and:

> . . . found lying between a thick book and a thin pamphlet. . . . They were so cleverly placed that no one would have expected they were there. He found himself afterwards unable to replace them so that they were equally invisible. The unconscious dexterity with which an object is mislaid on account of hidden but powerful motives is very reminiscent of "somnambulistic certainty."

Freud does not speculate on the nature of this remarkable "certainty," which was able to act in ways beyond the conscious ability to perform precisely a complex task.[1]

In his book *Zen in the Art of Archery*, Eugen Herrigel describes this strange certainty of the unconscious, as well as the difficulty involved in surrendering conscious control over the relatively simple act of target shooting with a bow and arrow.[2] The author spent six years with a Japanese Zen master, during which time he was taught to relinquish conscious control over the process of drawing the bow and loosening the shot. To encourage Herrigel to persevere, the master one night, in a practice hall lit only by a single candle, placed two arrows in the center of the target. The second split the first.

I first encountered this anecdote of Freud's as a college student at Penn. Even then I found this strange "somnambulistic" certainty awesome in its implications. It is now apparent to me that it is conscious will, the personal ego, that stands between ourselves and our fulfillment in art and life.

These are only two examples of the power, the certainty of the unconscious mind, made apparent in the simple tasks of tossing a bunch of keys and drawing a bow. The purpose of the Zen master, however, was not to teach his pupil to hit a target: he wanted him to learn to perform a simple task in harmony with the whole mind and, by so doing, alter and illuminate his life. Similarly, if architects could achieve that same spontaneous harmony as they work with compasses and square, the buildings that they erect would *necessarily* possess something of the beauty of those constructed in the past.

But how are we, who emerge from a milieu in which even the *existence* of the unconscious was denied, to achieve such harmony? How can we even begin?

First, we must recognize and accept the presence of the unconscious as an integral part of what we consider to be our individual self. An intellectual awareness, moreover, is not sufficient; what is required is a *knowing* of the existence of this deeper level of mind, and a willingness to enter into it. Such a knowing seems to have characterized those architects who built the cathedrals: it may even have characterized those great artists of our own time who, in abstract and action painting, are able to capture the essence of a spontaneous gesture.

Second, we need to cultivate introspection and meditation as a vital and necessary part of our personal and professional lives. These are the disciplines through which people of many cultures and times have been able to delve into the unconscious mind, particularly those deeper levels that Jung has called the "collective unconscious." In this way the balance between the rational and the intuitive understanding can be restored, and we may be granted insights into the roots of our instinctual behavior: into the interplay of male and female, or yin and yang, into our relation to the earth and to the larger cosmos, even into the purpose of our lives.

Finally, we must learn to trust our intuitive understanding. The intuition is our immediate access into "the wisdom of the heart." We must learn to rely upon it as a guide to the beautiful, and practice the intuitive way of grasping and integrating into a whole the innumerable factors involved in the art of building.

The Practice of Intuition

Above are the opening bars of Cherubino's song from *The Marriage of Figaro*. This glorious melody was written by Mozart in 1785–1786. The illustration is of a page in the original manuscript in the State Library of Berlin.

To the poet William Blake, harmony and melody were two different things. Harmony, Blake said, is based in mathematics and can be distinguished by the ear. Melody, without a physical or physiological basis, is pure meaning and results from the play of the imagination. Blake used the word *imagination*, but the image is fixed through the power of intuition.[3]

Architects use the word *intuition* to refer to any insight or inspiration that cannot be accounted for by logical or analytical conscious thought. It is understood by even the most materialistic practitioners of the art that, to a greater or lesser extent, we must rely on intuition to design all but the ugliest and most mundane structures. It is, unfortunately, the common assumption of those same practitioners that a building must first of all be "rational" and designed through a process of logical analysis. Intuition, they agree, may only then be called upon to determine the "aesthetics" of the project: for example, to regulate the proportions of a facade or to select finish materials for interior spaces. Few inquire into the nature of intuition or try to understand how it may function.

Intuition is here defined as the way in which we access the direct knowledge held in the continuum of the unconscious mind, including that of the deeper realms which has not and cannot be derived from experience. The intuitive understanding of any individual is normally partial, and often involved with specific material problems: the full revelation granted the mystic involves a higher level of awareness that is, in fact, a different qualitative dimension of existence. Nevertheless, the source of "knowing" from which the mystic vision arises is the same as that from which comes the flash of inspiration that can illuminate our art. The key to artistic creativity is thus the practice of intuition, through which we access the source, and then express in material form the truth we thereby perceive.

Intuition is both a skill and a gift, and it may be exercised on many levels of comprehension, from the most simple integration of disparate, mundane design material to the expression of a complex and spiritual truth. It is a skill because it may be learned, and through the practice of the skill, like any other, it will become more effective in the hands of the user. It is a gift, because some of us are by our nature more effective in applying intuition to the problems that we face, in either art or life. Only a few, at least in the West, are able to exercise intuition in the spirit of harmony with the total mind that was the object of the Zen master's teaching. One of these was certainly Wolfgang Amadeus Mozart. In that great soul, musical inspiration—by his own account—seemed to flow as easily and naturally as water runs downhill!

I quote at length from a letter of his, written in response to a question about his method of composing. (The emphasis is mine.)

I myself know no more about it and cannot account for it. When I am, as it were, completely myself, entirely alone, and of good cheer—say, traveling in a carriage, or walking after a good meal, or during the night when I can't sleep; it is on such occasions that my ideas flow best and most abundantly. *Whence and how they come, I know not, nor can I force them.* Those ideas that please me I retain in memory, and am accustomed, I am told, to hum them to myself. If I continue in this way, it soon occurs to me how I may turn this or that morsel to account, so as to make a good dish of it, that is to say, agreeably to the rules of counterpoint, to the peculiarities of the various instruments, etc.

All this fires my soul, and, provided I am not disturbed, *my subject enlarges itself,* becomes methodized and defined, and the whole, though it be long, *stands almost complete and finished in my mind,* so that I can survey it, like a fine picture or a beautiful statue, at a glance. Nor do I hear in my imagination the parts successively, but I hear them all at once [gleich alles zusammen]. What a delight this is I cannot tell! *All this inventing, this producing takes place in a pleasing lively dream.* Still the actual hearing of the tout ensemble is after all the best. What has been thus produced I do not easily forget, and this is perhaps the best gift I have my Divine Maker to thank for.

When I proceed to write down my ideas, I take out of the bag of my memory, if I may use that phrase, what has been previously collected into it in the way I have mentioned. For this reason the committing to paper is done quickly enough, for *everything is,* as I said before, *already finished;* and it rarely differs on paper from what it was in my imagination. At this occupation I can therefore suffer myself to be disturbed; for whatever may be going on around me, I write, and even talk, but only of fowls and geese, or of Gretel or Bärbel, or some such matters. But why my productions take from my hand that particular form and style that makes them Mozartish, and different from the works of other composers, is probably owing to the same cause which renders my nose so large or so aquiline, or, in short, makes it Mozart's, and different from those of other people. *For I really do not study or aim at any originality.*[4]

Mozart here indicates his perfect trust in his intuition; his ideas come, he knows not whence and he cannot force them. The "subject enlarges itself" and "stands almost complete and finished" in his mind. All this takes place in a "pleasing lively dream." "[E]verything is . . . finished" and needs only to be set down on paper. Finally, we note that Mozart has no concern for originality, a chief objective of the modern artist or architect. He knows that the inspiration that flows through his particular personality will result in music that is "Mozartish," but for that he doesn't seem to care. How different he is from modern architects, who attempt to justify every form that proceeds from their imagination with tortuous logic and an appeal to functional utility, and who are obsessively concerned that their work be new or different!

The spontaneity and directness found in the music of Mozart is often seen in quite humble works of architecture. We are all familiar, for instance, with the beauty of old barns, for many have been photographed. We may find the same unstudied grace in many other buildings remaining from the past if only we discard prejudice and look with open eyes.

While driving between Cambridge and Taylor's Island on the eastern shore of Chesapeake Bay, I stopped short and got out of the car at the sight of a white, wooden-framed little Baptist meetinghouse at the side of the road. It was utterly simple, a crisp, geometric shape against a blue sky. It made no pretense to be considered architecture; it was undoubtedly the work of a local craftsman. It sat there in tranquillity, being what it was, and it conveyed a sense of joy. The date on the historical marker was 1790, the year before Mozart's death, and the anonymous builder was long gone. He had lived at a time when creativity and craftsman-

ship were more nearly one: a time before the dominance of the rational intellect and the destructive effects of the materialist paradigm had made themselves felt and the intuitive understanding of proportion was lost. His achievement, the simple *rightness* of his little building, could not be duplicated today.

Today, the imbalance in our society between rational and intuitive knowledge, between logic and inspiration, has all but closed the door to the spontaneous creativity that is expressed in so many buildings of the past. If we are to recapture the sure touch of that earlier time, nothing less than a revolution in our way of thinking is required. It is not so much a return to "the old way of seeing," the title of Jonathan Hale's book, as a return to the old way of thinking.[5] We must, first of all, learn to *trust* intuition as our guide to the wisdom of the unconscious mind and put aside the elaborate rationalizations that are so much a part of contemporary design.

As a student I well remember how often, when we were assigned a building to design, we would quickly come up with an appropriate idea, which we would just as quickly discard because it was not the result of logical analysis. I also remember how, time after time, after weeks of struggle, we would return to the original idea. We had been *taught* to

Baptist Meeting House, Cambridge, Maryland. This little building has been owned by the same family for over two hundred years. Although it is now rarely used, it is lovingly maintained. Through the courtesy of the present owners, I was able to measure the building and make drawings that show the mathematical relations among the principal dimensions. These will be presented in chapter 10, Geometry and Number (starting on page 150).

distrust our intuition, distrust the simplicity and directness arising from the unconscious mind, and are still being so taught, not only in architectural schools, but in the larger institutions of our society as well.

Architects today are taught to regard their intuition with suspicion because its very existence is incompatible with the materialist paradigm. Intuition is considered acceptable only when applied to the "aesthetics" of a building. These are usually related to a "feminine" adornment of a rational "masculine" structure, and indeed, intuition itself is regarded as peculiarly feminine, as opposed to the "hard" masculine exercise of rationality. By the nature of our work, however, we can never lose complete contact with feminine intuition since design is inescapably an intuitive process. Even the mysterious aesthetic sense to which my professors at Penn referred is but another name for an intuitive knowledge of form and pattern: knowledge that, as we shall see, is the awareness of archetypal structures of geometry and number retained in the unconscious mind. Sadly, the exercise of intuition, once simple and direct, has been made difficult and complex by the materialist philosophical assumptions that deny the value of the knowledge so received.

As a result, we do not recognize, or wish to acknowledge, the extent to which we must call upon intuition to resolve even the practical problems associated with construction. The growing complexity of the varied systems that today comprise a building has led to the breakdown of our profession into separate disciplines to an unprecedented extent. The variety of materials, the complex structural designs, the systems of heating, cooling, plumbing, electrical service, and lighting require a coordination into a whole that usually cannot be accomplished through the exercise of logic and rational analysis. The word *analysis* is significant, for while analysis, or the breaking of a whole into component parts that may be studied independently, is the method of contemporary science and certainly a part of the design process, architects must think *holistically*. The holistic synthesis of even technical or engineering systems is possible only if the designer can draw upon the strengths and certainties of the unconscious mind.

More importantly, if we are to be artists and our buildings are to be successful as works of art, they must express spiritual truth. In order to accomplish this, we must refine and direct our intuition to the resolution of form. Paradoxically, we approach God through our experience of the world, in this case the experience of the environment that we reconstruct in material form. But the higher, mystical truth can be accessed only through an intuition that comes from the deeper, more profound levels of the mind.

The recognition of the need to rely upon intuition does not mean that intuitive insight will be immediately available to an architect. The habits of a lifetime are hard to break. Only after a determined effort can we learn to design in the serene confidence that our insight may be trusted. After all, it took Herrigel six years to learn to shoot an arrow!

The exercise of introspection and intuition may be seen as a journey of our conscious awareness through the vastness of our unconscious being. In this journey we are assisted by those who have gone before. We may draw upon the great systems of religion and philosophy, upon the teachings of the mystics, upon our personal experience and perhaps the experience of our former lives. The great art and architecture of the past has much to teach us, for in every age and in every culture the journey is always the same.

We may think of our intuition as a beam of light that we direct around an unimaginably enormous room. It is guided, by our learning and experience, to bring into conscious awareness the knowledge that we seek. Such knowledge may be mundane or profound. It may be readily obtained as a result of recent experience or, in the case of the deeper wisdom, many years of patient meditation and introspection may be required before we reach an insight.

The images we perceive are usually derived from the phenomena to which we have been exposed. For eclectic architects, these were usually the traditional architectural forms, and for modern architects, they are the works of the old masters of the Modern movement or more recent work seen in magazines.

But we are by no means limited to such images. Greatness in architecture and in art is found when to some degree the imagination has transcended the boundaries of the known to fix upon an aspect of a higher truth. In other words, intuition may be guided by the familiar images of our experience, but great art is not limited to them or even essentially concerned with them. Great art or architecture is concerned with those images that appear spontaneously from the depths of the subconscious and are common to all races and all times. Jung, who first identified these images in the course of his psychiatric practice, called them "archetypes."

The Theory of the Archetype

The pyramid is an archetypal form that appears in Mesopotamia, Central America, China, and most notably Egypt. The great pyramids of the Giza Plateau have captured the imagination of men for ages. In this photograph, the great pyramid of Khufu rises above the sands.

The theory of the archetype is usually thought to have originated with Carl Gustav Jung in the mid-twentieth century, but Jung himself is careful to point out that the idea, and even the term, is much older. It was Jung, however, who developed the theory and brought it into the structure of modern psychology. He thus made it an acceptable, although somewhat shady, part of the scientific-materialist interpretation of reality.

Jung considered archetypes to be not just material drawn from the contents of the collective unconscious, but a part of the organizing structure of the mind: the structure that makes thought possible and through which we perceive the world. Jung applied the term *archetype* to "archaic or . . . primordial types, that is, with universal images that have existed since the remotest times."[6] He went on to say, "The archetype is essentially an unconscious content that is altered by becoming conscious and by being perceived, and it takes its color from the individual consciousness in which it happens to appear."[7] Finally, he footnotes his definition to add, "One must, for the sake of accuracy, distinguish between archetype and archetypal ideas. The archetype as such is a hypothetical and unrepresentable model, something like the pattern of behavior in biology." Jung seems to be saying that he understands the archetype to be a recognizable psychic entity, or group of mental phenomena, that resides in the unconscious mind but appears with frequency and force in our conscious awareness and is a common heritage of humanity. In Jung's specific terminology, therefore, the archetype was the essential, indescribable complex of knowing, or, the "thing itself." It could be approached only indirectly by means of the archetypal *image:* the myth, mandala, mathematical revelation, artistic creation, or pattern of instinctual behavior through which the existence of the archetype was made evident.

For Jung, the identification of archetypes was initially a way of classifying and naming certain contents of the unconscious, particularly those that were involved in the process of clinical analysis. As he indicates, these contents are altered by becoming conscious and by being perceived: the very act of description would, of itself, break the archetype from the unconscious matrix and limit its significance.

In pursuit of the archetype, Jung fell into strange company indeed for a twentieth-century scientist-physician. He found archetypal ideas expressed in the myths and legends of all peoples: in Eastern metaphysics, in the works of medieval alchemists, and inherent in the formulations of the great religions of mankind. Jung had initially seen the archetype as a reflection of the historical experience of the species, rooted in instincts developed in the course of a Darwinian struggle for survival. As his studies progressed, it seems that he also began to see indications of a metaphysical reality that existed prior to human experience, even to that of the experience of the race, held in what he called the "collective-unconscious" part of the mind.

It is obvious that his well-known fascination with esoteric lore represented more than the interest that would be expected as part of a cool, scientific appraisal, but in the early twentieth century, when Jung began to develop his ideas, science was even more adamantly opposed to the recognition of anything other than a material reality than it is now. Moreover, early in his career Freud had cautioned Jung against falling into "the black mud of the occult." The resulting conflict is evident in Jung's writings as he oscillates between the deprecation of the archetype as no more than a way to categorize clinical phenomena and its acceptance as a possible key to understanding metaphysical reality and a higher truth. As Jung ventured further into the study of the occult, the identification of archetypes became a way in which he was able to bring to conscious awareness certain processes of the mind and something of the nature of the spiritual inner being.

In current popular usage, the term archetype *is used generally to refer to both the image and the underlying reality. For simplicity and brevity I follow the popular usage except where noted.*

There is a curious relation, apart from the common root, between the words architect *and* archetype. *The terms imply that the archetype is to be fabricated into formal reality by the architect.*

Great art and architecture reflect in form the archetypal, instinctive, and metaphysical awareness that is an inborn, a priori, comprehension of aspects of the ultimate reality. Architects of the distant past knew that this inherent, unconscious comprehension precedes, underlies, and conditions our conscious sensory perceptions. Their knowledge is visible in the temples of Egypt and Greece and in the cathedrals of France. Its presence has been clearly identified by R. A. Schwaller de Lubicz in his massive study of the Temple of Luxor. If it is the highest function of an architect to explore and express the eternal truths found in the collective unconscious, then a conscious awareness of the importance of archetypal images may enable architects to access more readily the deeper levels of spiritual understanding.

Archetypes, or, more specifically, archetypal images, may thus be seen as guides to the intuition: ways in which we may direct our intuition to bring forward from the unconscious mind, and particularly from the collective unconscious mind, the elements of a design that reflect underlying metaphysical truth, and that will express the essential harmony of man and cosmos in the fabric of a building.

Archetypes, however, are derived from many levels of awareness and understanding. At the most immediate level, we are informed by our experience as living beings reacting to our material environment. In our bodily existence, as postulated by Jung and Freud, we incorporate not only an a priori comprehension of the significance of form, but also the instinctual knowledge of the human race, and perhaps even that of our animal ancestors. We respond to the archetypal images of shelter that come to us as a part of this primeval heritage, and are thus related to the survival instincts of the species. The inclusion of this order of archetypal image is basic to the provision of an emotionally satisfying shelter. The following discussion of archetypes therefore begins with those architectural images rooted in the will to live and the instinct to survive.

After I began to critically evaluate the architectural forms of my own time and found them lacking, I realized that I had to discard the scientific approach and find a set of principles from which a new group of building types could evolve. The idea of the archetype offered a way in which I might come to an intuitive comprehension of human psychic and material needs that were basic and universal.

7
ARCHETYPES OF SHELTER

The Cave

Many years ago, when I was young, I experienced in an unforgettable way the primal, archetypal experience of the cave as shelter when I and another boy camped overnight on the Big Gunpowder River in Maryland. We had started out on a beautiful warm day in early spring, with a blue sky above us and only a few thunderheads in the distance. We had hiked up along the river on a tree-shaded path, never far from the sparkle and sound of the water, to a place where the river poured over a low natural dam of ledges and large rocks. Above the dam a deep pool reflected a wooded hill where stone slabs and ledges projected from the fallen leaves. When we leaped into the water from an enormous boulder, fish darted from under the rocks. Although we were only a few miles from Baltimore City, we were completely alone.

We built a fire and cooked our meal. We had no tent, so we laid our blankets on the soft earth of the bank, and as night fell we went to sleep. We were awakened by the crash of thunder and a rising wind. We snatched up our blankets and fled up the hill, looking for shelter among the rocks. A huge slab of stone jutted out from the hillside. There was just enough room for the two of us to lie side by side on the dry leaves in the depression under the stone. The rain poured down in sheets, running off the edge of the rock and roaring through the trees. The pool, the fire, the cave, and the falling rain formed an image of profound and lasting symbolic power.

Stone slab above the Big Gunpowder River, Maryland. This photograph was taken by the author in 2002. Nothing had changed during the sixty years since the night I sought shelter there.

Before the hut, before the tent, before any contrivance of humans to provide shelter against the weather, there was the cave. The cave is simply there, waiting to be used. It is not a human fabrication, nor is it the result of human effort. It was there before humanity, and sheltered the animal ancestors of our species, and it must be supposed that our primitive forebears utilized the natural shelters found on the earth eons before they were able to construct their own. The very term "caveman," however accurate archaeologically, reflects an intuitive understanding of the terms of existence of our predecessors. The cave, as shelter, is imprinted in the genetic fabric of our being.

The cave remains the archetypal image of shelter. It is the opening into the earth, and the earth is always thought of as the Mother. She is the source of our sustenance, the giver of life, and the place to which we must always return. In war she is not only our shelter, but also our hope of survival. Erich Maria Remarque writes of his experiences in World War I:

> To no man does the earth mean as much as to the soldier. When he presses himself down upon her long and powerfully, when he buries his face and limbs deep in her from the fear of death from shellfire, then she is his only friend, his brother, his mother; he stifles his terror and his cries in her silence and her security; she shelters him and releases him for ten seconds of life; she receives him again and often forever.[1]

If Earth is experienced as the mother, the cave must surely, in our unconscious imagination, be the womb: the place in the body of the mother from which we enter into the world, and according to Freud and his followers, the place to which we forever wish to return. The cave as an archetypal image reflecting the security of the womb is an image of tremendous power. It is an image that when ignored can only lead to feelings of insecurity and permanent dissatisfaction with our dwellings.

The profound archetypal significance of the cave is reflected in the structures we erect as places of worship. In the Christian East, the domed churches of the Orthodox faith are identified with the tomb of Christ, which is said to have been a natural or man-made cave.

In the West, beneath every great cathedral lies a crypt. The crypt is an underground chamber, often a burial place, within the foundations of a building, which itself may be constructed above a natural cave. The sites of many such crypts were considered holy long before the birth of Christianity. From the crypt, the structure of the cathedral rises to the stone vault far above. The vault itself symbolizes not only the roof

"Shelter" is here used in the broadest sense to include all buildings or natural formations that shield us from the severity of the climate and attacks of insects, animals, or our fellow men. It includes buildings erected for ritual or iconographic purposes as well. "Dwelling" refers to a shelter in which the functions of life, such as eating, sleeping, and procreating, take place.

The Baltimore Basilica by Benjamin Latrobe is an Orthodox dome onto which Latrobe has "grafted" a Roman temple to facilitate the Roman Catholic liturgy. The Modernists would cry "Pastiche!" but the simple massing of the forms is beautiful.

of heaven, but the roof of the cave and the tomb of the spirit as well, through which the divine light of heaven to which medieval man aspired poured through the stained-glass windows.

The sacred cave appears in other cultures and times. The Pyramid of the Sun in the once great city of Teotihuacán near modern-day Mexico City, for example, has at its base a winding, natural lava cave that leads to a group of radiating chambers, the center of which is directly beneath the apex of the pyramid.

A completely natural cave may also be sacred. In Yucatán, near the ruins of Chichen Itza, a huge natural room was used until recent times as a place of worship. There, an enormous stone pillar rises to support the roof, perhaps representing the Mayan concept of a sacred tree that supports the world. Around this limestone mass, ancient worshipers once placed beautiful pottery vessels, filled with food and flowers, as an offering to the god of the Earth.

The sacred cave at Chichen Itza, Mexico, was only recently discovered and opened to the public.

Nave, crossing, and choir in Chartres Cathedral.

Mies and his client, Dr. Edith Farnsworth, a nationally known nephrologist, had developed a close personal relation that led to the construction of the Farnsworth house. As the building approached completion, his ardor seems to have cooled. Dr. Farnsworth was understandably enraged and refused to pay his full commission. The resulting lawsuit and countersuit were damaging to them both.[2]

I once had a conversation with a builder who, with cynical contempt, said of his clients, "What these women really want in a house is a padded cave." His comment was meant to be disparaging, both of his clients and of the value of professional architectural design, but the women to whom he referred had intuitively perceived a profound psychological and emotional need that is deeply imprinted in the nature of our being. To ignore that need, or to rationalize away its existence, as all too many architects do, results in the construction of buildings that may be beautiful as artifacts, or as sculptures, but fail to satisfy the emotional and instinctive needs of those who will live within them.

The Farnsworth house, built by Mies van der Rohe in Plano, Illinois, also (discussed and pictured in chapter 2; see pages 19 and 24), is an

example of a house that fails in this way. The building is considered by many to be one of the most beautiful artifacts of the twentieth century. The care and attention of a famous architect were lavished upon its construction. Even Dr. Farnsworth, when she sued her architect, based her suit on mundane considerations such as the cost overrun, the lack of solar shielding, and the inadequate ventilation. She did not criticize the artistry of the design other than to refer to a "glib, false sophistication."[3]

Above and beyond the mundane considerations, however, the whole idea is flawed, and Dr. Farnsworth may have recognized this without being able to express the reasons for her dissatisfaction. The Farnsworth House, no matter how beautiful as an artifact, could never be satisfactory as a home, particularly one that was intended to be a refuge, a place where one could escape the stress and anxiety that are a part of modern life. The building absolutely denies the cave element, so necessary to satisfy our emotional and instinctive need for shelter.

The Glass House, designed and built by Philip Johnson for his own use in New Canaan, Connecticut, is an even better example. After completing the Glass House, Johnson found it necessary to construct another, separate building on the site. This second building was an enclosed box, an artificial cave, built at the side of a hill across from the first, completely glass-walled structure. When we stand within the first

The Farnsworth house (Plano, Illinois) from the west. When the curtains are drawn aside, the whole building is visually as open as the porch. It is usually photographed from the front, as on page 24, where the terrace (seen here in the foreground) balances the glass-enclosed mass and creates a transition from deck to porch to enclosure. Seen from other sides, the relation of porch to enclosure is awkward. The building, despite its formal and functional flaws, remains a widely heralded and lavishly praised symbol of the twentieth-century scientific vision of an ideal relation between man and the natural environment!

Philip Johnson began his architectural career as a follower and associate of Mies van der Rohe. He later embraced, in turn, every new architectural "ism" that became popular with the press and the public. (Photograph courtesy of the National Archives: Photograph no. 79-1769/C.)

Top: The Glass House, New Canaan, Connecticut. The brick core contains the bathroom and separates the sleeping area from the rest of the house. It is the only fixed floor to ceiling element within the glass cage. The Cave Building (below), a counterpoint to the Glass House, is just across the lawn and, according to the tour guide, is the one most used by Mr. Johnson. When Mies visited Johnson shortly after the completion of the building, he accused him of misunderstanding his details. A lively quarrel resulted, Mies walked out, and the rift was a long time in closing.[4]

building, we understand why it was necessary to construct the second.

The Glass House is a beautiful, carefully detailed gazebo, set down in a parklike setting, but there is no place to hide, no place to find shelter from a sudden assault of the elements or the attack of other men. It violates our instinctual need for refuge. To know that the cave is there, across the lawn, allows us to enjoy the lovely glassed-walled pavilion in a way that we otherwise could not. The quiet, the dark, and the peace of the second building are within a few steps should there be need of them.

And the cave is there also should we have need for silence and shelter from the sun, in order to explore through meditation and introspection the nature of our inner being.

Le Corbusier, the apostle of rationalism, turned to the cave for inspiration when, in the later part of his career, he built the church at Ronchamps in France. The massive shapes of walls and roof, the dimly lit interior, and the mysterious, non-geometrical space are evocative of the cave. The building can only be understood as an attempt to grasp the emotional and instinctive significance of the cave as a place of worship.

The Modern master who best understood the need for a cavelike space in the home was Frank Lloyd Wright. In the series of "Usonian" homes that he designed for people of modest means, he succeeded, to an unprecedented degree, in fusing the cave—the dark and sheltered place within these buildings—with the light and openness made possible through the use of walls of glass doors.[5] These brought the garden and the exterior space into the interior of the home. In so doing, he transcended ego and time to fuse the archetype of the cave with the archetype of the clearing and established a paradigm of shelter for the architecture of the new age.

Interior of the church in Ronchamps, France. Exterior views are shown on page 30. The irrationality of the building dismayed Le Corbusier's followers, who were unwilling to acknowledge a deviation from the Cartesian clarity of his earlier work.

The Clearing

The Palace of Vaux-le-Vicomte, fifty-five kilometers southeast of Paris. Designed from 1658 to 1661 by André le Nôtre and Louis Le Vau, it preceded their work at Versailles. The vista extends into the distance and what was previously forest has been replaced with acres of terraces and gardens. (Photograph courtesy of Yann Arthis Bertrand.)

A "clearing" is a space open to the sky through which we can freely move and see. In traditional Western architecture it is normally outside the enclosure of the walls and roof. It is an image of light and air, the counterpart of the cave. While the cave is both the ultimate and the most immediate archetypal expression of the feminine, or the mother, the clearing is an archetypal expression of the masculine aspect of our being. Both are psychically necessary and both reach back to a level of knowing that reflects the experience of the species.

The need for openness, for light and air, is expressed in countless ways. When suburban homes are built in a forest, for instance, most of the forest is usually quickly cleared away. As another example, consider the east coast of the United States from Long Island to Florida. It is a shifting reef of sand and yet it is covered with buildings. The hunger for space and proximity to the sea has overridden practical considerations.

Consider the great houses and châteaux of Europe. Can we imagine Versailles, for instance, without the acres of terraces and formal gardens that surround the main palace? Even the Petit Trianon, where a deliberate attempt was made to link the building more intimately to Nature, preserves an openness: nature, in the form of the true forest, is pushed into the near distance. We well know that the lawn of even a modest home is typically an object of devoted care.

As a result of technological improvements in the manufacture of

The New Jersey coast is solidly built up from one end to the other. Residents are not deterred by frequent storms or by the erosion of the beach, but continue to rebuild after each disaster.

The forecourt of the Petit Trianon, Versailles, France. Built between 1762 and 1768 as a refuge from the formality of the court, the trees surrounding it have been cleared in the front and pushed back from the structure at the sides and the rear.

The entrance of the eighteenth-century Chase house in Annapolis, Maryland, leads through a beautifully proportioned doorway to the central hall. There we look up the glorious stair to the great Palladian window at the landing.

glass, the relation between the interior, or cave, and the exterior, or clearing, has dramatically changed. In traditional buildings the opening, the transition between the interior and the exterior, was of the greatest architectural importance. The opening was where the cave changed to the clearing and where we experienced the dichotomy of day and night, of male and female, and the eternal dance of opposites that constitutes existence. The architecture of the past has therefore been an architecture of openings into solid walls of brick, stone, or wood; it was an architecture in which the wall served as an impermeable physical and visual barrier between the interior and the exterior space, and the openings were emphasized and embellished. Even in the eighteenth and nineteenth centuries, when glass became less expensive, it was used in windows and doors made up of small panes, and the network of mullions between them continued to define the wall.

The mass production of large glass sheets made it possible to eliminate the mullions, resulting in an unprecedented fusion of interior and exterior space. *Visually,* the solid wall was replaced by glass. The consequent interaction between the interior space and the outside world is the most striking change to be noted in the design of contemporary buildings in the West.

The points of transition, in the old architecture, afforded physical passage as well as visual access. Until recently, the windows and doors were always operable and were required for ventilation. In the twentieth century, systems of mechanical air circulation made it possible to have visual access to the outside world without direct physical access, and we now experience exterior space in most apartment buildings, hotels, and office structures passively, as an observer, not a participant. For this environmental isolation we will inevitably pay a price.

The interaction of cave and clearing did not, in fact, originate in the West, nor in milder climates was it wholly dependent upon the technology of glass. The possibilities had been thoroughly explored in Japan, where, under the influence of Zen Buddhism, the Japanese sought a greater spiritual identity with the natural world. Under the massive hinoki-bark roofs of such great houses as the Katsura Palace, walls of wood and paper, translucent when closed, could be slid aside to throw whole rooms open to the gardens outside.

The cavelike spaces of the interior rooms under the great, sheltering roofs became a part of the exterior world, and the interaction of man and nature was direct. I once read an account of a Japanese scholar, a Zen master, who in the cold of winter would slide open the translucent shoji panels and meditate on the beauty of the falling snow.

The remarkable Japanese architectural achievement directly influenced Frank Lloyd Wright, who worked in Japan as the architect of the famous Imperial Hotel in Tokyo. The work of Wright, in turn, influenced the architects of the International Style in their use of glass to open large areas of wall to the exterior space. Perhaps as a result of Wright's direct experience of the Japanese house, he never carried the new technology to its ultimate conclusion, as in the Farnsworth House and the Glass House of Philip Johnson. Wright never dissolved the wall: always, even when a wall became wholly glazed, it was defined by the plane of mullions and jambs, in the Japanese manner. Nor did he separate visual and physical access: he consistently used a wall of glass doors, rather than a glass wall with doors, even though this was not cost-effective and caused problems, never entirely solved, in sealing his buildings against extremes of weather. It is noteworthy that when Wright was able to dispense with large areas of wall entirely, as he did at Taliesin West, he compensated

Frank Lloyd Wright. (Photograph by Al Ravenna, courtesy of the Prints and Photographs Division, Library of Congress.)

In this Japanese house, horizontal mullions at the one glazed opening over the scholar's desk maintain the continuity of the wall.

This authentic Japanese "scholar's house" was constructed in the twentieth century and given to the city of Philadelphia by the people of Japan. It was carefully rebuilt within a Japanese garden constructed in Fairmount Park.

The same pattern of mullions defines the glazed wall in Falling Water, the famous house designed by Frank Lloyd Wright in Bear Run, Pennsylvania.

by anchoring the building to the earth by massive walls of stone, thus providing the psychological sense of shelter and the cave.

The introduction into the West of the fusion of interior and exterior—the cave and the clearing—so that the two melded and flowed together was Wright's great achievement. Wright was not the only architect to seize upon this technical possibility; some of his contemporaries worked with the same way of opening the house to the outside world. We may even see the idea expressed earlier in the banks of windows in French chateaux and English country houses, but it was Wright who brought the idea into the architectural vocabulary of the twentieth century.

When he spoke of his work to those clients who could perceive the advantages of what he described as "space, light, and freedom," Wright emphasized what he called a setting free from the "dominance of the cave." In this he spoke as a true child of his era, denying the significance of the feminine and mysterious in favor of masculine rationality. Intuitively, however, he recognized the psychological need for the cave, and incorporated into the flowing spaces of his open plans a corner, or an alcove, usually walled in brick or stone, often with a fire burning on the hearth, that balanced the area of glass and provided refuge and a sense of shelter. In spite of his own rhetoric, Wright knew that an architecture that ignores the images of both cave and clearing is invalid, and he incor-

porated this knowledge into his finest work. The need for this psychic balance was unfortunately not understood by his contemporaries, or by those whom he continues to influence.

The developing technology of the twentieth century was regarded with a peculiar romantic fervor by artists and architects. Images that resulted from the application of rational analysis to machine production were exploited for their own sake rather than for their inherent suitability to satisfy either material or psychic needs. A famous example is the Ville Savoy, designed by Le Corbusier, above and on page 8, with its resemblance to a contemporary steamship. Another example is the German Pavilion, originally erected by Mies van der Rohe for the 1929 Barcelona Universal Exposition, and rebuilt as a permanent monument of twentieth-century architecture in 1981–1986.

The Barcelona Pavilion, as it came to be called, was a work of great originality and power and was regarded with awe by the students of my time. The building totally destroyed the former identity of wall and enclosure. Sheets of glass and planes of what were apparently solid marble

Ville Savoy, near Paris, designed by Le Corbusier. The wall is an uninterrupted sheet of plate glass. The visible wall is at the other side of the interior courtyard. The ambiguity between the functional wall of glass and the visible wall is confusing and inharmonious.

The contrast between the Barcelona Pavilion and the Palau de Victoria Eugenia that rises above it on the hill is stunning—even shocking! The waving banner seems to herald the architectural revolution and call all good architects to the colors! This remarkable little building speaks of the endless technological optimism of the early twentieth century, but that has worn thin, and the Pavilion, in the cold light of the twenty-first century, is replete with problems, both practical and artistic. I now think that Mies led us down the wrong path.

In this view of the Barcelona Pavilion, the building reflection and transparency effect a strange sense of disorientation, perhaps expressive of the psychic and emotional disorientation of twentieth-century man.

walls were combined in a composition that denied the traditional function of the wall as shelter. In this building Mies used the marble walls to define a space that flowed *visually* to the exterior through the glass. The glass provided the necessary protection from the elements without a visual barrier and the wall enclosed exterior and interior space indeterminately.

The Barcelona Pavilion was a technical tour de force, and at the beginning of his career Mies demonstrated his lifelong obsession with the expression of science and technology in architectural form. Seventy years later, however, we find that while the materials retain their beauty, and the precision and clarity of the simple, unadorned planes is still exciting, the interior spaces strike one as curiously unpleasant. The negative effect results, at least in part, from the deliberate confusion of wall and window and the release of the form from the constraints of enclosure. Mies has achieved what Wright had proclaimed to be his credo: the setting free from the "dominance of the cave." The "Miesian" space is Cartesian and Apollonian, suffused with light, unlimited in its flow. But one also finds a loss of a sense of place, a lack of security in the experience of the building as shelter, and a psychic disharmony resulting from the rejection of the cave. The building, in a way, is a subtle attack on the psychic identity of the individual, who, in twentieth-century materialistic philosophy, is no longer at the center of the cosmos.

Wright, with all his faults of ego and hubris, with his showmanship and gimmicks, rarely failed to search for architectural solutions that would have a positive impact on those who would inhabit his spaces. Therefore, although the wall in his buildings tended to dissolve into the space outside, it always retained some measure of integrity and definition.

The Barcelona Pavilion, in contrast, was something of an architectural and technological stunt. Neither the pavilion nor the Farnsworth House expresses, in design, archetypal images of cave and clearing. But Wright, unlike Mies and most other Modern architects, lived in his own buildings. He understood, as do we, that a balance must be struck between the enclosure of the cave and the openness of the clearing.

The interior wall of the Pope-Leighey house in Alexandria, Virginia, designed by Frank Lloyd Wright, seems old-fashioned, but the experience of the space is reassuring.

The Garden

Adam and Eve in the Garden. (Photograph by Jean-Luc Fitoussi.)

Whenever men and women have been free from the fear of war or the threat of starvation and possess some degree of leisure, their dwellings have been set in gardens. In the fabled gardens of antiquity, in the gardens of medieval cloisters and the enclosed gardens of Islamic Spain, in the great Baroque and Rococo gardens of sixteenth- and seventeenth-century France, in the romantic gardens of eighteenth-century England, and in the gardens of China and Japan, the art of gardening has proceeded together with the art of architecture. There is no obvious reason why this should be so. No immediate survival factor can be identified. The love of gardening must therefore respond to a deep-seated, psychic need that is archetypal, and we find it expressed in the legends that anciently sought to explain the nature of the cosmos. The Book of Genesis, for instance, opens with a moving and poetical account of the creation of the world. In Genesis 2:7–8 we read:

And the Lord God formed man of the dust of the ground,
And breathed into his nostrils the breath of life;
And man became a living soul.
And the Lord God planted a garden Eastward in Eden;
And there he put the man whom he had formed.

In the biblical story, the first act of the Divine Spirit after the creation of man was to plant a garden. The unknown author has chosen to characterize Divinity as first and foremost a gardener, and the image of Paradise that has dominated the vision of men for millennia is that of eternal life in a garden.

The Garden of Eden was valued both for beauty and for fruit. We have kitchen gardens and herb gardens, but we now think of "gardens" as areas contrived and maintained in response to emotional and psychic needs rather than to contribute to our physical existence. The conscious search for harmonies of color and texture in foliage and flower, and the effort required to achieve pattern and structure in the placement and growth of plants, is not related to the direct necessities of survival. Gardening is an archetypal *symbol* of our dependence on the world of plants for our existence. In gardening we reestablish our identity as creatures of the earth, and as we work with plants to accentuate their inherent beauty, we unconsciously explore the structure of the universe.

In Japan the association of garden and dwelling was reinforced by the teachings of Zen, the fusion of Taoism with Buddhism. The religious emphasis on man, existing as a harmonious part of the natural world, fostered a respect, even a worship, of the beauties of the tangible material order. In Buddhist thought, that order, however illusory and misleading, was necessary to provide a metaphor through which to visualize and approach the ultimate reality.

Under the impetus of what was essentially a religious imperative, the Japanese achieved a near perfect fusion of dwelling and garden. The advanced technique of the sliding panel and the translucent paper wall opened the house to the garden in a way that was unknown in the West until mass-produced glass was available in large sheets.

The Japanese example can now be followed in the more rigorous Western climates by using large sheets of glass, and as the interaction between exterior and interior space, the cave and the clearing, becomes normal in the West, the exterior space will be cultivated as a garden. Modern and Post-Modern architects, however, particularly those who design in the International Style, tend to be hostile to the idea of a garden as part of the use pattern of their buildings. Although their work

The art of gardening involves the active, intimate, and loving association of plants with people. The scientific approach to plants is usually classification, followed by the analysis of forms and characteristics, and finally experiments and exploitation.

The astonishing fusion of garden and dwelling is shown here in the Philadelphia Japanese house. The exterior deck serves to unite seamlessly the cavelike interior to a landscape designed as a metaphor of the larger natural world.

features large areas of glazed wall that enhance visual access to the exterior space, the space itself is usually dominated by the same cold, rational, materialist philosophies upon which the designs of the buildings are based. The exterior space of the Barcelona Pavilion, for instance, Cartesian in its purity, recalls the denial of melody in the avant-garde music of the same time.

Le Corbusier built the Ville Savoy as a ship, detached from the earth and sailing across a meadow. The landscape is presented to the viewer within the building as a purely visual experience, unrelated to any need for stewardship. The Marseilles apartment house even more clearly rejects the earth and the life of plants. The building is again, typically, elevated above the ground, in this case on huge concrete columns. The playground for the children living in this structure is on the roof, where the barren space is dominated by the massive sculptural shapes of Le Corbusier's fancy (see page 106).

Not even a weed grows in the main courtyard of the Barcelona Pavilion. The plants and trees in the background are on the adjacent site.

I remember Louis Kahn's disparaging remarks when I wanted to put a tropical tree *inside* the enclosed courtyard space of a building designed as a studio project at Penn. This is a common practice now, but at mid-century it was a relatively new idea. Kahn didn't like the idea, and told me that a tree "wanted to be outside, in the sun and air." I believe that behind the poetry of the expression lay the hostility of the rational mind to a symbiotic and loving relationship between plants and people.

In recent years, as the technology of glass has revolutionized architecture and the wall has dissolved into window, we have seen a veritable explosion of interest in the creation of gardens, as essential parts not only of individual dwellings, but of larger public buildings as well. This broad-based movement owes little to the designs or theoretical formulations of architects, and runs counter to the accepted ideology of the Modern and Post-Modern movements. It responds instead to an instinctive and archetypal need to live with the presence of plants.

I incurred Kahn's displeasure by pointing out that the plant didn't care if it was inside or out: it only wanted to grow.

The "playground" roof of the Marseilles apartment house. I find it hard to believe that Le Corbusier seriously thought children would voluntarily play in this strictly confined, desolate, and dangerous space where nothing grows. (Photograph courtesy of Paul Raftery/VIEW.)

PRELIMINARY·SKETCH OF LOREN POPE HOUSE, FALLS CHURCH, VIRGINIA.

The Pope-Leighey house, designed by Frank Lloyd Wright. Once again, Wright stood in opposition to the prevailing trend. While to my knowledge he did not work with or share his responsibilities with landscape architects, his love of plants is inherent in all of his work. Some of his designs incorporate retaining walls and terraces as an architectural framework for the gardens to be developed later by the owners. (Illustration courtesy of the National Parks Service.)

The Pope-Leighey house as it was reconstructed on its present site in northern Virginia.

The new unity of cave and clearing has made the garden an essential part of the dwelling. What is now required is a fusion of the skills of the architect and the landscape architect. The separation of the two disciplines is artificial—what exists outside the walls is yours and what is within is mine—and is of a piece with the analytical specialization characteristic of our science. Some specialization is, no doubt, desirable: every architect need not have an intimate knowledge of plants, nor should an architect specializing in landscape be required to master the characteristics of construction materials. But since the success of our future buildings will depend upon the integration of cave, space, and garden, the training and practice of architects must be holistic in the sense that the total environment is recognized as the proper subject of architectural design. An architect or architectural team can then deploy the skills of what are now two separate disciplines in the service of a common purpose, and within a shared understanding.

The Presence of Water

The presence of water, both real and symbolic, is an essential physical and psychic element of existence. The surface of our planet is largely water: life itself is believed to have begun in the primeval ocean and evolved in such a way that terrestrial forms carry in their blood some of that water onto the land. A premise of Freudian psychology is that our awareness develops from an initial experience of floating in the amniotic sea and that the experience colors the rest of our lives. We may live for a while without food, but without water we quickly die.

In contemporary buildings the water necessary to sustain life is supplied by marvelous works of engineering that bring water from distant mountains, purify and distribute it through an incredible maze of pipes and valves, and make it available as needed at the touch of a hand. It is then carried away with our waste, to be returned to the rivers and seas. We no longer consider this marvel. We accept it as something that has always been as it is now.

Yet something of the immediacy with which we once experienced water is gone. I remember as a boy on my grandmother's farm in

The garden of the Dasien-in Temple in Kyoto, Japan. Here, in the absence of water, the Buddhist monks have created a symbolic sea, with raked sand to represent water. (Photograph courtesy of Douglas Hamilton.)

A gigantic water tank squats on the site of my grandmother's farm in Catonsville, Maryland. A car dealership sprawls across the foreground. I am told, "You can't fight progress." But is this progress? Does it have to be done this way? Reservoirs in Baltimore City, constructed a hundred years ago, are open to the sky and have enhanced the areas around them.

The predynastic temple dedicated to Osiris at Abydos in Egypt was designed to resemble an island in the sea. It was built of huge granite blocks floated down from Aswan, far up the Nile.

Maryland watching my aunt carry buckets of water to the house from the well outside the kitchen door. And I remember pumping water for a drink on a hot afternoon, the way it began to flow and then became a solid stream pouring into the dipper, cold and clear, with a slight mineral taste of iron. The house, the well, and the entire farm are now obliterated, and on the leveled plateau that once was a hill there stands, ironically enough, one of the largest water tanks in the world, from which chlorinated and "purified" water is distributed to the surrounding suburban region.

Near my home, a short road called Winespring Lane runs up through a little wooded valley. Until recently the Winespring flowed from a small grotto, a few yards back in the woods. The land on that side of the road has been "developed" for large and expensive homes. The spring could have been saved, but it and the grotto were bulldozed away, and it now exists as seepage into a ditch along the road. To the developer it was a nuisance—water was to be supplied through pipes from the distant city—but we who walked on that road and drank from that spring have lost something of the psychic and symbolic significance of water as the source of life.

The sacred nature of water has been recognized in all cultures except ours. That of ancient Egypt was dominated by the Nile and the annual flooding of the river. The Way of the Dead, the central, elongated plaza of the prehistoric city of Teotihuacán, near present-day Mexico City, is thought to have been composed of a series of reflecting pools, much like that of the Taj Mahal or those between the Lincoln Memorial and the Washington Monument. Rome, under the Republic and the Empire, was known for its aqueducts and fountains. There was a sacred well under Chartres Cathedral, and such wells are associated with many other religious sites in Western Europe. The well at Glastonbury is a noteworthy example.

In Mexico the sacred well at Chichen Itza is widely known, perhaps not so much for the human sacrifice reputed to have taken place there as for the strange beauty of its huge sunken pool. In the farthest and deepest part of the nearby sacred cave (see page 89), there is a pool of perfectly clear water, perhaps a Mayan "Holy of Holies," once surrounded by offerings.

In the hot and dry climates of the Middle East and Spain, the Moors used water as the central accent within courtyards. The pool surrounded by flowers is a common design motif in Oriental rugs. In the medieval West a well is often found in the center of a cloister. In the great Renaissance and Baroque houses and gardens, water, as pool, cascade, and fountain, completed the design. At Vaux-le-Vicomte and Versailles, for

Aerial view of Blenheim Palace, England. The lake is in the background. (Photograph courtesy of AeroPic, U.K.)

The sacred cenote, or sink hole, at Chichen Itza in Mexico.

instance, the vast systems of formal pools, basins, and fountains dominate the plans and vistas. As Baroque gave way to the Rococo and Romantic styles, water, in the form of lakes, ponds, and streams, remained an essential part of the extension of the inner space into the landscape. In a garden such as that of Blenheim Palace in England, there is a studied progression from the formal pools of the palace terraces to the famous vista across the lake constructed by the landscape architect Capability Brown.

In our contemporary culture, where so much of symbolic significance has been forgotten or suppressed, the sacred well survives only as a baptismal font, and if architects use water as a part of their designs, it is without conscious appreciation of its archetypal significance. Curiously, though, two of the most famous buildings of the twentieth century achieved their effect through very different emphases on water as a key element in the designs.

The best-known building designed by Frank Lloyd Wright is undoubtedly Falling Water, the spectacular house in south-central Pennsylvania cantilevered over a waterfall. The waterfall is, in fact, the reason for the building.

It was, of course, overkill. The imbalance of the elements involved in the stunt is decidedly uncomfortable, as is the building, but it restored Wright's reputation as a Modern architect. After the death of the owner, Falling Water was donated to a foundation and opened to the public. It has proved to be extraordinarily popular, and cars and tour buses arrive every day filled with visitors.

Can we imagine the Barcelona Pavilion without the pools that balance and complement the structure? Mies deliberately excluded any vestige of garden from the area defined by the travertine pavement and walls. He has instead caused the building to float, as it were, between the reflecting pool and the smaller pool in which he placed the bronze figure by Kolbe. There is no fountain, no movement; the flat planes of the water are rigidly confined, but they play beautifully against the simple geometric planes of the walls and roof.

The emotional impact that resulted from the successful use of water in the design of these two buildings was not understood or imitated by other architects. The evident and widespread psychic need for the presence of water as a part of the total environment stands apart from the rational ethos of the scientific architect. The client may be equally unconscious of the symbolic and archetypal significance of water, but often intuitively understands its importance and is willing to pay for it, whether it is for a shopping mall, a public plaza, or a private swimming pool.

Whether pool or fountain, natural stream, constructed pond, lake, or ocean, the deep-rooted need of human beings to be in the presence of water is evident. Notice the way homes tend to cluster at the immediate edge of a lake, a river, or the ocean, and the way land values shoot up at such locations, despite what often is their unsuitability for construction. Astute developers, such as the Rouse Corporation, which built the "new town" of Columbia in Maryland, or the developers of Reston, Virginia, have recognized the power of this emotional need and frequently *begin* major projects with the construction of a lake or pond (see page 114).

In gardens where a pond or pool is not feasible, the presence of water is sometimes simulated. For centuries the Japanese have symbolized the presence of water in gardens without a natural water supply by using river gravel to simulate streams and ponds. The garden of the

The Barcelona Pavilion (right), designed by Mies van der Rohe. Statue by Kolbe.

Falling Water, in Bear Run, Pennsylvania, has been widely praised by both critics and the public since its construction in the 1930s. The little waterfall, however, is overpowered by the thrust of the white concrete decks, and the building rises triumphantly, arrogantly, above the natural features of water and rock. It expresses the boundless hubris of twentieth-century man: the world is to be conquered and subjugated by technology. The individual ego, in this case Frank Lloyd Wright's, is supreme.

Wilde Lake in Columbia, the Maryland town developed by the Rouse Company. Consistent with our modern tendency to rationalize everything in terms of a utilitarian function, the attraction of water is often held to be its use for sport or "recreation." But aside from a few rental rowboats, this little lake is unused. Restaurants and office buildings nevertheless cluster around its shores.

Dasien-in Temple, shown at the beginning of this section, represents a purely symbolic and spiritual use of water as a source of psychic re-creation. In contemporary Western gardens it has become possible to simulate the flow of sizable streams through the use of pumps, and as pumps have become cheap and reliable, this has become a regular practice in landscape design.

While the importance of water is accepted, and water is consistently introduced into the design of gardens by landscape architects, it is not often appreciated by architects. Water usually relates only indirectly to a building through a garden or a view, and architects tend to regard anything outside the building envelope as beyond their sphere of concern. This illusion is consistent with the fragmentation of art and life that is so much a part of the modern scene. The proper concern of an architect should be the entire living environment, projected through the space directly controlled by the design into the larger world beyond.

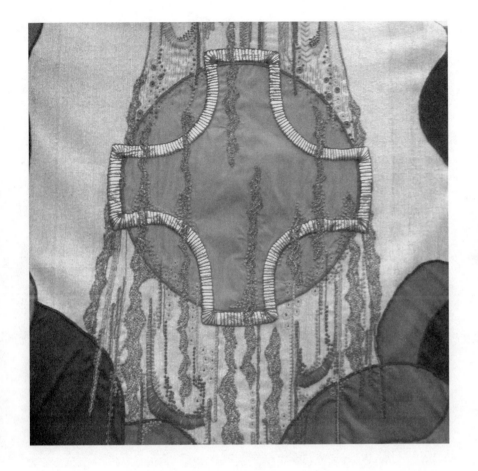

The four elements are represented in this detail of the back of a magnificent twentieth-century chasuble in the Washington National Cathedral. The sun at the center represents fire, the white fabric stands for air, and the artist has embroidered lines of rain falling upon the earth. On the front, rain and snow are shown falling into the sea. (Photograph courtesy of the Washington National Cathedral.)

The Four Elements

I have identified four archetypes of shelter for purposes of discussion, but I have in no way defined what is a complex, psychic reality. The words *cave, clearing, garden,* and *water* are only intended to call to mind certain principles that architects should seek to express as they proceed with a design. The emotional satisfaction that their inclusion may provide is distinct from beauty. They do not resolve the problem of form since they may be incorporated into a design in an infinite number of ways. They are *functional* realities rooted in the survival instincts and the experience of the human species.

Those acquainted with esoteric philosophy will be aware of the parallel between these four, functional archetypes and the phenomena selected by the ancients to describe the physical world, the matrix of all sensuous experience. Earth, air, fire, and water were not identified, as modern science naively believes, to describe "elements" in the sense that we use the term today, as materials containing specific atomic characteristics. They were used rather as terms applied to principles or forces that characterized different aspects of our experience of the material world.

Earth—solid, dark, and inanimate—clearly relates to the cave. Air relates to space and light, or what I refer to as the clearing. Fire refers not so much to the open fire burning on the hearth, a feature of all of Wright's Usonian homes, as it does to the transforming energy of the sun pouring down on the world of plants. These, in turn, provide the energy that sustains our life, expressed symbolically and actually by the garden. Water is water, the ultimate source of our being. In identifying the psychic, instinctive needs to which architects should respond, I have inadvertently followed the ancient system: the forces that were once identified as earth, air, fire, and water are reflected in the identification of the archetypes of shelter.

In reviewing my experience when I camped overnight without a tent and was caught in an evening thunderstorm, I realize that all of the archetypes of shelter were present: the refuge under the slab of rock; the openness to the sky and weather; the fire, not only warming our bodies and cooking our food, but also evident in the energies of the living forest about us; and finally the river and the rain.

8
ARCHETYPES
OF DESIGN

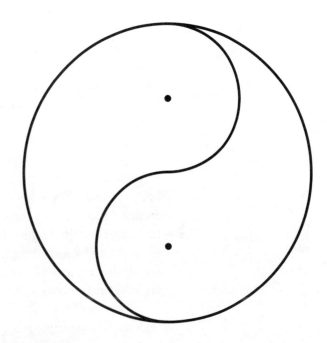

The Principle of Duality

Duality represents the basic dichotomy of being, the eternal dance of opposites. It is the way in which we comprehend the world. It represents the idea of distinction, that is, *difference,* and through the perception of difference we are able to determine both quantity and quality. As one divides into two, the original and fundamental creative act Schwaller de Lubicz calls the "primal scission," the universe comes into being.[1]

The principle of duality is beautifully symbolized by an ancient geometrical diagram, an archetypal image wherein two identical tangent circles are circumscribed by a third, centered on the point of tangency. The diagram represents duality within unity, and numerically the division of one into two.

The symbol has been prominent in Eastern philosophy, in which the term *yin and yang* designates the multilayered concept of the two aspects of the primal unity. Yin and yang refer to the paired concepts of active and passive, of light and dark, of sun and moon, of cave and clearing, of fire and water, and of odd and even numbers. It is also male and female, mother and father, and is intimately connected to the act of procreation.

The forces symbolized by yin and yang represent the pulsating rhythm of existence. If they are unbalanced, it is impossible to achieve harmony in our lives or in our art. Today our world is perishing from

The ancient yin-yang symbol is an archetypal image of the duality of existence.

the dominance of paternalistic values, those associated with the masculine, logical, and calculating aspect of our minds. And while we proceed to order our lives, our society, and our environment in response to the imperatives of rational thought as opposed to intuition; while we deny the significance of the mystical understanding; and while we refuse to recognize the instinctive basis of our behavior—then the images and dreams of the repressed feminine part of our nature struggle for expression.

Sigmund Freud was the first modern investigator of the subconscious to demonstrate the all-pervasive sexuality inherent in our daily lives, but we have always been haunted by the male-female, atavistic, and archetypal content of the sexual image. It is inevitable that this should find expression in architectural form. Tower and vault, column and lintel, solid and void, all may be seen as images of the fundamental male-female duality, as well as the dichotomy of darkness and light, earth and air, cave and clearing.

In the architecture of the past, the images are often explicit. The male-female principle is found in the design of the great medieval cathedrals where the images of the phallus and the vulva are so clearly visible that, in our post-Freudian era, it is almost incomprehensible that they could still be ignored. The Gothic or pointed arches, particularly in the aisles and in the portals through which we enter into the dark, mysterious body of the church, replicate the vulva, and the spires reaching into the sky express the phallus.

Not only in Gothic architecture, but also in great architecture everywhere and in every time, the dance goes on: in the ornament, in the plan, in the opposition of cave and clearing, of garden and pool. Think of the Taj Mahal, the splendid phallic dome reflected in the yonic sheet of water in front of it; or the fountains of Versailles, where the rigorous and abstract geometry of the landscape plan comes to life only when the fountains hurl their plumes of water into the sky, to fall back into the system of pools that extend into the distance. Active and passive, male and female, the principle is always the same. Ignored and misunderstood in our contemporary culture, it cannot be suppressed, and appears even in the work of the scientific architects of the present time.

The tall office building, the "skyscraper," is said to be the structural form most characteristic of our age. Supposedly it developed as a logical response to the high land values in the central business districts of American cities. It is more likely that it reflected the masculine hubris of the business elite. As architecture it owes much to the poetry of Louis Sullivan, Frank Lloyd Wright's mentor. In Sullivan's greatest building, the Auditorium Hotel, a phallic tower reaches up above the roofline, and

At left above, the south portal of Chartres Cathedral. At right, the south tower.

The Taj Mahal from the reflecting pool. (Photograph courtesy of Peter T. Kandel.)

Interior of the Auditorium Hotel in Chicago, designed by Adler and Sullivan.

The Richards Medical Research Building at the University of Pennsylvania, designed by Louis Kahn. The dominant fire-stair tower at left is partially concealed by trees. The stairs themselves are dark, mean, and poorly finished.

In the interior of Chartres Cathedral, the south aisle recedes through the space defined by the feminine pointed arches into the dimly lit distance. The experience is one of mystery and wonder.

within the body of the building is the unmistakably feminine, arched vault of the auditorium itself.

The buildings of Louis Kahn, that misplaced rationalist, serve as another example. The well-known addition to the Yale Art Museum effectively contrasts the feminine, cavelike space created by the coffered, concrete floor slabs with the thrust into light of the stairway space and its symbol of the divine trinity. In the University of Pennsylvania Medical Building, Kahn used the stair and elevator towers on the exterior of the wall as the masculine, phallic image to oppose the horizontal, sheltering image of the spandrels and floors. Even Le Corbusier, in designing the Ronchamps Church, included some masculine elements—the bell tower and the curious and ugly little towers at the entrance that evoke an image of the phallus—in what was essentially a feminine building (see page 30, bottom). It is this *partial* success, this still flawed imbalance of the contrasting poles of the principle of duality, that remains a problem.

As a final example of this imbalance, consider the use of light in contemporary architecture. Light and dark are basic expressions of duality: they also represent male and female, or yin and yang. The dark, mysterious image of the cave is as necessary to our lives as the blaze of Apollonian light. Yet today every space must be illuminated to the standards of a contemporary office or a scientific laboratory, and there is a separate discipline, that of "lighting engineer," set up to maintain these standards. Books have been written to ensure that even a contemporary residence is uniformly lighted, without dark corners or evident contrast. This is all apparently logical and scientific, but beneath the arbitrary standards lies a fear of the dark, itself a rejection of the feminine.

Contrast our present attitude to that of the master masons of the Middle Ages when the great Gothic cathedrals were dedicated to "Our Lady," and were *designed* to be experienced in the dim light that passed through the stained glass far above. We now have electric lights at the religious services held in Notre Dame in Paris. This is not due to the technical achievement that makes electric light possible. Even in the Cathedral of Chartres some of the stained glass was replaced with colorless panes so that the bishop might be more clearly seen. And today no modern church architect would consider deliberately designing a church in such a way that the lighting would enhance whatever mystery remains in the rituals. Contemporary architects are no longer able to perceive the imbalance of light and dark in their designs.

What is to be done to reestablish the ancient balance of the fundamental duality, the archetypal yin and yang? If architects should consciously attempt to incorporate the concept of duality in their plans and elevations in the form of obvious symbols representing the phallus and the vulva, their efforts would be wholly wasted. Symbols are valid only when they emerge as archetypes from deeper levels of the mind. Only then do they represent a part of our being and evoke the presence of the sacred in a building.

It is, rather, that a fundamental change in the attitude of individual architects is required, not just in relation to the balance and harmony of yin and yang in architecture, but in all aspects of life. When architects accept the principle of duality, it will permeate their minds, guide their intuition, and enrich their work. In a time when masculine values of Apollonian light and "hard" rationalization exclude the feminine, the mystery and the dark, architects must pursue an understanding of the *balance* and the *integration* of what are now seen as warring opposites, and constantly seek to express duality within a harmonious whole.

Hierarchy

The concept of hierarchy is inherent in the structure of the human mind and reflects our objective experience of the world. The world is organized in visible hierarchies, and the hierarchical principle is exemplified at every level of comprehension. The suns and stars of our galaxy comprise an inconceivably immense flattened spiral. Around our sun, and probably around every sun, orbits a host of lesser bodies—planets, comets, and far-flung stellar dust—and in turn a greater or lesser number of moons circle the planets.

In the realm of physical reality too small to be visible to the naked eye, the principle of hierarchy is present in the organization of matter itself. The molecule, once thought to be the smallest possible particle, is found to be made up of still smaller particles called atoms, in solids, geometrically arranged in three-dimensional patterns called space-lattices. Atoms, in turn, are constituted of further strange and incomprehensible

In this artistic evocation of the birth of a solar system, a cloud of debris swirls about a newly discovered sun. A hierarchy of planets coalesces from the dust and debris in the manner in which our own solar system is imagined to have been born. (Image courtesy of NASA.)

A table of organization, in this case that of a public agency.

hierarchies of "particles" that orbit about their nuclei at discrete levels of energy.

In the biological realm, the realm of life, hierarchy is manifest in both plants and animals. The basic unit, the cell, is itself composed of a multitude of complex smaller elements. Agglomerations of cells form larger structures, which perform specific functions. In the human body these constitute the blood, the brain, the heart, the liver, the spleen, and other discrete organs. These are subservient in turn to the larger purpose and together constitute the whole man.

Humans, too, are organized into societies, which are also structured in systems of overlapping hierarchies. The most basic cohesive group of individuals is the family, composed of mother, father, and children. In all societies before ours families were grouped into clans by kinship relations, or into tribes and villages. The loss of these supporting structures in the great industrial cities of our time is regarded as one cause of the social disruption and alienation characteristic of many aspects of modern society.

Today we exist within other larger hierarchies, devoted to other ends. There are business hierarchies and political hierarchies, with their own elaborate tables of organization. These were originally derived from military hierarchies established to ensure efficiency in war. In medieval Europe there were the intricate systems of feudalism, and in our complex industrial society there is usually some hierarchic variation of city, state, and nation. As individuals, we are aware of our separate responsibilities to all these various levels of organization.

Architecture should be similarly assembled according to hierarchical principles, not only in the design of an individual building, but also in the broadest sense, the design of the total human environment. The planet Earth, the home of man, constitutes the largest and most comprehensive architectural element, and there is evidence that it may have been organized across continents and seas by some remote antediluvian civilization. Today, our plans are limited in scope to those for nations, regions, and cities. These direct human efforts in ways that profoundly, but indirectly, affect our lives.

Architects, however, are involved primarily in the planning and design of that part of the environment in which we actually live. This includes townscape and cityscape, where they confront the chaos of our materialistic culture and try to bring some measure of order and amenity into the world.

The traditional architectural task, however, remains the design of an individual building and its site. Here, too, hierarchical principles should prevail. The spaces allocated to active human use and interaction should be dominant, while the spaces devoted to minor or service functions should be subordinate or concealed. The ornament must follow the principal characteristics of the structure and the space. Greater importance should be given to that which is understood to be more important in actual, recognized fact. Normally, the greater subsumes the lesser; the structure supports the space.

Awareness of this hierarchic principle is so natural that it would seem unnecessary to discuss its application to Modern and Post-Modern architecture, but unfortunately the principle is often violated. Intuitive understanding is replaced by a logical analysis based on faulty assumptions, or an eccentric form is selected and then justified by specious arguments. An example of the former error is the use of air ducts and piping as ornament or decoration, as in the Pompidou Center in Paris. It was

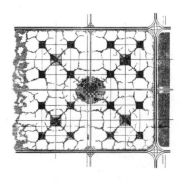

This development policy diagram from the Baltimore County Master Plan breaks a hypothetical town into a hierarchy of functions and functional areas. Note the emphasis on the system of interconnected linear parks.

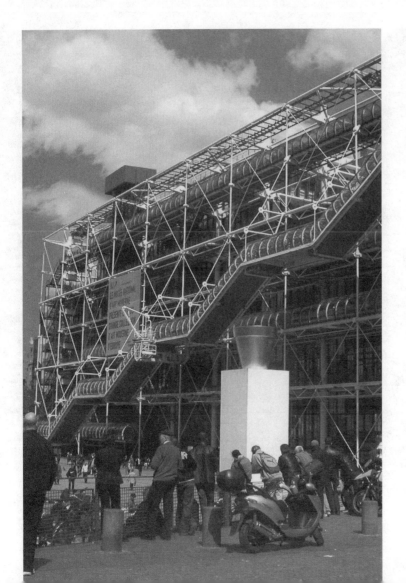

The Pompidou Center, Paris. The maze of plumbing, ductwork, and structural bracing effectively hides the enclosing walls. The architectural critic Ada Louise Huxtable called it "muscular."[2] *Intestinal* would be a better word, for the building has been turned inside out. Note the ridiculous gilded flowerpot on its pedestal in the foreground. It is as empty of meaning and as inane as the building itself.

argued that since the mechanical systems now comprise a third of the cost of a building, they should be exposed and their function boldly indicated by various colors of paint. But we understand intuitively that mechanical systems are, or should be, hierarchically subservient to the purpose of the space. Even those who commission the buildings and do not question the reasoning of their designers must know at some level of awareness that something is wrong.

The Marine Biotechnology Building of the University of Maryland in Baltimore is another telling example. The nature of the tasks to be performed within the structure require extensive air venting to the exterior. The architects therefore decided to wrap oversized exterior vents around the side of the building. The effect is novel but bizarre: The vents dominate the appearance of the building and the intuitive comprehension of hierarchies is turned on its head.

Pompidou Center, Paris, interior view. The image of a warehouse.

The Marine Biotechnological Building, in Baltimore.

I have already spoken of the zigzag space-frame towers designed in the 1950s by the students of Louis Kahn. While Kahn, in actual practice, never did anything so strange, he and Paul Rudolph sought forms in which vertical phallic elements dominate the facades of their buildings. In the Richards Medical Research Building at the University of Pennsylvania (see p. 121) and in the Yale Art and Architecture Building designed by Paul Rudolph, fire stairs and elevators have been grouped into dramatic towers that overpower the visual impact of the spaces actually used by people. Kahn attempted to justify this odd arrangement by means of a far-fetched rationalization of "slave" spaces and "master" spaces, but in the actual work it appears that the slaves are the masters.

Further examples can be found in the pages of any current architectural magazine. The archetypal principle of hierarchy is not so much misconceived as ignored in favor of a narrow rationality that too often proceeds from an error in judgment. To intuitively and correctly gauge the hierarchical position of a particular architectural element and accord it its proper place is to design in accordance with the principles of life and the nature of the universe. It is to search for the expression of the eternal harmonies that lie behind the multifaceted appearance of the world.

Kahn labeled the dwelling spaces in a building the "master spaces." He then proposed to group all other functions—mechanical, fire stairs, and elevators—in "slave" spaces that would be expressed in the exterior volumes of the building. This gave an architectural importance to the service functions and distorted the hierarchical principle in the work.

The Nature of Materials

When I attended Penn in the 1950s, students were required to take a course entitled "Materials and Methods of Construction." A similar course was taught at other major architectural schools. The materials that were the subject of the course, the steel and stone, the bricks and mortar, the glass and the thousand and one other materials used in building construction, were discussed only in terms of their physical characteristics. Textbooks and class lectures dealt with such matters as the properties of structural lumber, the compressive strength of various kinds of brick, and the steel shapes rolled by the mills. It was not realized then, nor is it now, that it is necessary to consider the archetypal and associative characteristics of materials as well.

There is, for instance, a chain of human relationship to stone that can be traced back to the beginning of culture, when the cave was shelter and stone the principal material used in making tools. Stone is an archetypal symbol of hardness, durability, and weight. We say "hard as a rock" and "heavy as stone." The logo of one of our largest insurance companies, Prudential, *is* a rock, and the company relies upon the image of durability and stability in its advertising.

Stonehenge, on the Salisbury Plain in England. The careful cutting and fitting of the uprights and lintels into cone and socket joints demonstrates that the builders could have carved a regular form and finished the surfaces if they had so wished. Evidently, however, these "Sarsen" stones that comprise the central group of this great monument were deliberately left as rough blocks. Whatever the intention of the builders, the nature of the material is beautifully expressed. (Photograph courtesy of Kristian H. Resset, Wikimedia Commons.)

We understand something of the physical properties of various kinds of stone, such as granite, limestone, marble, and sandstone. We know something of their geological history and how they were formed, but the ancients knew far more about their esoteric qualities. They went to astonishing lengths in order to provide particular kinds of stone for different locations and purposes. They must have been aware of obscure but significant differences that are now forgotten. The bluestones of the Stonehenge outer circle, for instance, were brought from as far away as Wales, while the Egyptians ignored nearby quarries to bring red granite from Aswan, 500 miles south along the Nile. In the great pyramid of Teotihuacán, near Mexico City, a thick layer of mica was uncovered; no one now knows what it was used for, but it came from faraway Brazil!

Within the limits of our present knowledge, we do know that stone is *heavy*, very heavy, and a wall built of stone is apt to collapse unless it is relatively wide in relation to its height. We know this not only intuitively but as a result of our own experience as well. Most of us have played with rocks and stones as children, and we have also seen many a crumpled pasture wall in an old abandoned field. In Modern architecture, however, we routinely misuse our materials, particularly stone and brick.

Old stone pasture wall in Hartford County, Maryland.

A friend who had bought a stone house erected in the 1950s recently asked me for architectural advice. The masonry work was excellent and the material was a hard and durable quartzite. The builder, however, had constructed broad bands of windows—one was over twenty feet long—that were surmounted by another four or five feet of stone wall. The practice of suspending large areas of brick or stone above a band of windows is now so commonly seen in large steel-and-concrete buildings that it no longer attracts comment or notice. Seeing it in a private home makes one realize that such construction defies logic and experience. A mass of masonry placed above a void without apparent support looks wrong and there is nothing that can be done to make it look right.

A mile from where I live, a large and impressive house by the Bauhaus teacher and architect Marcel Breuer features an exterior, unglazed "window" set in a stone garden wall much like the one in the previous example. The effect is equally disturbing.

This willful misuse of material was a common error shared by the leaders of the Modern movement. The stone walls of the Barcelona Pavilion, for instance, are actually thin walls of steel framing upon which a cladding of marble sheets has been hung. The pavilion is unusual only in that the height and placement of the wall make it appear to be extraordinarily thin, solid masonry: the practice of using stone as a veneer on the face of a steel or reinforced-concrete structure is commonplace. The

The interior courtyard of a stone-and-glass house in Baltimore County, Maryland, designed by Marcel Breuer. The builder of the stone house cited above could have derived the idea from this nearby Breuer building.

stone is used for its durability and for its emotional associations, but to haul it aloft and tie it to the structural members of a high-rise office building indicates a fundamental misunderstanding of the archetypal image of the material.

Brick and concrete are different types of artificial stone. Concrete block is cheaper than brick, and since its invention, most masonry walls have been made of block faced with brick. There is some deception in this practice, but at least the walls are all masonry. It is, however, possible to lay up bricks as a thin 3½-inch skin, braced by metal ties to a wall of wood or steel. "Brick" houses of the last fifty years have typically been built using this combination of a single thickness of brick with a wooden wall. Over time, the structural stability of such composite construction has been questioned, but the psychic disharmony resulting from the misuse of the material is not even considered.

For the last century, brick has been applied routinely to surface the facades of large structures framed in steel or concrete. A recent fashion has seen the construction of buildings with a skin of brick applied adja-

cent to a glass curtain wall in such a way that the fragility of the brick skin is evident. This kind of architectural stunt derives its effect from the deliberate violation of an archetypal image.

Together with stone and brick, wood has been used for millennia in every possible way. It has been used structurally, as a facing on both the interior and the exterior of buildings, as roofing, and for floors. It is infinitely variable, in species, in the characteristics of the individual tree, and in how it was cut from the original plant. A good carpenter loves his material and always seeks to recognize the characteristics of the various pieces of wood with which he works.

Wood once grew as a living tree, and we recognize this fact when we speak of the "warmth" of wood and seek to incorporate its beauty into objects of daily use. Through the use of wood we renew our ties to the forest and the world of plants upon which our lives depend. Wood, therefore, may engender archetypal associations that go far beyond the structural values of wood understood only as lumber. In the construction of a Japanese teahouse, a small building dedicated to

In the Barcelona Pavilion, Mies van der Rohe chose to express a deliberate contradiction between what seem to be load-bearing stone walls and the actual, steel-column supports of the roof. And then we find that the stone walls are not really stone, but present only the appearance of stone! The building begins to resemble a conjuring trick, as do many of its successors.

Brick is here used to give the impression of a thin, unsupported skin *over* a part of the glass. GBMC Physicians Building in Baltimore County, Maryland.

the ritual preparation and consumption of tea, one wooden post was always prominently placed and left unfinished, just as it was cut from the tree.

Metals such as gold, silver, lead, copper, and bronze were known and used in antiquity and even assigned astrological significance. Today, gold alone retains some of its ancient meaning. Gold was the metal of the sun and we still find it beaten into thin leaves and appropriately applied as gilding on domes. Iron and steel, aluminum, glass in large sheets, and plastics are materials that became widely available after the Industrial Revolution. The wealth of associations and the depth of personal experience through which we relate to stone and wood are not present when we consider these relatively new materials. However, even now we are collectively developing the chain of associations through which we will come to an unconscious and intuitive comprehension of these materials, as well as the more familiar ones of our experience.

Materials *must* be understood as having not only a material significance but a psychic one as well. Stone is not just stone and wood is not just wood. Each material, more particularly those with which we, as a species with a living and continuing tradition, have used through past millennia, possesses an esoteric and archetypal significance that we can comprehend through meditation and introspection.

I remember Louis Kahn speaking to his studio class one day when I was at Penn. He was talking about the misuse of materials that he had recognized in the design of one of his students and repeated several times, "A brick wants to be a brick!" It didn't make sense to the class then and probably wouldn't now, a *brick* wanting to be a brick! Yet it makes perfect sense if *we* want a brick to be a brick. And we do. We want, or expect, that materials will be used not only according to their weight and measure, but according to their symbolic and archetypal significance, their psychic meaning, as well.

To recognize the psychic significance of materials is to forever reject the kind of gross misuse that has become so common that it is considered acceptable. It is to design with a reverence for the materials that have come from the earth and have been shaped by human intent. It is to establish a harmony with the earth and the cosmos.

9

THE RESOLUTION OF FORM

Form and Function

The archetypal concepts discussed in the preceding section arise into awareness through both the individual and collective psyches. A work of architecture cannot be successful unless they are accepted and become a part of the design. But architects must also study the way in which the biological needs for shelter are to be met: the mundane characteristics of materials, the technical means available to construct the building, and finally the architectural program. These, too, are requirements that must be recognized, considered, and satisfied within the fabric of the building.

Since all of these psychic and mundane demands, needs, and requirements may be satisfied in an infinite number of ways, they do not alone determine the form of a building and the form of the spaces its walls define. The form also functions to communicate the temporal experience and the spiritual insight of its architect, and it is this that constitutes the organizing principle. Put in a different way, form embodies principle, and principle is based on the personal history of an individual architect, a knowledge of space and time, which is both a priori and learned, and an intuitive insight into harmony and proportion that is the basis of beauty. It is the synthesis of inspired principle and technical means that operates within the definition of form to create that which we call great architecture.

Testing a dome section, Geodesics, Inc., Raleigh, North Carolina, 1955. Fuller taught that the form of a building evolved from the objective, impersonal analysis of the structure and the utilitarian function. It wasn't that simple—even for Fuller.

Form: the observable consequence of pattern in space. A cat is a vital form; a triangle is an abstract or ideal form.[1]

—JOHN ANTHONY WEST

133

Architects, by the nature of their craft, and by the necessities of their social role, are supposed to express, in the definition of solid and void, and in the reality of material construction, that which is beautiful and true. In the search for beauty in form, the contemporary scientific architect has been misled and effectively hobbled by his adherence to the outworn materialist definition of reality, and by a naive and misleading concept of function.

"Form follows function" was a rallying cry of the Modern architects who led the way into the acceptance of the International Style. The aphorism is attributed to Louis Sullivan, the great Chicago architect, but it apparently originated with Horatio Greenough, an American sculptor, writer, and art critic. Greenough wrote in the early part of the nineteenth century, but his ideas go back even further to the Enlightenment, and to Edmund Burke and David Hume. Burke and Hume proved to the satisfaction of their peers and their Utilitarian successors such as Jeremy Bentham and Count Rumford that form had no inherent meaning.

Sullivan, who was a master of color and ornament, understood the slogan to refer to the psychic or spiritual functions, as well as to the mundane requirements of a building. His scientific successors, however, in accordance with the doctrine of the materialist paradigm, recognize only simple utilitarian functions as the appropriate basis of architectural design. This brings them face to face with the puzzling problem of the place of "aesthetics," of which I have spoken in discussing the architectural schools.

An architecture limited to the resolution of *utilitarian* functions denies any significance to architecture as art other than that of titillating the undefined "aesthetic sense" of the observer. Yet, as we have seen, it is this same aesthetic sense upon which much of the studio courses at the schools are based, and upon which much of the professional standing of practicing architects is determined.

An ideological gap, therefore, exists between aesthetics and utilitarian functionalism, and in response "architectural theory" developed as a separate discipline within academia in the latter half of the twentieth century. Architectural theorists, with few exceptions, are fully committed to the materialist paradigm, and therefore must tacitly agree that aesthetics are peripheral to the real purpose of construction, which is seen to be that of providing utilitarian shelter. Most maintain that form should be based upon the logical analysis of the purely material functions of a proposed building. The theoretical literature that has appeared over the last half century reflects this view, as it seeks to define a philosophical basis for the method of design taught in schools and advocated in the profession.

Since the architectural revolution, the functions to be considered by a Modern, scientific architect have been held to be those limited to the biological necessities of the human organism on the one hand and the technology of enclosure on the other. Styles have come and gone, but the same approach, labeled "biotechnical determinism," underlies them all. Its more extreme advocates maintain that through the application of ever sharper tools of analysis and logical determination, the form of a building will emerge as an objective reality, without the intuitive or egoistic involvement of an individual architect. The examples cited in support of this idea are taken mostly from the various engineering disciplines. Objects such as ships, locomotives, aircraft, and bridges are said to have emerged from these without the intervention of either the aesthetic intuition or a preconceived mental image or pattern fixed by prior experience. While some architects and theorists feel that buildings should somehow express ideals such as political responsibility, gender equality, and income redistribution, the search for beauty in form is considered irrelevant.

Beauty is recognized neither as an objective value nor as an architectural goal. Those qualities that tradition defines as "beauty" are expected to proceed naturally from the complete analysis of the program and the logical conclusions drawn by the designer. In its extreme form, reliance on both personal intuition and the knowledge of an array of typical forms that can be adapted or directly applied to a new use are rejected as incompatible with the process of scientific analysis and resolution.

The exemplar of the biotechnical approach is often held to be R. Buckminster Fuller, the inventor of the geodesic dome and the octet truss. Fuller's work was and is widely misunderstood, not least of all by Fuller. I remember a conversation in 1958 with Jerry Batey, one of the young designers working for Fuller at the offices of Geodesics, Inc., in Raleigh, North Carolina. Jerry could not see any logical reason why a geodesic configuration should be superior to a lesser circle configuration, and later went on to successfully build lesser circle domes for the Spitz Planetarium Company. Logically, Jerry was right, but the lesser circle domes were never as beautiful as the geodesic ones. It was only years later that I realized that Fuller's domes were beautiful because they exemplified an a priori mathematical truth that was only distantly related to the biotechnical analysis of the architectural problem. The existence of such a truth could only be denied by the architectural theorists, since in accordance with the principles laid down in the eighteenth century by Burke and Hume, forms, no matter how they are derived, are held to have no significance in themselves.

Alan Colquhoun, a well-known architect and theorist, quotes designer and educator Tomas Monaldo, who admitted at a seminar held at Princeton University that in cases where it is not possible to classify every observable activity in an architectural program, it might be necessary to use a typology of forms in order to arrive at a solution.[2] But he added that these forms were like a cancer in the body, and that as our techniques of classification become more systematic, it should be possible to eliminate them altogether. I assume that the quotation accurately reflects Monaldo's thought. In any case, it is unfortunately consistent with the attitude of those materialists who embrace the biotechnical position.

The Post-Modern architects and theorists of the latter part of the twentieth century have rebelled at the rigidity and emptiness of the bio-technical approach. They have sought an architecture that through language, symbols, and historical allusion would convey meaning. But they all agree that our reaction to the various shapes and spaces that we experience as architecture is learned behavior, grounded in the social situation. To these theorists, a key word has become *semiology*, the science of signs, whereby a building, itself a decorated shed bereft of significant form, is to communicate its reason for being. And in the absence, or rather the exclusion, of the Divine, architectural theory has sought to locate an appropriate ethic in the interaction between the architect and the social context within which the work has been produced. A building is thus intended to comment, by means of its decorative trappings, on its social and political context, as well as on other buildings. This "ethical function of architecture" (the title of Karsten Harries's book) in this context represents a humanism in which the spark of Divinity, that most vital element of the human being, is ignored.

Architects do not and cannot work in the way that the scientific functionalists propose. Nor can they successfully apply a pastiche of signs, symbols, and pre-Modern ornament to a utilitarian shed.

In the process of design, architects gather as much information as they can about the way in which a building or building complex will be used. They become aware of the constraints of structure, the available construction techniques, the control of climate, the nature of the available materials, and the predisposition of clients. To assume that this information will somehow organize itself into a coherent form requires a leap of faith that is not only *un*scientific but illogical as well.

There are an infinite number of ways in which functional determinants may be winnowed out by the process of analysis and resolution. And there are an infinite number of ways in which they may be incorporated into an architectural form. How, then, are they to determine the form of a building?

The difficulty has been admitted by some theorists, who propose to fill the gap between function and form with a reliance upon personal intuition. The significant functions are supposedly seized upon intuitively by the designer and comprehensively organized in terms of the relative importance of a hierarchy of forms to express the purpose and meaning of a building. In chapter 6 we have seen that intuition is, indeed, an essential part of any artistic creation, but in the search for form, intuition requires guidance. Without understanding its place in the phenomenon of mind, it may all too often be misused, and lead to an egoistic eccentricity. In any event, the admission of intuition creates an additional problem for the theorists in that intuition lacks a "rational" explanation and is therefore regarded with scientific distrust. Moreover, forms derived through intuition may or may not be related to the logical analysis of biotechnical functions.

The effect of contemporary architectural theory has been to confuse and obfuscate the real issue, which is that an architecture dedicated to the reflection of a higher reality is incompatible with our material science. The new academic discipline, nevertheless, has been highly successful, but not in the sense that it has provided insight or guidance to students or practitioners. It has been successful as a scholastic enterprise, winning scholarly approval, grants, and the support of the educational establishment. The theorists have found an apparently impregnable position in this particular ivory tower. Their texts are written in a dense and specialized jargon that is impenetrable without a sustained effort on the part of the average reader to decipher them. It is a well-known, if regrettable, fact that few architects read more than the captions in the architectural periodicals. They are, after all, visually oriented by aptitude and training. They are unlikely to study the dismal writings of the theorists, unless, as was the case with Venturi, they are presented with some sort of catchy flair and they deal with their immediate concerns.

The theories of functional determinism are clearly inappropriate and misleading: at best they lead to buildings that reflect the proper concerns of engineers. The various other "isms" that followed Modernism have, one by one, come to a dead end or been subsumed by the commercial culture. But in their search for forms expressive of beauty, grace, and that indefinable quality of greatness, where are architects to turn for inspiration? As for the slogan "Form follows function," if the supreme function of architecture—and all the other arts—is that of opening the mind to higher levels of understanding and awareness, the aphorism is valid only in a limited sense. It is valid in that the material functions of a building are the *parameters* within which an architect must search intuitively for the expressive power, the beauty, and the deeper significance of the architectural form.

The sentence below was not carefully selected but taken more or less at random from the pages of a collection of essays on architectural theory:

"Architecture's urban vocation was theorized in this structuralist-formalist discourse as a liberal reconciliation of heterogeneity and autonomy or of fragmented individual forms and events against a coordinating grammatical ground which in its canonical form, that of Colin Rowe's 'collage city,' manifested itself both physically and conceptually in a planimetric grid."[5]

Architectural theory remains unread and continues to flourish since, in the absence of a transcendental architectural ethic, it is reassuring to students, faculty, and administration, and to actual practitioners as well, to know that the theorists are there, supporting what is universally taught and commonly accepted.

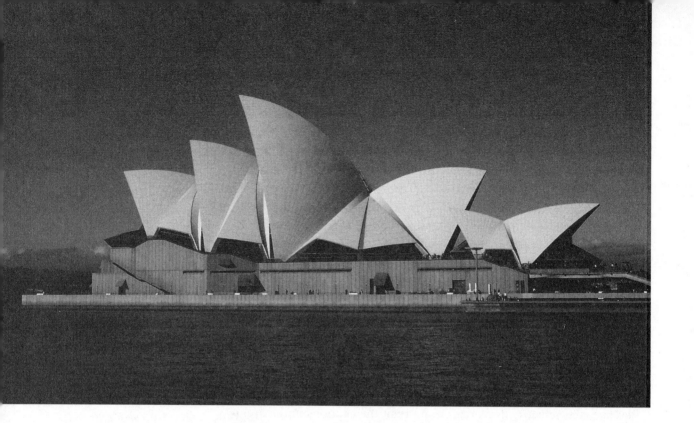

The Search for Form

The Sydney Opera House, in Australia, a form of a "fantastic or unusual kind," was to have been an example of the then technically daring and fashionable concrete-shell construction. It could not be built as designed and, at huge expense, the shell form was imitated in standard concrete construction. In spite of this fiasco, the building was praised lavishly by the critics and the press. It is also popular with the general public, which detests glass boxes and responds to a romantic image. (Photograph courtesy of Enoch Lau, Wikimedia Commons, GNUFDL license.)

It is widely accepted, even by architectural theorists, that as architects search for forms that satisfy the functional requirements discussed above and are aesthetically pleasing—perhaps even beautiful—they must rely upon the intuitive knowledge held in the unconscious mind. But intuition requires some measure of direction; it needs a field, as it were, within which it can operate to crystallize the imagination. In a flash of intuitive insight, a great artist or architect may in the manner of a Mozart visualize a synthesis that transforms disparate functions into beauty. Yet even a Mozart must be supported in his art by the system of expression, the widely accepted meanings associated with certain formal structures or patterns by which the intentions of the artist become comprehensible, to others and to himself.

In the jargon of contemporary architectural theory, this has been called "relying upon a typology of forms." In this context it means adapting formal arrangements of the past to the functional problems of the present, and thus achieving a continuity of expression. Historically, the knowledge of a "typology of forms" was an essential part of the skills of an architect, and when architectural design was directed through the inherited forms of the past, the changes in style appeared incrementally. Architecture was, until the architectural revolution, a communal effort, proceeding in time through centuries and evolving through the creative efforts of many individuals. The revolution aborted the process and limited the available prototypical models to Modern or Post-Modern buildings of the immediate past. Contemporary architects thus find themselves riffling through back issues of architectural magazines, looking for some novel form that could be made to fit the utilitarian requirements of a proposed building.

Forms selected in this way are seldom adopted without changes: No two programs or sites are the same, and change is valued for its own sake, since contemporary architects are taught they must be "creative." Creativity, however, is rarely involved in a synthesis of the spiritual and temporal functions discussed in the preceding chapter, but rather in the choice of the model, the success of the adaptation, and whatever novel twist may be given to the project. And in actual practice, the structural and mechanical engineers are left to struggle with the so-called biotechnical functions after a form has been selected.

Those identified as leading architects or architectural firms have a somewhat different problem. While they may pay lip service to the principle of biotechnical function, their need to be different, to be continuously "interesting," and to justify their eminence is more pressing. As "leaders" they are unable to borrow freely from readily identified predecessors and are forced to seek novel forms. These forms have also been derived, but not from recent buildings, nor from the natural forms of shells, minerals, and plants.

They are derived from sources like machines, manufactured products, and models of obscure mathematical equations. The latest round of museums and concert halls designed for the cultural establishment reflects various modes in abstract sculpture and painting. The influential architect and theorist Robert Venturi and his associate Denise Scott Brown have even recommended that architects turn to Pop culture, Las Vegas, and the "A&P parking lot" for inspiration.[3]

Forms thus derived may or may not be related to biotechnical functions, or, indeed, any function at all. Colquhoun, for instance, points out that, paradoxically, "in most of the projects where form determinants are held to be technical or operational in an avant-garde sense, rationalism and cost are discarded for forms of a fantastic or expressionist kind."[4]

In other words, function as the determinant of form in such projects is abandoned, and the form, however derived, is presented as the expression of an individual ego. Such forms, widely hailed by the media, may or may not be beautiful, but beauty, in any case, lies beyond the

The contemporary architect and engineer Santiago Calatrava says that he derives the forms of his buildings and bridges from his observations of natural forms, particularly palm trees. Perhaps this is so, but even in his "palm tree designs" there is a striking resemblance to the plastic combs that women now use to pin up their hair.

The Rosenthal Center for Contemporary Art in Cincinnati by Zaha Hadid. The center received the usual glowing review granted buildings on the "cutting edge"—in this case by Paul Goldberger in *New Yorker* magazine.[6] But the form is clearly nonfunctional. It has been derived from twentieth-century abstract painting and sculpture and is deliberately dissonant within its urban environment. (Photograph courtesy of Roland Halbe, 2002.)

scope of the functionalist theory and the materialist philosophy that lies behind it.

The personal and idiosyncratic forms evolved by architectural leaders and imitated by their less famous contemporaries are not long lasting. In the search for the novel and "interesting," such forms, even if they are powerful and expressive, or even beautiful, are quickly discarded in favor of those that are more immediately fashionable. The International Style, with all its faults, was a fully articulated style, but since the rise of Post-Modernism and its successors, a widely intelligible style such as Gothic or Renaissance has never had a chance to crystallize.

The continuity of architectural tradition has been shattered, and the efforts of Post-Modern architects to use classical motifs as decoration to enliven the cold facades of scientific modernism have been unconvincing and unsuccessful. A new architectural style is required, based on forms and ornaments that will arise from the interplay of climate, materials, and technique with the psychic insights of the artist. Within such a style, creativity could proceed naturally and spontaneously. The forms of the past, even the recent past, would no longer need to be adapted to fit a foreign function, but would be set free to serve as inspiration to the achievements of the present.

The style should be both local and universal. It should be local in that it will respond to regional environments and indigenous traditions and universal in that the underlying principles should be everywhere the same. It cannot be the product of a single organizing mind. It must, rather, emerge and evolve as it becomes widely understood that the idea of function goes beyond the concerns of simple biotechnical materialism.

The creative architects who formulate the new style must go beyond utilitarian and technical knowledge to an awareness of the complex of experiential associations and symbolic meanings that lie behind the visible form. They will, as they must, rely upon intuition to synthesize disparate functions into form. Buildings created within such a new vocabulary would necessarily be decent, comprehensible, and satisfactory as human shelter, but we must remember that there is still no assurance that they will possess the indefinable qualities of beauty and truth. Beauty would continue to depend upon the skill and intuition of the individual architect, an intuition that is now undirected and uninformed by any guiding principle other than a destructive personal egotism. Great architecture, however, must satisfy universal archetypal and instinctive demands of the psyche.

Architects once had an unfailing "touch" whereby they were able to imbue even the least of their buildings with creative fire. What has happened to that touch? How was it lost in the age of scientific materialism? We now wonder at the beauty of buildings such as the Ephrata Cloister and ask ourselves what the anonymous architect knew that we have forgotten. Can we, in this age of rampant materialism, recover some of the principles that guided his hand?

We can! The message of the past is everywhere the same: There is an objective basis that underlies the great architecture of every culture and

A hodgepodge of Post-Modern ornament in the Sainsbury Wing of the National Gallery of Art, London, 1991. Venturi, Rauch, and Scott Brown were the architects. It is difficult to imagine what was in their minds when the Doric columns, paste-on arches, and arches that are not arches were assembled. Do they represent an honest if misguided attempt to satisfy the desire of the client to link stylistically the new wing and the old building? Or do they constitute a cynical comment on the folly of expecting any kind of integrity in what Venturi would call a "decorated shed"?

Frank Lloyd Wright sought, over an exceptionally long lifetime, to create a personal vocabulary of space and form, but although he had his own school of followers, he was unable to effectively communicate his vision.

The Ephrata Cloister was built in southern Pennsylvania in 1741–1743 by Conrad Beissel (1691–1768) and his followers. Beissel was a musician, and the "solitary," as the celibate brothers and sisters were called, found God in the comprehension of harmony and melody. Their intuitive grasp of the archetypal mathematics of music is expressed in the serene beauty of their buildings.

every age, and that basis is mathematics. It is not, however, the familiar, scientific mathematics of pure quantity. The work of many scholars, architects, archaeologists, and, above all, brilliant amateurs has established beyond question that the essential principles upon which the great buildings of antiquity were erected are to be found in the *esoteric* comprehension of number and geometry. These are the principles that have been lost in the age of the materialist paradigm, and it is these principles that our architects must understand and recapture if they are to construct buildings worth comparing to those of the past.

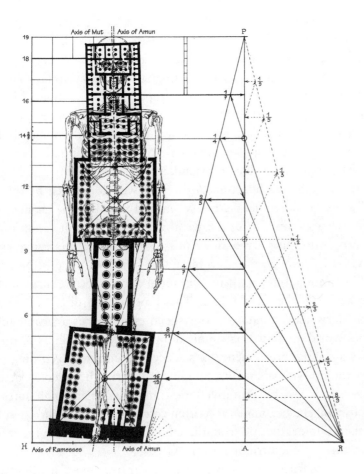

Axis of Mut | Axis of Amun

Axis of Ramesses | Axis of Amun

Schwaller de Lubicz here demonstrates how the mathematical ratios of the human body are incorporated into the design of the great Temple of Luxor, Egypt, the Temple of Man.[7] (Image courtesy of Inner Traditions International, Rochester, Vermont.)

The Mathematical Basis of Architecture

The ancient numerical and geometric sciences and the art and architecture of antiquity were founded upon a conviction that man and Cosmos were one, and the structure of our minds reflected the structure of the universe. The old adage "Know thyself" thus represents the practical application of this identity: Through self-knowledge, through introspection and meditation, one can know God. Works of art sought to express the ultimate harmony of the cosmos, and something of this harmony was understood to be comprehensible to man through mathematics.

In this ancient tradition, which may go back to the beginnings of human awareness, number and geometrical form are archetypal metaphors for the structure of the universe, and the laws of geometry are the actual laws by which the universe is organized. In recent years, careful measurements have revealed that the buildings of antiquity were established across the world and through the millennia upon an identical canon of number, geometry, and proportion—the same canon that underlies the great cathedrals of the twelfth and thirteenth centuries! In the architecture of today, that canon is forgotten or ignored, and even the idea that there could *be* a canon, or any system of number and geometry that would have objective significance, is never considered.

Yet the great architecture of the past was dominated by the forms and ratios of sacred geometry! When and how did the change occur? Under what circumstances did we abandon the ancient canon of order and proportion to pursue an eventually trivial and ineffective egocentric vision? Although the deathblow was struck in the post-Newtonian world of rational materialism, a gradual decline seems, surprisingly, to have begun in the *distant* past. This long decline directly contradicts the modern understanding of our social evolution as a steady advance from a world inhabited by simple hunter-gatherer peasants to one that enjoys a unique preeminence in science and culture. According to this conventional wisdom, civilization evolved through the construction of villages, followed by primitive cities, and finally national states were established. The beginning of written communication occurred in Egypt and the Middle East, and from there humanity advanced to the rational, analytical thought attributed to the Greeks.

The scenario is obviously wrong, for the most mathematically advanced and complex monument of which we know within our purview is the Great Pyramid at Giza, built at least 4,650 years ago at what is believed to be the dawn of civilization. Even in ruins, stripped of its polished white limestone casing, it is awesome. Before the ninth-century act of vandalism that left it as it is today, it must have been totally astounding, like some post–space age artifact, a pure, huge, gleaming form in the desert. And we still do not even know why or for what purpose it was built!

Although some parts of the mathematical and technical knowledge that made the Great Pyramid possible were retained in Egypt and employed in the construction of the unsurpassed architecture of that country, the pyramid has never been equaled, and a steady decline in quality occurred through the following millennia. Nevertheless, enough of this knowledge remained to inspire Pythagoras and Plato, and the Alsatian scholar R. A. Schwaller de Lubicz was able to deduce the basis of the design system through his study of the Temple of Luxor, built

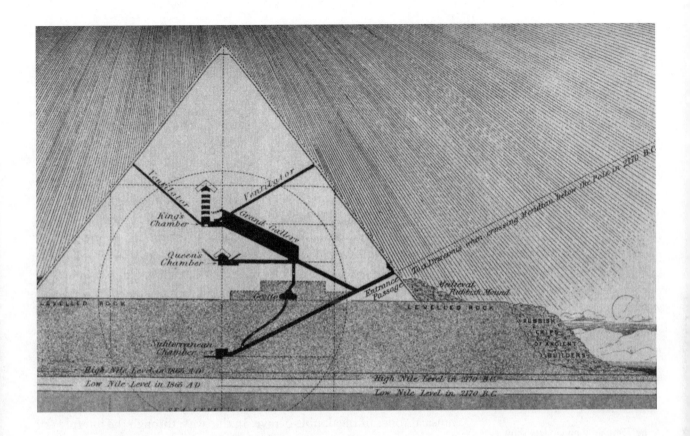

1,500 years after the accepted date for the construction of the pyramid. According to Schwaller, an institution he called "The Temple" had preserved the essential information, and continued to preserve and disseminate it to Greece and Rome until the coming of Roman Christianity and the final destruction of the Egyptian religion.

Some of the ancient knowledge either was preserved in the West, through the Dark Ages, or was reintroduced from the Near East, where it had been preserved under Islam, for it burst forth in a wholly unprecedented way in the twelfth and thirteenth centuries. Not only the great cathedrals, but also hundreds of lesser churches, together with bridges, halls, fortifications, and other structures, were erected all across France, and to a lesser extent in other European countries as well. This was one of the greatest public-works undertakings, relative to the size of the population, of which we have knowledge. The artistry of these buildings, particularly that of the cathedrals, reflects the same advanced knowledge of the esoteric significance of number and geometry that had characterized the works of ancient Egypt.

While contemporary archaeologists resolutely hold to the "tomb and tomb only" theory, there is no evidence that the Great Pyramid in Egypt was ever used to house a corpse. No one really knows why it was built or even how it could have been constructed. The drawing above appeared in *The Great Pyramid*, first published by the Victorian scholar Piazzi Smith in 1880.[8]

145

The moving force behind this immense building boom seems to have been the Knights Templar and the Brotherhood of Solomon, the mysterious group of craftsmen who built for the Templars. The Templars were based in the East and had direct knowledge of the remains of the great civilizations of the eastern Mediterranean. The esoteric knowledge could, therefore, have been transmitted by them. The destruction of the Templars by Philip IV of France with the connivance of the pope and the revocation of the special privileges granted the Brotherhood coincided with the beginning of a period of architectural and economic decline that was only arrested two centuries later in the Italian Renaissance.

By then, much had been lost; how or why we do not know. The buildings of the later Gothic period lack the geometric simplicity and authority of their predecessors, and the early Renaissance architects no longer possessed the understanding of Phi, the golden proportion, although they retained and used the square root of two. By the time of Andrea Palladio,[9] even that irrational root was regarded with distrust. Palladio indicated that square rooms might be extended by the length of the diagonal, but in actual practice he would admit into his canon of proportion only those ratios that were found in the system of musical harmony. Within this limited canon he achieved remarkable results. Palladio used whole-number ratios in architecture as analogues to the musical tones of the double octave. In this way, through the interplay of number and proportion, he was able to create buildings and spaces that were harmonious and, even in their complexity, symphonic.

Palladio's system was unfortunately reduced to a formula by his followers. And after Isaac Newton, with the publication of the *Principia Mathematica,* the theory upon which the architecture of the later Renaissance rested was gradually abandoned. There was no place in Newton's mechanical universe, the world of Burke and Hume, for the tradition of sacred geometry and the esoteric meaning of number. Even the identity of number in tones and space, and the interweaving of ratios into melodic and harmonic wholes, was dismissed by post-Enlightenment science as of little value. It was eventually lost to architecture as well, although architectural practice was, until recently, so conservative that some use of geometric principles persisted into the twentieth century through the influence of the Beaux Arts schools of France and their imitations in other countries.

With the advent of the new, scientific architecture and the birth of the International Style, even Beaux Arts disciplines were discarded, although Le Corbusier himself experimented with Phi.[10] He was evidently fascinated with the generative power of the root, but failed to see

The Templar commandery shown above is located on a minor road between Chartres and Orléans. It is maintained by the French government.

One of the four great staircases arranged in perfect symmetry around the famous Villa Rotunda in Vicenza, Italy. The monumental impact of this elegant private home designed by Andrea Palladio is as remarkable as the beautiful and harmonious proportions of every part of the structure.

its esoteric significance and actually attempted to establish the sacred function as the basis of a rational system of manufactured building components! Le Corbusier's attempt to use Phi essentially represented the end of the tradition. In our materialist world, mundane geometry as a part of a useful and logically rigorous mathematical science is still acceptable. It is taught in our public schools and is recognized as the means by which architects construct their plans. Sacred geometry, however, valued for the religious and philosophical insights that it might afford, is ignored by both architects and the larger society, or greeted with simple incomprehension.

Yet to any unprejudiced eye, the buildings of the pre-Modern world, designed when architects understood the esoteric meaning of geometry and number, are markedly superior to anything that we can now achieve. Geometry and number were then the means by which a building and all its separate parts attained balance and harmony. A building conceived and erected according to the principles of sacred geometry was intended to replicate the order of the universe and exert an immediate creative effect upon the human beings within its walls. The reality of the spiritual and emotional effects that were achieved cannot be doubted, for we still respond to the beauty of these buildings even when we find them in ruins. Chartres Cathedral, for example, is considered to be the greatest achievement of the medieval masons. Even in our materialistic age the pilgrims continue to come, no longer to worship the statue of the Black Virgin or to adore the reputed shift of the Virgin Mary, but simply to experience the wonder of standing within these walls.

It is astonishing that so little effort has been made by architects to understand how these sublime effects were achieved, much less to replicate the principles that made them possible. And when we have traced some of the ways geometry and number were used in the arts as the basis of the patterns of space and form that we find so beautiful, it is difficult for our logically conditioned minds to grasp our predecessors' philosophical approach to form and number. In sacred geometry and in arithmetic, which in its early form encompassed all numerical knowledge, geometric forms and their associated numbers were considered to have a meaningful association with both the world of sensory perception—which is the world of material reality—and the higher, spiritual world. Geometry and number were thus seen as archetypal symbols of the ultimate reality that encompassed the form of the cosmos and the purpose of existence. They were intermediaries between the human and the divine.

It is the philosophical understanding of what is rightly called "sacred" geometry that lies beneath the profound spiritual and emotional effects achieved in the buildings constructed by our ancient predecessors. In the buildings of the past, geometric forms and numbers were consciously manipulated by architects and carefully placed in association with other forms and numbers in order to express an insight into a higher truth. Such manipulation could not have proceeded from a basis of rational analysis, or even from a more profound and guided intuition. It must have been based on a systematic body of knowledge, a mathematical science of esoteric number and form. Architects today, in the absence of that knowledge, and relying upon their intuitive vision, may unconsciously incorporate the beauty of mathematical truth into their work, but to again create buildings that compare to those designed by our predecessors, we must acquire the systematic knowledge, the lost tradition, of the mathematics of form.

Is it possible to recapture the lost esoteric knowledge of geometry and number? Can we again design our buildings, cities, even our landscapes in accordance with the ancient canon? Fifty years ago the possibility, even the desirability, of doing so would have been denied. But now the certitudes of our belief in a mechanical universe are no longer with us, and in archetype and myth, in religion and philosophy, and even in science itself, we have begun to seek a deeper reality. As that reality is further explored and becomes an accepted part of our culture, esoteric mathematics will again be recognized as the basis of art and architecture.

Architects who have studied the esoteric significance of geometry and number, and comprehend the essential forms and ratios, are equipped with an awareness of the function of the mind itself. The patterns derived from this awareness are the patterns of the universal mind, and an architecture arising from sacred geometry will possess truth and beauty, for it will incorporate these patterns into material reality.

10
GEOMETRY AND NUMBER

Recovering the Ancient Tradition

The great temple of Luxor in Egypt was a half-buried ruin when seen across the river by Napoleon's soldiers as they marched up the west bank of the Nile. It was excavated and partly restored in the nineteenth and twentieth centuries and carefully studied for fifteen years by the alchemist and scholar R. A. Schwaller de Lubicz. From his studies, Schwaller was able to deduce the existence of a "sacred science" upon which ancient Egyptian architecture—and civilization—had been founded. The photograph above shows the temple as it appeared when Schwaller was alive. (Photograph courtesy of Inner Traditions International, Rochester, Vermont.)

Information concerning the esoteric meaning of geometry and number is not readily obtained, since it is neither valued in our society nor taught in our schools. Those who want to pursue the subject must rely upon the work of a few individuals who have dedicated much of their lives to its study. While knowledge of the ancient science has never been entirely lost, much of what we now know has come to us quite recently, principally through the work of R. A. Schwaller de Lubicz and his followers.[1] Schwaller de Lubicz has demonstrated that the numerical philosophy ascribed to Pythagoras, and upon which Plato's philosophy was based, was at a far earlier time known to the ancient Egyptians, and was an essential determinant of form in the unsurpassed architectural works of their civilization. When Plato and Pythagoras studied in Egypt, they learned their philosophy from a living tradition. Although that tradition no longer exists, in a remarkable intellectual feat Schwaller was able to reconstruct some of the ways in which the Pythagorean philosophy was applied to a building. At Luxor, his careful and detailed measurements revealed the existence of the underlying geometrical and symbolic principles on which the structure was based. He further deduced from his work at Luxor and elsewhere in Egypt the esoteric significance of numbers. The results of his studies have been made available in a massive two-volume work called *The Temple of*

Man,[2] as well as in a number of shorter books, but nothing less than a virtual revolution in our way of thinking is required before we can grasp the more abstruse ideas.

Though *The Temple of Man* remains the most comprehensive and profound exposition of the Pythagorean philosophy, those who seek the ancient knowledge may more readily approach the subject through the study of other books that have been written on the subject. *Serpent in the Sky: The High Wisdom of Ancient Egypt,* by John Anthony West, remains the most definitive, if not the only, work that has been able to make Schwaller's arcane and difficult interpretation of ancient Egyptian art and culture available to the average reader.[3] West not only introduces the reader in a clear and lucid style to the underlying philosophical basis of Schwaller's thought, but also provides a running commentary on the antics of conventional Egyptologists as they try to evade or negate the importance of his work.

Sacred Geometry: Philosophy and Practice, by Robert Lawlor,[4] dedicated to R. A. Schwaller de Lubicz and his stepdaughter Lucie Lamy, will be particularly valuable to architects and artists. Lawlor has wedded a penetrating discussion of the Pythagorean philosophical principles to a series of exercises in the construction of the most important geometric figures with straightedge and compasses. As the exercises are performed, the underlying principles are made clear. The brief introduction to the principles of sacred geometry here on pages 154–161 is based largely upon my own study of *Sacred Geometry.*

Those who delve into the ancient science will find that their first tentative efforts at incorporating meaningful geometric form into the design of a building can be astonishingly rewarding. With only a few principles in mind, architectural problems can be solved with remarkable and unexpected ease. The development of a design will sometimes flow of its own volition, and an architect will at times feel a curious detachment from the work, almost as if he were a spectator watching a dance of form and shape inadvertently set in motion. As architects proceed to free themselves from the preoccupations of ego and personality, they will visualize these formal patterns more clearly and, as for Mozart, the eternal truths and harmonies that are the basis of beauty will emerge.

Nor is the ancient science to be valued merely for the enhanced ability it affords in the creation of art. The diagrams, patterns, and numerical formulations of sacred geometry have a life of their own, and once they seize the imagination, they can lead in unexpected directions. The

R. A. Schwaller de Lubicz, perhaps the greatest philosopher of the twentieth century. (Photograph courtesy of Inner Traditions International, Rochester, Vermont.)

John Anthony West has led the fight to have Schwaller's ideas accepted.

mystic and seer Rudolf Steiner wrote of his experience as an elementary school student when a book on geometry fell into his hands:

> For weeks at a time my mind was filled with the coincidence, the similarity, of triangles, squares, polygons. I racked my brain over the question: Where do parallel lines actually meet? The theorem of Pythagoras fascinated me. That one can live within the mind in the shaping of forms perceived only within oneself, entirely without impression upon the external senses, became for me the deepest satisfaction. I found in this a solace for the unhappiness my unanswered questions had caused me. To be able to lay hold of something in the spirit alone brought me an inner joy. I am sure that I learned through geometry to know happiness for the first time.[5]

Obviously, there are few among us who possess the insight of even a young Rudolf Steiner, and we cannot expect the truth to fall so effortlessly into *our* hands. Robert Lawlor reminds us that Plato said the soul's fire must gradually be rekindled:

> You amuse me, you who are worried that I impose impractical studies upon you. It does not only reside in mediocre minds, but all men have difficulty in persuading themselves that it is through these studies, as with instruments, that one purifies the eye of the soul, and that one causes a new fire to burn in this organ which was obscured and as though extinguished by the shadows of the other sciences, an organ whose conservation is more important than ten thousand eyes, since it is by it alone that we contemplate the truth.[6]

Saint Bernard, the great Cistercian, has said: "What is God? He is length, width, height and depth."[7] It was Saint Bernard who provided the "rule" for the much maligned and heretical Knights Templar, the warrior monks of the Middle Ages. They in turn were closely associated with the Brotherhood of Solomon, the craft group who were the builders of the great cathedrals.

The Templars are believed to have been the financiers that made possible the construction of these mighty works. Modern Masons trace their origins at least as far back as the Templars and the Brotherhood. It is a curious fact that in the "Charge" to a successful candidate for the Second Degree of the Masonic Order we find, somehow preserved through the centuries, the following admonition:

In the wake of my first visit to Chartres, I found the books of John Anthony West and Robert Lawlor tremendously helpful: West's because it opened the door to an alternative culture with a different attitude to meaning and purpose in life and art; Lawlor's because it showed me how the Pythagorean philosophy of number and geometrical form could be applied to the practice of architecture. Without the work of these two men, I might not have found my way.

The "rule" was the code of behavior, dress, and diet and the regimen of daily life that governed a particular monastic society. It is significant that it was provided by St. Bernard, who corresponded with Abbot Suger, the builder of Saint-Denis, the first great church in the Gothic style.

The Apprentice Pillar in the interior of Rosslyn Chapel, seven miles south of Edinburgh. Rosslyn Chapel was constructed in the fifteenth century under Templar influence, but after the formal suppression of the Order. It is considered to be the last great Gothic building and is still revered by Masons. (Photograph courtesy of John Mullen, Wikimedia Commons.)

. . . the science of Geometry . . . is established as the basis of our art. Geometry or Masonry, originally synonymous terms, being of a divine and moral nature, is enriched with the most useful knowledge. While it proves the wonderful properties of nature, it demonstrates the more important truths of morality.[8]

At the "high noon" of Western architecture, reflection and meditation upon geometric form was evidently required of a master mason, the architect of that distant time, and was thought to make possible a measure of insight into the divine itself. I have found that even in our materialistic age, the ancient science may afford a sometimes terrifying glimpse into the eternal and infinite nature of existence.

I might have supposed that accepting a discipline of geometry and number would result in feelings of restriction and confinement. In fact, the opposite took place, and I experienced feelings of freedom and ease.

Principles of Sacred Geometry

The well-known Pearly Nautilus shell replicates exactly the form of the golden spiral, discussed on page 158.

A comprehensive or detailed explanation of the occult, or esoteric principles of sacred geometry, is certainly not within the scope of this book and I have already referred readers to the inspiring book by Robert Lawlor.[9] Here I can only provide a brief introduction to a way of thinking in which philosophical concepts are related to numbers and geometric forms. It is my hope that the interest of architects will be aroused and they will seek out Mr. Lawlor's book, take up the study of the ancient science, and incorporate its principles into their work.

The circle is not only the most basic geometric form: It is the symbol of undifferentiated unity, and in esoteric philosophy represents the cosmos prior to the fundamental creative moment when it divides in two. Schwaller de Lubicz found that in the system of ancient Egyptian thought, this was believed to be the single unique event that brought the universe into being.

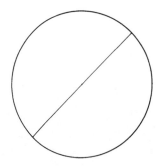

If the diameter of a circle is considered to be "one," the traditional number of Deity, the relation of the circumference to the diameter is a ratio called pi. This essential ratio is "irrational" in that it has no fractional expression. In other words, there is no number, no matter how small, that will evenly divide both parts. For computation we use 1: 3.1416, plus as many decimals as are required for a satisfactory approximation, but we have in no way succeeded in describing the ratio by a *number*. It is a "function" in that one quantity depends upon the other. The Pythagoreans referred to the irrational functions as "unutterable," a term that exactly describes the situation.

The circle is essential for the construction of other geometric figures. The instrument by which a circle is drawn, the compass or compasses, has long been venerated by the Masonic orders. In Western art, God the Creator is often shown with compasses in his hand.

Regular polygons are those that can be circumscribed: that is, drawn within a circle so that all the intersections of their equal sides touch the circumference. Similarly, the regular, or Platonic, solids are those in which the vertices of regular plane figures touch the surface of a sphere. In sacred or philosophical geometry, the circle is therefore the determinant of the archetypal form of both the regular polygons and the Platonic solids, and in the process of constructing these various figures, they may be seen to develop and grow from the circle.

When we draw a second, identical circle so that the center of each is on the circumference of the other, the area of overlap is called the Vesica Pisces (see page 156). The Vesica is a powerful archetypal form. It not only represents the link between the two circles: it also implies the existence of "three," namely the two circles and the Vesica they define in the area of overlap. Moreover, lines drawn connecting the centers of the circles with the intersections of the Vesica define equilateral triangles. Three is the smallest number of lines that can define a plane geometry figure, and the triangle is the most basic of the straight-line figures that comprise the regular polygons.

As additional Vesicae are drawn, a succession of polygons arises, beginning from the triangle, which unfolds to define the square, and proceeding through the pentagon, hexagon, octagon, decagon, and dodecagon. Robert Lawlor remarks that the form of this construction suggests the tree, with the initial Vesica representing the seed.[10]

The length of the vertical axis of the Vesica, by the Pythagorean theorem, is the square root of three, which is also the length of the diagonal of a cube with edge and side of one. If a series of Vesicae are drawn,

The circle and its diameter. The circle is always feminine: It represents the mother and the womb.

In sacred geometry, number means a ratio of integers, but in modern mathematics inexpressible quantities are called irrational numbers.

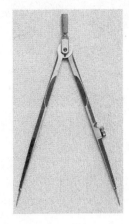

The compasses (as this instrument is known by the Masons). This one was made for me in 1954 by T. Alteneder & Sons in Philadelphia.

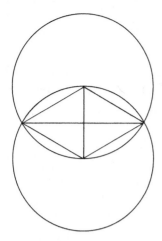

The fishlike shape of the Vesica was considered particularly significant in medieval art and architecture, since the fish was the zodiacal sign of the Piscean Age, the time of Jesus. In medieval art Jesus was often shown depicted seated in the Vesica, mediating between the two circles symbolizing God and man.

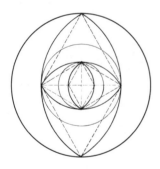

The Vesica Pisces progression.

alternating with their enclosed and enclosing circles, the relationship of their successive axes is that of a geometric progression wherein

$$1:\sqrt{3}::\sqrt{3}:3::3:3\sqrt{3}, \text{ also written as } \frac{1}{\sqrt{3}} = \frac{\sqrt{3}}{3} = \frac{3}{3\sqrt{3}}$$

Keith Critchlow has demonstrated in his study of the ruins of the once great Glastonbury Abbey that such a progression is the basis of the architectural design of Saint Mary's Chapel, built to enclose the site of the original mud-and-wattle church believed to have been founded by Joseph of Arimathea.[11] Jonathan Hale has shown the use of the Vesica in a little office building in Chelsea, Vermont, dated around 1825, where an ordinary structure in an urban street affords grace and repose through this geometric form.[12]

As the circle represents the original, vast, undifferentiated unity, the spirit and the sky, so do the square and the associated number four represent the earth, or the material order. The cross represents the square: a cross with equal arms defines a square, and Jesus upon the cross represents the perfect man crucified upon the square of materiality.

The square, considered as unity, is divided by the diagonal into two equal parts. The process is analogous to the primal act of creation, whereby the one (unity) becomes two, and the diagram is thus an expression of the act.

The ratio of the side to the diagonal by the Pythagorean theorem is one to the square root of two, written as $1:\sqrt{2}$. Since the diagonal is potentially the side of a larger square of twice the area, and the side is potentially the diagonal of a smaller square of one-half the area, the square may readily be transformed into a series of dimensions, infinitely large and infinitely small. Dimensions that thus oscillate between side and diagonal will inherently be in harmony, for they are all related by the square root of two.

The square is of particular significance to architects. The power of the form itself and the series of proportional, geometric dimensions that grow from it define a framework within which further invention may proceed. This principle is exemplified in the little Baptist Meeting House pictured on pages 81 and 166.

The double square, a rectangle consisting of two identical squares having a common edge, can be readily generated from the square. The ratio of the two sides of the rectangle is two to one and the diagonal is, again by the Pythagorean theorem, the square root of five, another irrational function.

The two-to-one ratio of the double square is related to music through the octave. If a note is sounded on a stretched string, and that string is then divided in half, the note sounded on either section of the string will be the same note, only one octave higher; in other words, as the length is halved, the frequency of vibration is doubled. This two-to-one ratio was considered to be the most important, next to that of unison (or one-to-one), by Saint Augustine, who was himself a musician. As a result of his influence and that of Saint Bernard, it is the ratio of the double square that dominates the design of the medieval cathedrals. Even the idea of "the four corners of the earth," prominent in medieval theology, did not refer to a square, but rather to a double, or two-to-one square.

From the double square, the marvelous and mysterious function written in our alphabet as *Phi* and customarily designated by the Greek letter Φ may readily be developed. Phi represents the only way in which a line segment of given length can be divided so that the ratio of the smaller part to the larger is equal to the ratio of the larger part to the whole. For example, in the diagram below, Phi = a/b = $(a + b)/a$ = 1.618 or, more precisely, 1.6180339.

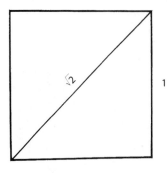

The square and its diagonal.

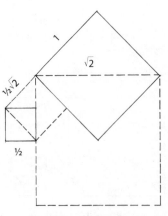

A sequence of squares.

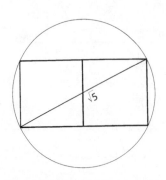

The double square. The idea of the earth as a flat double square was a vulgarization of the mystical understanding of the square as the symbol of material order.

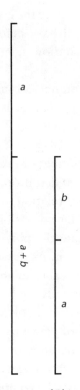

An illustration that represents the ratios of Phi—otherwise known as the golden proportion.

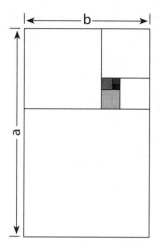

Successive golden rectangles and their squares.

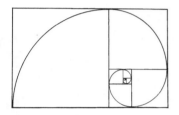

The golden spiral is generated from the succession of rectangles.

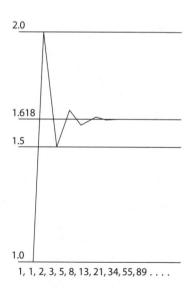

2.0

1.618

1.5

1.0

1, 1, 2, 3, 5, 8, 13, 21, 34, 55, 89 . . . .

The Fibonacci series and Phi. Note how rapidly the quotient of any two successive numbers approaches Phi as the numbers become larger.

This unique ratio, 1.618, an irrational function rather than a number, is called the *golden proportion*. It defines the architecturally significant *golden rectangle*, a rectangle in which the ratio of its long side to its short side is Phi.

As a consequence of the unique mathematical properties of this geometric figure, a square added or subtracted from the rectangle defines another golden rectangle. If successive rectangles, so generated, are connected in a continuous curve, they define a *golden spiral*, the form so well represented in nature by the Pearly Nautilus, shown on page 154.

The Phi function is intimately related to the Fibonacci series of numbers, named for the Renaissance mathematician who called attention to its properties. In a Fibonacci series, a number is selected: the next number in the series is the sum of that number and the preceding number. For instance, the most common series, beginning with one, is as follows: 1, 1, 2, 3, 5, 8, 13, 21, 34, 55, 89, 144, and so on. It is a remarkable fact that in a Fibonacci series, any number divided by the preceding number yields an approximation of Phi, which becomes more exact as the numbers grow larger.

Through the Fibonacci series we see the golden proportion expressed as number in nature. As I write, I have before me the seed head of a common, commercially grown sunflower, purchased at random from the local farmers market.

I have carefully counted the number of intersecting spiral rows that determine the location of the individual seeds. There are 55 to the right and 89 to the left. As seen above, these are Fibonacci numbers, and 89 divided by 55 gives the number 1.618182, a close approximation of Phi, which is 1.618034 at the same number of decimals. Such an experience of the pervasive presence of the golden proportion in natural phenomena forcefully calls attention to our relation to the world of numbers and the form that lies beneath the surface of visible things.

It is impossible to overestimate the philosophical and architectural importance of the golden proportion. As the information presented here can only begin to describe this magical ratio, members of the lay public as well as architects are urged to carefully study chapter 5, Proportion and the Golden Section, in Robert Lawlor's book *Sacred Geometry*. Johannes Kepler, the discoverer of the laws of planetary motion, is often quoted as saying, "Geometry has two great treasures: one is the theorem of Pythagoras, the other the division of a line into mean and extreme ratios, that is, the golden proportion. The first may be compared to a measure of gold, the second to a precious jewel."[13]

Sunflower seed head, the organic design of which is composed of Fibonacci numbers.

It is evident from the remains of the great buildings of antiquity that the golden proportion has been known and applied to architecture and allied arts since the beginning of civilization. It is found not only in the ancient architecture of India and of Egypt, Mesopotamia, Greece, and Rome, but also in that of China and Japan, and even in pre-Columbian Mexico. The double square, favored in medieval Europe, is related to the golden rectangle through the $\sqrt{5}$ diagonal. The golden rectangle itself persists in the great medieval cathedrals: in Chartres Cathedral, for instance, it becomes the shape that defines the passage of the aisles. It was prominent in the art of the Renaissance, and continued to exert some influence over architectural design until the final demise of Beaux Arts education. It is only in our time, the time of the materialist paradigm, that the golden proportion has been relegated to the status of a mathematical curiosity and the ancient subject of sacred geometry itself, with its vast philosophical and religious implications, ignored by both architects and the larger society.

Not only the golden proportion, but all of the basic forms described above possess a characteristic group of esoteric associations. Each stands

An aisle at Chartres Cathedral.

for a complex of intuitive wisdom. It is a remarkable fact that the key ratios pi, Phi, and the roots $\sqrt{2}$, $\sqrt{3}$, and $\sqrt{5}$ involved in the description of these basic archetypal forms are all "irrational." They cannot, therefore, be captured in the web of numbers or described in words. They are, as the Pythagoreans said, "unutterable," and yet they can be perfectly visualized through geometry. Some idea of the esoteric significance of these "functions" may be obtained through Robert Lawlor, who writes:

> The irrational functions (which we will consider rather as supra-rational) are a key opening a door to a higher reality of Number. They demonstrate that no matter what quantities are applied to the side and to the diameter the relationship will remain invariable, for in essence this functional aspect of Number is neither large nor small, neither infinite nor finite: it is universal.[14]

Architecture, unlike painting, is involved not only with the geometry of plane, or two-dimensional forms; it is an art of exterior and interior volumes that are generated through the study of planes. A building and its associated landscape are designed, first of all, as a plan. A *plan* in architecture is a projection to a plane passed horizontally at or above a floor or ground surface of a proposed building. Volumes are then produced by raising vertical planes from the horizontal plane of the plan. The projections drawn upon these vertical planes are called *elevations* and, together with the plan, they define architectural volumes.

Until recently, architectural volumes were limited to variations of the sphere, the cone, the rectangular, and the triangular prisms. Now there are volumes based on mathematical formulas such as the parabola and hyperbola. Other "free-form" volumes are based on the imaginative fancy of the architect, and represent a contemporary fad that will not long survive. Sacred geometry, however, is concerned with a group of volumes other than those used in the design of buildings.

These are the five archetypal, or Platonic, volumes that were described in the *Timaeus,* but they must have been known since man first began to contemplate the mysteries of geometry. They were recognized in the British Isles 2,000 years before Plato: Full sets of five have been found at Neolithic stone circles in Aberdeenshire, Scotland.[15]

The cube, tetrahedron, octahedron, icosahedron, and dodecahedron are the only possible solids in which both the edges and the interior angles are of equal size. Plato distinguished the first four from the dodecahedron, in that the four may be assembled from only two basic right-angle triangles, the 45° and the 30°–60° triangles. It is, perhaps,

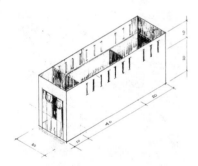

Elevations raised upon a plan. The drawing illustrates the proportions of King Solomon's Temple, as given in the Book of Kings. The volumes are all expressed in ratios of simple, whole-number integers.

The five Platonic solids. (Illustration from *Time Stands Still*, courtesy of Keith Critchlow.)

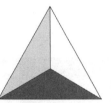

Tetrahedron

Cube

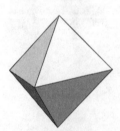

Octahedron

Icosahedron

Dodecahedron

not a coincidence that these are the two triangles with which architects have traditionally drawn their plans.

Plato identified four of these solids with the four elements: the tetrahedron with fire, the cube with earth, the octahedron with air, and the icosahedron with water, thus affording additional insight into their archetypal significance. He is noncommittal regarding the esoteric meaning of the fifth form, the dodecahedron, stating that God used it "for embroidering the constellations on the whole heaven." He evidently regarded the shape as one having particular importance, but his meaning is obscure.

Observe the interplay among the five forms and how the shape of one is implicit in the shape of another. Robert Lawlor in *Sacred Geometry* demonstrates how the other forms may be developed from the icosahedron, which is itself determined by applying the golden section ratio to the diameter of a sphere.[16] It is ironic that R. Buckminster Fuller, regarded as the epitome of the scientific architect, achieved fame as the inventor of the octet truss and the geodesic dome, forms that betray his fascination with the ancient Platonic solids. The truss (see page 39) is composed of interrelated octahedrons and tetrahedrons, while the geodesic domes were based upon structural members connecting the vertices of either the icosahedron or the dodecahedron.

The beauty of these forms, and of the buildings based upon them, results from our intuitive recognition of the archetypal, mathematical truth they display. When architects refer to this truth, they do so, vaguely, as "good proportion." But we were not taught, and few of us understand, the mathematical basis of proportion. The plane and solid geometric figures discussed above exemplify mathematical ratios and proportions. It is now necessary to explore more rigorously the meaning of *proportion* and how an understanding of mathematical proportion is essential to the creation of great works of architecture.

The Meaning of Proportion

This beautifully proportioned house in Vicenza, Italy, was built by Andrea Palladio on a bridge over a small, slow-moving stream. The perfect rightness of the proportions is apparent without the aid of a geometric analysis.

Proportion is the essence of architecture, yet few architects are aware that it refers to mathematical properties. When we speak of good proportion or poor proportion, we casually assume that proportion is determined only by individual intuition and lacks an objective base. We no longer accept, nor are we aware of, what has been widely understood in every culture except our own: that proportion is governed by mathematical laws that can be systematically studied through geometry. Nor do we any longer recognize that knowledge of these laws is necessary to achieve harmony in the art of building, and can even lead beyond, toward achieving the mystical insight that has been said to be the purpose of our existence.

The study of proportion begins with the idea of ratio. A ratio may be mathematically expressed as *a/b*. A proportion represents the equivalence of two ratios and is usually expressed as a *four-term proportion*, or *a/b = c/d*. Comparisons based on four elements are termed *discontinuous four-term proportions*, and are what Plato called "particular knowledge," which he says is of a vulnerable character open to dispute and arbitrariness.

A *three-term proportion* exists when the ratio of the first term to the second is the same as that of the second to the third, or *a/b = b/c*. In a three-term proportion, the elements are bound more tightly, and it is the three-term proportion that is the principle concern of architects. Plato regarded the three-term proportion as essential knowledge, the knowledge through which the mind is able to comprehend the world. Through the study of mediation, the ways in which the mean term in a three-term proportion was determined, he said that it is possible to comprehend the laws that govern the creation of all things.

A *two-term proportion* may be regarded as a special case of the three-term proportion: that is, when one term (*b*) of a three-term proportion is to the other (*a*) as the other (*a*) is to the sum of the two (*a + b*).

$$\frac{a}{b} = \frac{a+b}{a} = \Phi$$

This, of course, is the golden proportion, discussed on pages 157–158. When one of the two terms is assigned a numerical value, the other is a multiple of the function Phi.

$$\frac{a}{b} = \frac{a+b}{a} = \Phi \text{ also written as } a = \Phi b$$

In addition to the geometric proportion illustrated above and at right, two important types of three-term proportions may be identified through introducing the idea of difference. These are termed *arithmetic* and *harmonic*.

Robert Lawlor writes:

> The most important and mysterious character of the harmonic proportion is the fact that the inverse of every harmonic progression is an arithmetic progression. Thus 2, 3, 4, 5, is an ascending progression while the inverse series 1/2, 1/3, 1/4, 1/5, is a descending harmonic progression. In music it is the insertion of the harmonic and arithmetic means between the two extremes in double ratios—representing the octave double—which gives us the progression known as the "musical" proportion, that is 1, 4/3, 3/2, 2.[17]

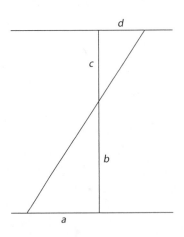

Lines intersecting parallel lines define triangles having the same shape but not the same size. The ratio of side *a* to *b* is the same as that of *c* to *d*, or *a/b = c/d*.

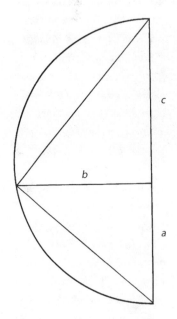

The large right triangle is divided into two similar right triangles. Therefore, side *a* is to *b* as *b* is to *c*, or *a/b = b/c*.

The term harmonic *in mathematics refers not to the general meaning of the word, but specifically to the third of the three possible types of proportional systems.*

An arithmetic proportion such as 3, 5, 7 shows an equality of difference but an inequality of ratio. Thus 7 – 5 = 5 – 3, but 7/5 does not equal 5/3. In a geometric progression such as 2, 4, 8 there is an equality of ratio but an inequality of difference, since 4/2 = 8/4, but 4 – 2 does not equal 8 – 4. The "harmonic" proportion is more complex. In the progression 6, 8, 12, for example, the difference of the first two terms, 2, is to the first term 6 as the difference of the last two terms, 4, is to the last term 12. The equivalency is 1/3 = 1/3. Given any two dimensions, the mean terms of each type may be found in the following ways:

Arithmetic: b = (a + c)/2
Geometric: b² = ac
Harmonic: b = 2ac/(a + c)

The harmony of proportionate whole-number ratios is directly felt through music. The relation of musical harmony to number was recognized and demonstrated by Pythagoras, who is generally credited with the discovery, but it is, in fact, much older, since we find musical proportions represented in Egyptian sculpture and architecture. Near the end of the sacred mathematical tradition in architecture, the designs of Palladio were based upon ratios of the numbers that define the musical harmonies.

Goethe, when confronted with the buildings of Palladio, is supposed to have exclaimed, "Architecture is frozen music!" Most of us have heard the saying, but have always assumed that it referred to some vague aesthetic effect. It refers, however, to the fact that the same mathematical principles are the basis of the two arts.

These principles can be demonstrated by means of the monochord. A *monochord* is a single string stretched over a sounding board that can be stopped, or varied in length, at specific intervals. When the string is plucked, harmonies audible to the ear are found at intervals that are precise ratios of whole numbers. The most significant ratios, as expected, are those of 1/2, or the octave; 2/3, or the musical fifth; and 3/4, the musical fourth. The progression known as the *musical proportion* is therefore determined empirically to be 1, 4/3, 3/2, 2. Almost all musical scales are thus based on combinations of the numbers one, two, three, and four. Architects who rely upon these harmonies are not translating musical ratios into architecture, but rather making use of a universal harmony apparent in the ratios and proportions of music.

The created world exemplifies proportion and harmony in all its aspects. We see mathematical law expressed in the form of a shell, the crystalline shape of a mineral, and even in the proportions of the human body. Modern physics is said to demonstrate that matter itself is composed of geometric patterns of light energy. To express the laws of proportion in a building, landscape, cityscape, or in any other created work, is to design in harmony with the cosmos itself.

The forms, ratios, roots, and transformations of number and geometry were regarded by ancient philosophers as analogues to the essential processes of life and a key to the construction of the cosmos. One may look at these arithmetical or geometrical systems in the context of modern mathematical science and have little or no insight into the nature of their esoteric significance. If, however, we accept that these analogues are "true" in the sense that they reflect an intuitive understanding of reality that cannot be put into words, we have a basis upon which we may construct architectural forms that are ageless because they are eternally true.

The Il Redentore Church in Venice, Italy, designed by Andrea Palladio, is a symphony in stone. It demonstrates the beautiful harmonies of the musical proportions.

I found this iron pyrite octahedron (upper left in photo above) at the French Creek mine in Pennsylvania when I was sixteen years old. The occurrence of such perfect geometric forms in the mineral kingdom is still, to me, a matter of wonder.

We thus have in our hands the key to an architecture that will be free from the narrowly defined functionality of the twentieth century and the fashionable eccentricities of individual architects. If architects become familiar with the arcane material that has come down from the past, and through study and meditation guide their intuition to an awareness of the deeper significance of number and diagram, the archetypal patterns and forms of sacred geometry will come into their work unsought.

Architectural Examples

Baptist Meeting House, Cambridge, Maryland. In this front-on view, the beautiful proportions of the elevation are evident.

When I measured the Baptist Meeting House shown above (first illustrated on page 81), I found that the principal dimensions were very close to those of a proportional series that would have resulted from the application of the square root of two to the interior width of the building. (The importance of this ratio was discussed on page 156.) While the correspondence is not exact, it is too close to be ascribed to coincidence, and within the limits of accuracy to be expected if the unknown builder had laid out the structure by using arcs of string lines.

The 25-foot width was the key dimension, and would have been determined by the expected size of the congregation and the distance that could easily be spanned by simple wooden rafters. From a 25-foot baseline the unknown builder must have laid out on the leveled ground what I call the primary square. An arc was swung from the diagonal of the square to define the interior length of the building (mathematically $\sqrt{2} \times 25$), and the balcony for the slaves was located at the edge of the primary square, shown in the top figure on page 167.

The √2 geometry was then carried into the interior elevations and the volume of the building. The height of the wall from the floor to the sloping part of the ceiling was made one-half the width of the building, and the one-to-one—or 45° slope of the roof from the top of the wall to the apex of the ceiling above the tie beams—defined another square with sides equal to ½√2.

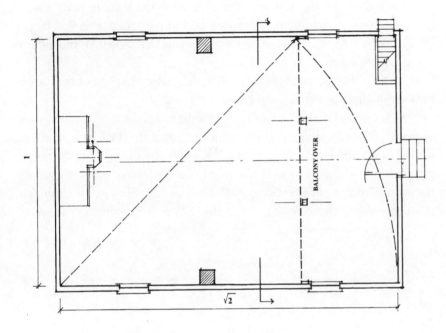

PLAN: The measured width of the room is approximately 25 feet, here taken as one.

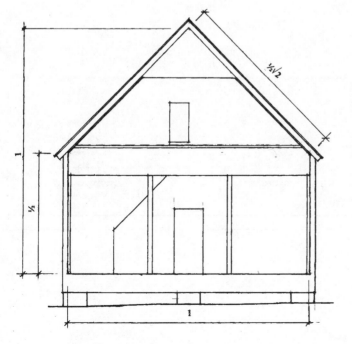

SECTION: The end facades are as easily understood and as beautiful as the section, since they repeat the same proportional series. The measured dimensions are within an inch or two of those obtained by multiplying 25 feet by the proportional numbers shown.

The series of dimensions is as follows:

a = height of wall		½
b = ceiling from wall to apex		½$\sqrt{2}$
c = width and height of room		1
d = length of room		$\sqrt{2}$

Not only is a/b equal to c/d, a four-term proportion, but $a/b = b/c = c/d$ is a three-term geometric progression, and the series is related by the oscillation of the square root of two between the diagonal and side of successive squares!

But how did the anonymous builder solve the problem of the important south elevation facing the road?

I first noticed that the two 6' × 3' windows are double-square, superimposed, 3' × 3' square frames and these, plus the 1½' × 3' shutters, also define a square. More remarkably, when squares are drawn on the elevation, as shown in the illustration below, their diagonals intersect the centers of the upper frames! And when the left diagonal is extended, it is centered on the chimney as the chimney emerges through the roof! The principle of the square has organized the elevation.

The interior of the Baptist Meeting House in Cambridge, Maryland.

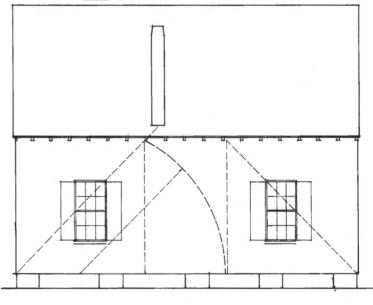

South elevation.

But what of the overall proportions of this building facade? On the south elevation, on page 168, I have constructed a golden rectangle, the right side of which almost perfectly coincides with the side of the remaining square. The ratio of height to length is therefore $1:1+\Phi$, and by the remarkable proportionate characteristics of Φ, $1+\Phi$ is equal to Φ^2. The overall proportion of the facade may therefore be expressed simply as $1:\Phi^2$!

Now I understand why, at a glance, I found the building beautiful! But did the unknown builder lay it out using these geometrical principles, or could he have intuitively selected proportions that would be in harmony without knowing the reason why? We can never be sure, but the repeated correspondence of building dimensions with geometric principles makes it probable that he consciously understood the construction, if not the philosophical implications, of the forms he chose.

In the late nineteenth and early twentieth century, architects trained in the Beaux Arts tradition continued to produce designs in which proportions related to number and geometry. The house shown on page 170 was built in 1904, not long before the beginning of the modern architectural revolution. Although by that time neither sacred geometry nor the theory of musical proportions was taught in the schools, I found harmony and beauty in the spaces of the principal first-floor rooms. A set of "as-built" plans fortunately had been drawn at a later time, and the dimensions were derived from these.

The entry is a perfect square, 14' 6" × 14' 6". Since the ceiling height of all the rooms is 11' 1", the ratio of height to width is almost exactly 4:3, that of the musical fourth.

The dimensions of the parlor are 9' 2" × 13' 2". The 11' 1" ceiling height is again almost exactly the arithmetic mean (11' 2"), and the series 9' 2", 11' 1", 13' 2" is therefore almost exactly a perfect arithmetic proportion, and one of the three proportional series recommended for the dimensions of rooms by Palladio!

The average width of the living room is 14' 4", the length is 28' 6". The ratio is therefore almost exactly that of the double square or, musically, of the octave. Further, when we compare this average width to the 11' 1" ceiling height, we again find the ratio to be within two inches of the musical fourth!

The 14' 8" × 22' 0" dining room was even more interesting. Not only is the ratio of the 22' 0" length to the 11' 1" height almost exactly 1:2, or the octave, but the ratio of the width to the height, 14' 8" / 11' 1", is almost exactly that of the musical fourth, and the series of the

Beaux Arts house built in 1904
in Roland Park, an Olmsted-
designed development in what
was then suburban Baltimore.

Floor plan of the 1904 house.
The drawing was made from a set
of as-built prints and checked in
the field.

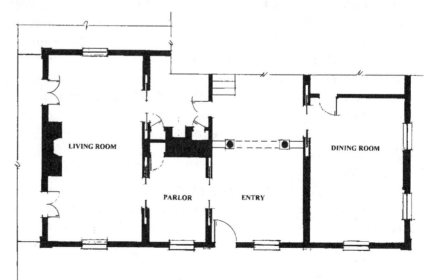

LIVING ROOM

DINING ROOM

PARLOR   ENTRY

three principal dimensions—11' 1", 14' 8", 22' 0"— is less than an inch from being a perfect harmonic progression, the third type of proportional series recommended by Palladio!

Moreover, if we examine the relative size of the rooms in terms of their floor area, we find them to be in rough arithmetic proportion. The actual areas in square feet are Parlor 121, Entry 210, Dining 319, and Living 416, while an exact arithmetic series would have been 116.5, 216.5, 316.5, 416.5.

Did the unknown architect actually use a knowledge of mathematical and musical proportional systems in the process of design? The convergence of numbers and theory is not exact, but very close. It is, however, possible that the architect worked from an intuitive proportional sense, developed and refined from the intensive study of buildings designed by earlier architects who *did* know and use mathematical principles. Unlike architects today, the eclectic architects of the nineteenth and twentieth centuries were familiar with a wide range of famous buildings that had survived from the past. Even without understanding the principles involved, they must have known the ratios and proportions used by their predecessors as visually apparent shapes that were then expressed in their own work.

I designed the Masonic lodge room shown on page 172 in year 2000, in conscious awareness of the esoteric principles of sacred geometry and in the hope that Masons would adopt the plans as a guide to the construction of their own lodges, and thus enhance the significance of the rituals. While only the overall proportions and shapes of this hypothetical lodge room were completed, in an actual building the fenestration, ornament, and details would follow the same mathematical and esoteric principles.

The double square, with its 2:1 musical ratio of the octave, was selected as the shape of the "working floor," the area within which the Masonic rituals are performed. Since all lodge rooms are oriented to the four cardinal directions, the double square, if centered on the altar, can represent the two hemispheres of the earth, separated at the meridian on which the altar is located. The equator, the Tropics of Cancer and Capricorn, and the zodiac can be visualized as if they were spread out upon the floor.

The width of the traditional border around the working floor was determined by the construction of a circle with a perimeter equal to that of one of the squares. To achieve equivalence between the yin and yang of the material and the spiritual realms was a principle concern of sacred

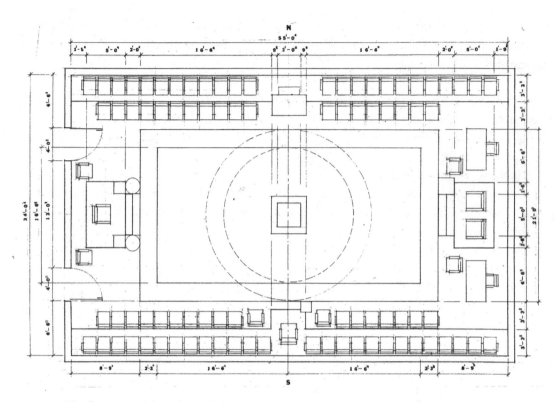

The floor plan of the Masonic lodge room. The altar is always located at the center of a Masonic lodge. The plans and elevations are available without charge to Masons through the Masonic Service Organization in Washington, D.C.

At right, the meridian of the altar divides the working floor so that it may represent the two hemispheres of the world inscribed in a double square. The proportions of the room unfold from this figure. Note the path of the ecliptic and the signs of the zodiac that may be visualized upon the floor.

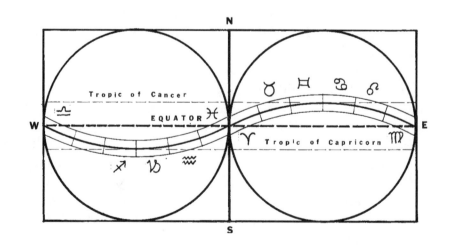

geometry. As we shall see, this circle will be expressed as the circle of the heavens above the square of the earth. The method chosen is based on the 3–4–5 Pythagorean triangle. If 22/7 is accepted as the value of pi, the equivalence is exact.

For functional reasons, the width of the working floor and hence the side of the original square must be between 15 and 20 feet, and if set at 16' 6", the diameter of the circle becomes 21 feet. This is a number in the Fibonacci series, and if we allow 6' 6" on each side of the room for seating, the overall width of the room becomes 34 feet, another Fibonacci number. If we assign the value "one" to the 21' width of the floor and border, the ratio may be expressed as 1:Φ. Furthermore, if we in turn multiply the 34' width of the room by Φ, the ratio of the width of the working floor to the length of the room becomes 55', or, in relation to the 21' working floor, 1:Φ²! All of these dimensions may be constructed geometrically, and the geometric construction is actually more meaningful since we can see the beauty of the mathematical figures as they unfold.

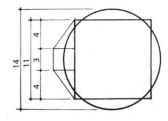

The construction of the squared circle.

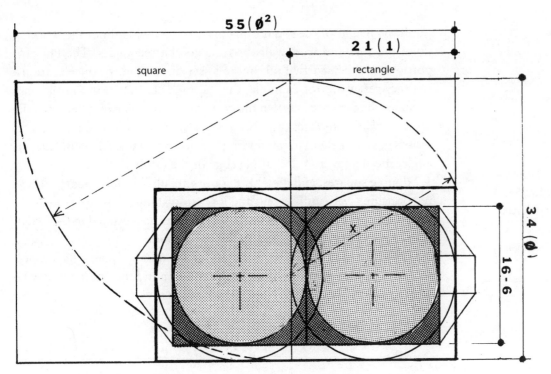

The semi-diagonal of the double square (line x above) defines a golden rectangle. A square (at left) added to the rectangle (at right) produces another golden rectangle, in which the short side of the second is equal to the long side of the first.

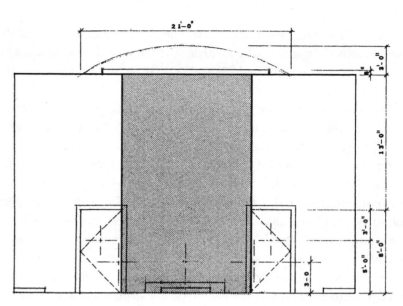

West elevation. The total area of the doors is a close approximation of one divided by Phi to the fourth power!

By using Fibonacci numbers instead of those directly derived from Phi, the dimensions of the room are expressed as whole numbers closely approximate to Phi. For example, if we were to multiply the 21' width of the room by Phi, the length would have been 33.999' rather than 34 feet. The difference is indiscernible to the eye. See page 158 for a discussion of the Fibonacci series.

If the height of the room is made equal to the width of the working floor, the east and west walls become golden rectangles. The Phi proportions are then carried out in the lesser dimensions of the elevations. On the west wall, for example, the 13', or $1/\Phi$, dimension in the plan becomes the distance between the doorways. The eight-foot height of the doors is also a Fibonacci number and an approximation of $1:1/\Phi^2$. This results in still further Phi relationships: The central panel is a golden rectangle, the shapes from the inside edge of the doors to the walls become 1:2 double squares, and the 4' × 8' doors are also double squares. These relationships were unforeseen, and it is astonishing to see how the use of the golden proportion in the major dimensions has resulted in the extension of the proportional series to the minor ones.

The final series is symmetrical about the number one, which represents the combined width of the working floor and the border. It may be written $1/\Phi^2:1/\Phi::1/\Phi:1::1:\Phi::\Phi:\Phi^2$, or alternatively

$$\frac{\frac{1}{\Phi^2}}{\frac{1}{\Phi}} = \frac{\frac{1}{\Phi}}{1} = \frac{1}{\Phi} = \frac{\Phi}{\Phi^2}$$

One is the traditional number of deity.

The ceiling represents the dome of the heavens—either an actual dome or one to be constructed within the space afforded by a dropped ceiling—and it should be adorned by the stars of the zodiac. Its diameter is 21 feet, or one, and as determined above, its perimeter is equal to that of one of the original two squares. If located above such a "square of the earth"— defined on the floor and centered on the altar— we see a symbol of the perfect equivalence between heaven and earth, as expressed in the ancient Hermetic aphorism "As above, so below."

The room has been linked to the cosmos by orientation, by the double square centered on the altar, and by the circle of the heavens, commensurable with the square of the Earth. Moving through these concepts and binding them into a unified whole is the proportional series based on Phi, the golden section.

The preceding three examples trace a historical progression in the definition of architectural form. In the first example, the unknown carpenter or builder designed his little eighteenth-century church with complete trust in the proportional system that had come down to him either through oral tradition or through one of the builder's manuals that featured a section on geometry.

In the second example, we see the preservation of numerical proportions through the Beaux Arts system of architectural education and the eclecticism of nineteenth- and early-twentieth-century practice. But even then the system was in decline and not widely understood. Its use by an

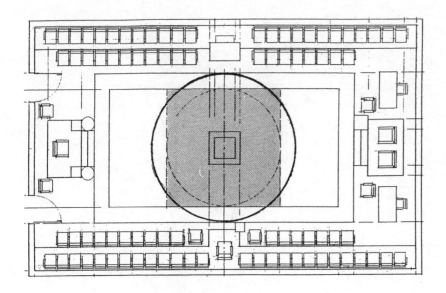

The circular dome of the sky above the square of the earth.

architect working in the early twentieth century was therefore exceptional, and a short time after the building was erected, the remnants of the old canon of proportion were swept away by the onslaught of "scientific" design.

The final example represents the beginning of a new architecture in which esoteric insight will be given expression in space and form. In this architecture man will be linked to the cosmos through sacred geometry and the canon of proportion. Architecture will again become a magical interplay between the mathematical symbol and the reality of our physical existence.

11
ARCHITECT AND COSMOS

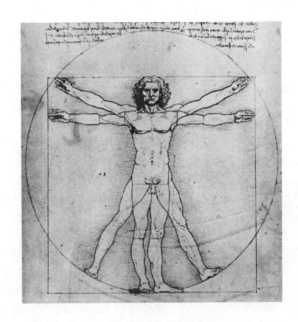

Man as the measure of all things. In this famous drawing, Leonardo da Vinci summarizes the anthropocosmic understanding.

Anthropocosm

The Gospel of Saint John, the most Gnostic of the four that comprise the official canon, opens with the following dramatic sentence: "In the beginning was the Word, and the Word was with God, and the Word was God."

This is the most profound statement in the Bible regarding the creation of the cosmos. The comprehension of the text may elude us, but we are intuitively aware that something of great significance has been expressed. The translator, working in the time of King James, chose to use *word* for the Greek "logos." Logos implies an active principle and would be more accurately translated as "verb." What, then, is the word, or verb, of which Saint John has written? According to the anthropocosmic understanding, it can be only the marvelous transforming power of Phi, the golden proportion.

Schwaller de Lubicz, through his studies of ancient Egyptian architecture and hieroglyphic texts, has identified a theological principle he calls the primal scission: the original division of the ultimate unity of God, the creative act that brings the world into being.[1] In mathematical analogy the number one, divided proportionally, becomes two and three, comprising the duality of the two parts and the transforming function that initiates the division. This Trinity was understood by the Egyptian

A hurricane approaches the east coast of North America, a spiral vortex in the atmosphere of the earth. (Photograph courtesy of NASA.)

Gnostics to represent God the Father, or One; the Feminine Holy Spirit, or Two; and the Son, the Transforming Principle, or Three. The scission cannot be equal and static in the manner in which we conceive of the division of a cell into two equal parts. It must be asymmetric, dynamic: it can only be Phi, whirling in the form of a spiral from the infinitely small to the infinitely large.

We thus see Phi—a comprehensible mathematical fact and one visible in the ruins of ancient Egyptian temples—in its deeper significance as a symbolic representation of the origin of the cosmos. This is a characteristic example of the way of thinking that underlies the anthropocosmic comprehension of the world.

In anthropocosmic thought, archetypal myth and metaphor, especially mathematical metaphor, are the means whereby we explain the meaning of existence. Our individual consciousness is considered to be akin to the divine consciousness. It is therefore possible through archetypes of myth and symbol to direct our intuition to the apperception of the divine unity.

I do not pretend to grasp the essence of the anthropocosmic understanding and can only present some of the obvious characteristics that are available to the conscious intellect. Of these, the most significant is the idea that the universe is ultimately the pure flow of a divine consciousness that has no beginning and no end. It is an endless expanse of formless spirit that becomes manifest through material reality. All of existence is thus intimately connected. There is an evolutionary progression from the simple to the complex. Man, as the highest and most complex life-form of which we know, is the culmination of the purpose inherent from the beginning of all things in the conception of the cosmos. The purpose of our lives, through cycles of reincarnation and karma, is to become aware of our divine identity, to be reborn as a body of light and rejoin the ultimate unity that we call God.

The idea of *anthropos,* or the divine man, has been formulated differently by many cultures, but remains the basis of all the great religions. Even when suppressed and unavailable to the conscious mind, as it was under the hegemony of the Roman Church, it persisted as an intuitive awareness that continued to inspire the Christian mystics. It is the philosophical expression, the theoretical basis, of the realization of the divine unity that has been sought—and found—by individual mystics of every religious persuasion.

Even we who possess a lesser understanding may find it possible to follow those who have achieved the mystical insight, and ourselves intuitively comprehend something of the purpose and meaning of existence.

We may then consciously express something of that comprehension in art and architecture by means of symbols.

Within a pre-Modern temple, church, or home there are symbols derived from natural phenomena, such as the acanthus leaves of the Grecian capitals, the lotus capitals of Egyptian art, and the vines that twine through the ornament of American architect Louis Sullivan. Animals, real and fanciful, are represented, and humans are depicted as beautiful or grotesque. There are astronomical phenomena, such as the zodiac, the sun, moon, and planets. But preeminent among the symbolic possibilities are the mysterious systems of number, geometry, and mathematical thought that were once incorporated not only into the systems of ornament but also into the very fabric of a building. These systems are mysterious because the relation of mathematics to reality is not understood, although in one way or another we assume a relationship to exist. Scientists today see this critical relationship as one of pure quantity. Ancient scientists, according to Schwaller, saw numbers and diagrams as metaphors of the cosmos, both the microcosm of the individual consciousness and the macrocosm of the spiritual and material whole.

The great drama of existence, according to the anthropocosmic vision, is the transformation of man to cosmic man: the rebirth of the individual spirit in a total awareness of God. It was the function of the ancient temple, and the Gothic cathedral, to lead the worshiper into an awareness of his own divine identity, to make explicit in architectural form and ornament the insights gained through the study of sacred geometry. The plan of the great Gothic cathedrals, for instance, was that of the cross, the cross of materiality upon which the divine man-god suffers.

In Egypt there is one great temple designed to represent the human body. It is the Temple of Luxor, the building so carefully studied by Schwaller de Lubicz. Cosmic man, both in the architecture and in the ritual bas-relief designs, is in the process of being born.

In India the tradition of temple design based on the image of the cosmic man is still alive, not only in actual construction but also in the form of the mandala, the sacred painting that replicates the plan of the temple. The Hindu architectural sutra declares that the universe is present in the temple by means of proportion.[4]

Our science has demonstrated a singular incapacity to offer any valid explanation for existence or for the phenomenon of mind. Ancient science and mathematics did provide an explanation, and the spiritual results of the application of ancient science to art and architecture are undoubted. Even now the architectural works built in the light of the

Ornament of the Carson, Pirie and Scott Department Store in Chicago, designed by Louis Sullivan. I see entwined in plant forms and vines an abstract, geometric face—the "green man" of ancient and medieval Celtic art.

The brilliant reconstruction of the Temple of Luxor as the "Temple of Man" by Schwaller de Lubicz is shown in the figure on page 143. The correspondence between the principal divisions of the human body and the principal divisions of the great temple is exact and beyond dispute.[3]

This image of the Tibetan Buddhist Mahakala Yantra Mandala is at once a plan of the Temple, a plan of the Earth, and a plan of the Universe. It is here reproduced in black-and-white courtesy of the astrologer/architect A. T. Mann.

ancient understanding affect us emotionally, can change our lives, and can continue to influence the spiritual development of those who are willing to approach the remains of that art and architecture and seek their meaning. Thus, when we introduce the symbolism of number and sacred geometry into the design of a building, we are following a long-trodden path. We are expressing in architectural form something of the nature of the cosmos and the purpose of existence. To do so consciously and deliberately is essentially a religious act that can transform the awareness of both the architect and all those who will experience the results of his work.

Yet the introduction of symbolism, particularly the symbolism of sacred geometry and number, is not to be accomplished simply by means of rational calculation. An architect must be familiar with at least some of the esoteric properties of the mathematical and geometrical systems upon which he must rely, but the vision or the insight that comprehends the final whole must wait upon inspiration. The architect then becomes a shaman or priest: his work possesses a magical power to alter the states of consciousness of those who live, work, and worship in the spaces that his pencil has defined.

Magic and Symbol

Prehistoric painting from a cave at Lascaux. The use of magic and symbol is evident in these great Neolithic works of art. (Photograph courtesy of Wikimedia Commons.)

The interconnection of all things in a continual flow of divine consciousness is inherent in the idea of *anthropos*. Consequently, a symbol, a rite, a musical phrase, or an architectural form that synthesizes a complex thought becomes an agent of transformation that can effect change in the spiritual and material realms. This is the essence of magic and, perceived in the light of the anthropocosmic understanding, magic is real.

Today we define magic as "the pretended art of producing effects or controlling events by means of charms, spells, or rituals supposed to govern certain natural or supernatural forces."[5] The key words in this definition are *pretended* and *supposed,* for they indicate the skepticism and disbelief with which the efficacy of magic is regarded in the age of the materialist paradigm. Magic to us means either the effects achieved by a conventional trickster magician on the stage, whereby the laws of material causality seem to be suspended, or it is a reference to a past belief in magic in order to describe a certain kind of "aesthetic pleasure."

Jonathan Hale wrote in his fine book *The Old Way of Seeing* about the magic of old buildings. The subtitle is *How Architecture Lost Its Magic (And How to Get It Back)*.[6] But magic to Hale is visual delight in pattern, in the interrelation of forms, in the liveliness of a townscape or facade. He is aware of the mathematical basis of the forms that he finds so attractive; he appreciates the power of a symbol such as the Vesica Pisces that he sees on a passing tire truck; he realizes that the magic of which he speaks arises through the intuition from the depths of the unconscious mind. But even he, in our mundane world, is reluctant to make the final connection and admit that magic is truly magical: that shapes and symbols have the power to alter personalities and affect even the real world of materiality.

Yet a belief in magic as a way of effecting change in the totality of the spiritual and physical reality has been, until the last few centuries, a consistent feature of human society. Even the Church, which would accept no rival to the institutionalized magic of its own rituals and anathematized all other magic as "sorcery," attested to the sincerity of its belief by the dreadful penalties imposed on anyone suspected of the detested crime. And evidence of the practice of magic and even sorcery, which has come to mean magic in the service of evil, is found among the earliest archaeological records of man.

In 1879 a small child exploring a low and relatively inaccessible part of a cave on her father's estate in Spain while he searched for prehistoric artifacts cried out in amazement at the sight of magnificently painted animals emblazoned across the limestone walls. This was the first find of the magical cave art of Cro-Magnon man.[7] Initially disbelieved, the discovery was followed by others at Lascaux and elsewhere in southern France and northern Spain. Typically, "experts" dismissed the paintings and sculpture as part of some obscure religious rite having to do with "primitive superstition." Only when the obvious parallels were drawn between this art and the art that primitive societies create today was it realized and accepted by many that the paintings were probably made in an effort to ensure success in the hunt through the systematic application of magic.[8]

Today, secure in our rational materialism, we deride our ancestors for their folly. But during the nineteenth and twentieth centuries, a number of explorers and anthropologists lived intimately with primitive tribes, and even took part in their ceremonies and hunts. They testify

According to Robert Lawlor, in his book *Voices of the First Day,* Joseph Campbell has related this Australian Aborigine ritual dance to similar imagery found in the Stone Age cave paintings at Lascaux.[9] (Photograph courtesy of Robert Lawlor.)

that, for some reason unknown to them, the magical rites do, in fact, work to ensure success in the hunt, or for whatever other purpose they may be intended. Our own rationalistic society, far removed from the supposed naiveté of our primitive ancestors, regards such information with hostility and sees it as a threat to the ruling paradigm.

Magic, nevertheless, still persists, and is recognized by those willing to consider the evidence without prejudice as a body of inexplicable but real phenomena that can effect change not only in the personality, the emotions, and the soul, but in the world of materiality as well. Despite the continuing denial of those bound to the materialist paradigm, there is convincing evidence that certain gifted individuals can bend spoons, cure illnesses, foretell the future, dowse for water, and produce the incomprehensible coincidences that Jung called "synchronicity." It may even be that such talents are latent in us all, and if we accept the anthropocosmic premise that the universe is ultimately a flow of pure thought, it is perfectly understandable, even necessary, that the mind of the individual or the group can effect change in both the spiritual and material aspects of the universe.

If magic is indeed real, it is as applicable to the form of our dwellings as to our success in the hunt. When, therefore, we speak of the "magic" of architecture, we are using a term that has a far greater significance than that of describing a pleasurable aesthetic sensation. The magical form of a building, a landscape, or a garden moves in a subtle way to change the world.

The practice of magic is intimately related to the selection of symbols, and the symbols that link man to the cosmos are among those that are manipulated to produce the magic of architecture. A symbol is a synthesis, a representation of some aspect of thought or life that embodies a complex of associations in such a way that the awareness is concentrated upon the particular force or function that it represents. The symbol serves to concentrate the mind: in the case of the prehistoric cave art or the buffalo dance, for instance, it serves to establish an identity between the hunter and his prey. Similarly, an architect might use the Phi proportion or the musical proportions recommended by Palladio to symbolically link the microcosm of the individual mind to the macrocosm of the ultimate unity.

Architectural theorists, in their obsession with semiology, tend to confuse symbols and signs. Jung, however, wrote that symbols are produced spontaneously from the unconscious, although they may be consciously elaborated later. He contrasts the ankh, ancient Egypt's symbol of life, the universe, and man, with an airways insignia, which he identifies as a consciously contrived sign, not a symbol.[10] Similarly, we would say that the famous "duck" building to which Venturi referred in *Learning from Las Vegas,* and the golden television antenna atop his Guild House in Philadelphia, are signs, whereas the use of the Phi proportion in a building is a symbol of the creative function itself.

The symbols used in architecture are of many kinds. They can be trivial or profound. They may involve the form of the whole building, as well as selected parts and the ornament. They may even belong to the past and no longer be consciously understood by either architects or their public. As late as the early part of the twentieth century, and even today in Post-Modern buildings, the symbols evolved by the Greeks and Romans continue to be used, not for their inherent meaning, which has been forgotten, but to reflect a previous, more vital tradition.

The symbolic means that affect our most profound understanding, engage our deepest emotions, and link man to the cosmos are archetypal. They cannot be completely forgotten: they are always present in every culture, even our own, for they arise from our common heritage in the collective unconscious mind. These symbols are predominantly numerical and geometrical.

The ankh, the ancient Egyptian symbol of life.

Here the ankh is shown in abstract form to emphasize the constituent forms of the circle and the cross.

Piazza d'Italia, New Orleans, designed by Charles Moore. The building, or rather the pavilion, is a colorful and clever pastiche of Renaissance and Roman forms, the meaning of which has long been lost. (Photograph courtesy of Piazza d'Italia.)

The ratios and proportions, the numbers and diagrams of sacred geometry are thus archetypal symbols. They are regarded by those who accept the mystic doctrine of the anthropocosm as metaphors of an a priori knowledge of the structure of the universe. This knowledge arises through the identity of man and the cosmos. Robert Lawlor writes,

> Our brains and bodies necessarily shape all our perceptions and have themselves been shaped by the same seen and unseen energies that have shaped every perceivable thing. Body, Mind and Universe must be in parallel, formative identity.[11]

The same numerical and geometric proportions that are the laws of creation are therefore visible in our own bodies. This remarkable correspondence fascinated the artists of the Renaissance. The famous figures drawn by both Leonardo da Vinci and Albrecht Dürer show the human body, with outstretched limbs, enclosed within a circle. The genitals divide the body in half; the navel, by one over phi. Dürer also has drawn the front and side view of a striding man in which the body is entirely divided in accordance with the division of unity into the unique arithmetical, geometric, and harmonic proportions. The Fibonacci series may be recognized in the varying length of the bones of the human arm and hand.

Nor are symbols, mathematical or otherwise, to be considered as if they existed only in isolation. Taken together, they may constitute a language: a "language of the heart," to use a phrase of Schwaller de Lubicz, who identified the existence of such a language in the temples of ancient Egypt. There the hieroglyphs, the ritual carvings, and the geometry of space and number combined to lead the mind to the higher spiritual awareness. In Egypt, there was what might be called a "science of symbols."

Hieroglyphs were a key element of this science. According to Schwaller, they constitute a sacred language, the inner meaning of which could be only written and not voiced. This language was separate and apart from the common speech, represented by the demotic script. The hieroglyphs were used by the priesthood and were carved into important monuments to express complex trains of associative symbolic ideas.

We, of course, have no such sacred language. All of the symbolic means available to architects are now severely limited. Venturi refers to buildings as "decorated sheds," but even if we accept his limited and disparaging definition, with what are we to decorate these sheds? The scientific architecture of the mid-twentieth century ruthlessly excoriated

These dimensions have been confirmed by exhaustive biometric studies of the average measurements of the human body. It has been found that at birth the navel divides the child exactly in half, and as maturation proceeds, the navel moves to the location of the Phi division and the genitals divide the body in half.

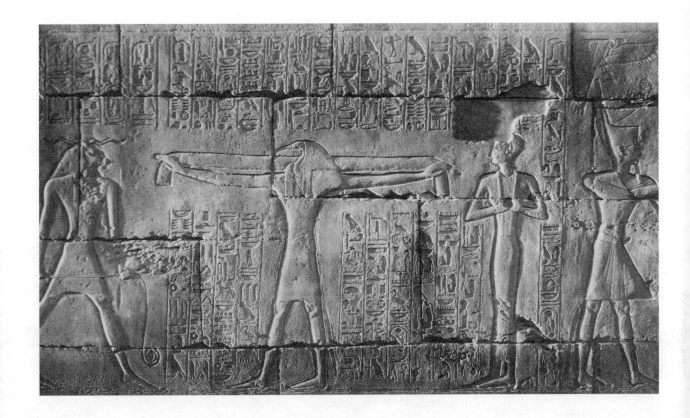

all that remained of the symbology of the past. The Post-Moderns want to replace it with a mélange of arbitrary borrowings from a symbolic language no longer understood, together with the signs and insignia of our commercial culture. This is to admit failure and abdicate our responsibilities.

Instead, we must seek to enrich our architectural vocabulary with a reconstituted symbology based upon the intuitive perception of meaningful archetypes. Although we may be guided by careful studies of the past, such as those undertaken by Schwaller de Lubicz at Luxor and John James at Chartres, an assemblage of associative symbols will be difficult to comprise.[13] The danger is that idiosyncratic forms drawn from the personal unconscious of individual architects will substitute for the timeless images of the collective unconscious. The magic of architecture can best be worked through the power of symbols that may be comprehended both consciously and subliminally by everyone in every age.

Fortunately, we have available for our study and use the disciplined symbology of number. Schwaller de Lubicz writes: "There is a

Thoth, Master of the Net. Wall relief from the Temple of Karnak, Egypt. Schwaller de Lubicz writes: " . . . to penetrate the thought of the Ancients we rely on the architecture and the geometry that guides it, rather than on descriptive texts. It is the gesture that speaks and unveils."[12] (Photograph courtesy of Inner Traditions International, Rochester, Vermont.)

unique impulse, original and constant, and number reveals its modes to us through the varieties that make up Nature. Number is therefore the essential—but also the last—word explaining the Universe."[14] He adds, "The functional character of numbers is not relative or accidental, it is cosmic, the conscious revelation of our innate knowledge."[15]

The esoteric symbology of number is revealed through the ancient science of sacred geometry, which is common to all peoples and all cultures and has long been understood to link man to the cosmos. Through the study and comprehension of the sacred science of mathematical symbology, architects can organize the fabric of a building, a garden, or a landscape in a way that is truly magical, and will lead the mind to the comprehension of a higher truth.

Our science is a science of objects. The source of life, the mystery of being, is inaccessible to our science. The new science, like the ancient one, will comprehend the significance of myth and symbol. Schwaller writes:

> We thus have symbol and function as elements for making predictions about things and as a descriptive writing. "Understanding" will necessarily belong to the domain of a new state of consciousness that surpasses the three dimensional state.
>
> Now, the object of such a science is positive and the power of its application is magic, in the sense that causes are no longer particular but cosmic, and the phenomenon is subject to a knowledge of cosmic conditions, neither more nor less so than the sowing of a garden. In this way science *is* knowledge.[16]

St. James the Greater, from the south portal, central door at Chartres Cathedral. The anonymous medieval sculptor of this magnificent work was unconcerned with personal fame. He worked at whatever had to be done each day: statues, moldings, or even plain walls. When faced with a challenge such as this, he serenely relied upon the inspiration that he devoutly trusted would flow from God.

The Parameters of Inspiration

The anthropocosmic vision implies that an inspired artist or architect becomes a channel through which the accumulated insights of the collective unconscious find expression. This idea is diametrically opposed to the post-Renaissance cult of the individual that continues to shape the imagination of architects, their clients, and their critics in contemporary society. Today, those architects who are regarded as the leaders of the profession are expected to find the source of their creativity within the individual self. One result of this expectation is the uncritical acceptance of a personal egotism that has proved profoundly destructive to the beauty of our buildings and of our environment.

Self-expression is both the key word and the ideal held up as a mirror for emulation. Any piece of trash is acceptable if it is regarded as an authentic expression of the "self," by which is meant the individual conscious ego. I am not referring to the true self, which even according to the Freudian jargon contains the "superego." The true self represents an aspect of the soul.

Today we tiptoe around the other key word, *inspired,* which reflects a quality that we once expected in our buildings. The word *inspired* refers to spirit, hence the spiritual. It is derived from the Latin *spiritus,* and refers to "the life principle, especially in man, originally regarded as an animating vapor infused by the breath, *or as bestowed by a deity* [my emphasis]."[17] In the context of the anthropocosmic understanding, therefore, architectural inspiration is the flow of symbolic form from the collective unconscious into material reality.

This inspired flow of archetypal ideas is shaped and composed by the individual creative mind through which it passes. Mozart cannot explain why the ideas that come to him are "Mozartish," nor is he concerned about whether or not they reflect his personality. I believe that this sublime unconcern is one reason for the profound beauty of his work. For Mozart, his reward was not fame, or public acclamation, or even the pleasure of composing, but instead the joy that he must have felt as the truth and beauty he received as inspiration emerged into conscious awareness.

For architects, the joy of creation is to be found in the flow of geometric pattern as it emerges onto the drawing board, and later as the forms become evident in mass, space, and ornament. It is the work itself rather than any hope of fame that must be the goal. Schwaller de Lubicz writes:

> For Western man, it has become very difficult to discern the true from the false. And so he attaches all value to the product of his work, which, however, contributes absolutely nothing to his reality; that is, to the widening of his consciousness, the aim of his existence. He has forgotten that it is only the love that he puts into his work, only the quest to live at one with the life of the material that he fashions, which can augment his humanness.[19]

To submit to the discipline of mathematical truth, to incorporate symbolic images arising from the collective unconscious, is to augment our being.

Yet even the mathematical and geometrical systems upon which we must base the symbolic art and architecture of the future are subject to modification by the intuitive sense. They are by no means to be thought

Diorite head of the Buddha. I saw this carving in a flea market in Zurich and was compelled to buy it. I often stop and meditate before it, fascinated by the interplay of geometric forms. At such times I feel the presence of its creator and am aware of the spiritual insight that he achieved.

of as formulae, but rather as the framework within which artistic creation is to proceed. These modifications may even be deliberate disharmonies, or what John Anthony West calls "lawful inexactitudes."

One of my friends is a sculptor by day and a drummer in a jazz band by night. Some years ago, when still a beginner, he had the opportunity to back a well-known and respected musician. He was careful to keep an exact beat, which drove the musician to outspoken exasperation. The beat, he said, was like a machine, it was not "living," nor did it not reflect the nuances of the emotional flow of the melodic line. "You've got to speed it up and slow it down, man! You've got to feel the way it wants to be!" The changes wanted were virtually imperceptible, but critical to the flow of the musical ideas.

In my home I have displayed an ancient Chinese head of the Buddha. I often stop to marvel at the tranquillity and power that emanates from the work, and study the mathematical pattern that underlies the form. Within the overall geometry there are subtle distortions of symmetry: The right side of the head is distinctly larger than the left, the top-knob is skewed back to compensate, and the left-front facial plane is larger than the right. The geometric organization is so powerful that it can absorb these deliberate irregularities within the overall structure, but they give the piece tremendous force as they play within the serene geometry of intersecting ovals and triangles.

When Mozart wrote his music, the mathematical structure within which he worked was already there. The vibrational patterns of sound respond to mathematical laws, but even those laws had been amended by his predecessors. The system of musical notes within which he wrote had been "tempered," adjusted slightly but imperceptibly, to make possible the complex harmonies and the polyphonic compositions that are the glory of Western music. Yet within that structure and that system, what marvelous effects he achieved! The notes and intervals were not considered confining—they were liberating. Within the mathematical structure that he had inherited, his imagination was free to roam.

In the *Quattro Livre*, the "Four Books" on architecture written by Andrea Palladio, he disclosed his method for determining the proportions of rooms. Alas, as might be expected, his successors quickly converted his system into formulae, and the magical interplay, not only of geometry and number, but also of the subtle changes in what we might call "the beat," was lost.

In the preceding chapter I have called for a science of geometric symbology that would constitute an essential part of the framework, the "beat" within which artistic and architectural creation would proceed.

The poet William Blake made a distinction between harmony and melody. Harmony is directly accessible to the senses, for it is an expression of number and geometry. The laws of harmony must be observed, but within any harmonic system the imaginative possibilities of combination and recombination are infinite. Melody, Blake thought, is pure meaning, pure imagination, although considered mathematically and physiologically, it has no meaning. Blake wrote that the heavens themselves are only an instrument upon which is played the music of the Imagination.[18]

And yet it is equally true that mathematical law runs like a living flame through every material manifestation of the spirit of God.

The famous Villa Rotunda, in Vicenza, Italy, designed by Andrea Palladio. The beautiful interior rooms are seldom seen. Palladio says the dimensions of rooms should be determined by three different sets of ratios. He gives examples of each, but although he obviously understands the mathematical principles of these ratios (briefly described on page 164), he does not choose to disclose them.[20]

But such a science must not be absolute, nor should it be precisely regulated by quantitative mathematical formulae the way our material science is based on sense phenomena. It must respond to the subtle flow of pattern in the living human body and mind. This science must be acceptable to modification. It must feel right to the intuitive sense.

The deeper intuitive sense, the "wisdom of the heart," must be granted the authority to modify even the precision of the archetypal and geometrical truths within which it finds expression. But these truths must be accepted as the parameters within which the imagination is free to play.

12
A TIME OF TRANSITION

Principle and Process

In the preceding chapters I have identified a group of architectural principles that are so basic, so closely related to the needs of the human psyche, and so fundamental to the organization of space and form that they will be found to underlie any meaningful process of design. Although they are not identified in the schools or in the theoretical literature, and stand in opposition to the materialist paradigm, a few architects will be led through intuition, reflection, and study to express these principles in their work. But between a principle and its expression in form lies a technical process, the way in which the form of a building takes shape, first as a conception, then on the drawing board, and finally in visual and tactile fact.

As the work of sculpture responds to the tool and the material, so does the work of architecture respond to the technical process of creating a building. This process involves not only the methods of construction, but also the way in which the thought in the mind of the designer is expressed and communicated to all those engaged in the work of construction. Today, as in the past, this is done primarily through drawings and models initially conceived in the mind of an individual architect.

Traditionally, architectural design has followed a series of stages, from free-hand pencil sketches through preliminary plans and elevations made with T-square and right-angled triangles, to the dimensioned and

An architect's drawing board in the late twentieth century was not very different from the trestle board of the medieval master mason. The T-square has been replaced by the parallel rule with its wires and pulleys, compasses and pencils are made of metal instead of wood, and triangles are made of plastic, but the process of drawing a plan was the same. However, both the architect's tools and the process of drawing have drastically changed with the advent of the computer.

annotated working drawings used on the site. Until the last few centuries, the final stage was the direct supervision of the work by its creator. It was during the Renaissance that architects became "gentlemen" who drew the plans and did not dirty their hands with the work. This ideal permeated through the class structures of Europe into America and to the rest of the world, and has been reinforced by the productive efficiencies achieved by the division of labor characteristic of an industrial economy. In a large firm today, most architects work with paper plans and specifications, and are largely isolated from actual construction. The designing architects, in whose minds the buildings are originally conceived, become specialists in the production of preliminary plans. The working drawings, including those drawn by the engineers, the specifications, the perspective illustrations made for the press or for the client, and even the construction supervision are all produced by other specialists. The original designer goes on to other preliminary plans and may never see the building that he has conceived!

When the great cathedrals of medieval Europe were constructed, the system could not have been more different, for then the architect was the builder and in direct control of the entire project. The master mason of the Middle Ages came up through the trades, and was familiar with the various tasks of the men whom he supervised. When he picked up his pencil, there was a depth of meaning in every line that he drew. A line, for instance, that represented a wall of stone was understood in all its technical reality—the material in the quarry, the fabrication of the separate blocks with mallet and chisel, and finally the union of blocks and mortar into a solid mass. While sketches, diagrams, paper plans, and models were then, as now, the methods whereby an original idea was shaped into a finished design, the medieval architect understood in body and mind the implications of every line. That understanding has been lost and the paper abstraction has become an end in itself. Architects are thus alienated, set at one remove, from the environments that their abstractions define.

But even the paper abstraction has become further alienated from the direct intuitive creativity of the architect's mind. The primary tool has long been the pencil, but the pencil was once used to produce freehand drawings. Architects learned to draw; drawing, in fact, was recognized as a required skill of a cultivated man.

The contemporary architect relies upon "hard" lines even for preliminary drawings, whereby the pencil line is directed and restricted by straight-edged tools that ensure a uniform quality, but which inevitably restrict the imagination. An example of the effect of this restriction may

Yet even in the high Renaissance, Palladio was trained as a stonemason.

Drawing is a skill, a simple skill, and can be taught. Some of us are more adept at it—have more aptitude—and some might possess genius, but anyone can be taught to pick up a pencil and transfer ideas to paper. But we are no longer so taught! In our slightly mad concentration upon the discursive media, we are left to find our way by trial and error, and our children are brought up on coloring books.

be found in the ornamental design of Frank Lloyd Wright. His T-square and triangle systems of ornament have been justly celebrated, but cannot be compared to the freely designed ornament of his mentor and predecessor, Louis Sullivan.

Creative architects in a time of transition must learn to draw, but they also need to reconsider the properties of the tools used to produce the "hard" lines needed for the working drawings. Traditionally these have been T-squares or parallel rules, which together with right-angled triangles are used to establish a Cartesian system of lines that cross at right angles. Compasses are used to turn circles, and scales are used to set out dimensions on paper. Of the right-angled triangles, only the 30° and 45° fixed triangles are commonly used; adjustable triangles graduated in degrees are used for any other angular dimension. The 45° and 30° triangles are indeed important: They present the sacred roots of two and three, and are the two triangles mentioned by Plato in the *Timaeus* as the only ones necessary to construct the first four regular solids.

There are, however, other triangles whose use we could explore. There is the right triangle representing in side and base the proportions of Phi; there is the double square, square root of five triangle; and the

Left: The doorway of an early house in Oak Park, Chicago, designed by Frank Lloyd Wright, is beautiful in its classical grace and dignity. *Right:* The ornament of Louis Sullivan is imbued with a dark, creative fire. The inspired "melody"—to use William Blake's word—plays within the parameters of the underlying geometric form. (Carson Pirie and Scott Department Store, Chicago, built in 1904.)

sacred Pythagorean triangle with sides of three, four, and five. And why are compasses so seldom used, and why do most architects use a circle template instead? What we see in the selection of tools is a reflection of a loss of interest in the geometric basis of the art. Even Wright, who occasionally broke out of the Cartesian right-angled grid, seems to have been limited by his training in the use of the two conventional triangles to the exclusion of other possibilities, such as those afforded by the Phi proportion or the Pythagorean triangle.

A triangle is not just a simple tool for drawing right-angled lines; it represents significant ratios and proportional series. To have in one's hand a triangle that represents the Phi proportion, for instance, is to be constantly reminded of the Phi principle. To use the compass is to express, by the act of drawing a circle, the sacred nature of that essential form.

The computer represents yet another layer of abstraction and alienation from the reality of actual construction. With the widespread use of the computer, the creative capacity of the artist's mind is directed not only to the paper plans rather than to the physical reality of construction, but also to the effective use of the machine that produces those paper plans. The hand-drawn plans, even if they were not free hand, at least bore the imprint of the artist's pencil, the physical touch of his hand, and the documents themselves were an artful product. The computer product, by contrast, is regular and even: There is no touch, no personality. Like a commercial cake mix, it is always edible but never very good.

People who are good with computers are not likely to make good architects. To computer people, creativity lies in using the computer: Manipulation of the machine has replaced the skill of drawing, and a rational, mental process has replaced an intuitive, artistic way of thinking. The real issue for computer people is their ability to operate the system.

Properly used, the computer can be an asset. Many of us remember the long hours spent in the tedious and time-consuming task of producing working drawings and writing specifications in the detail required for the legal documents that architectural plans have become. Before the computer, minor changes had to be correlated across sheet after sheet, and seemed an endless drudgery. The computer is able to effect such changes quickly and easily, and if the preliminary plans and elevations, the ornament and details, are produced directly under the architect's hand, that material can be computerized without destroying the integrity of the artistic concept. A few architects now work in this way, but the thrust of our technology-obsessed society is toward an ever greater reliance upon the machine as the primary design tool.

In the absence of an ethical imperative, the future of Modern architecture is the computer, and this can now be seen in the schools. On a recent visit to Penn, I was struck forcibly by the dramatic change in the working environment that has occurred in the past fifty years. When I was a student we all worked together in one vast, naturally lighted room where we were able to learn from each other. When I returned I found the school in a new, dismal, scientifically designed building, where the students worked in small classrooms with computers. The emphasis in the school had shifted from the camaraderie of equals and the interplay of ideas to the relation between an individual and his machine. The same shift has rapidly occurred in most architectural offices as well: Proficiency in the use of the various CAD (Computer Assisted Design) programs is now demanded for entry-level positions, a factor that influences the methods taught in the schools. And as we have seen, graduation from an architectural school has become a virtual requirement for obtaining the coveted license. The system ensures that the most promising aspiring young architects are locked into a method that represses the full exercise of their talent.

The few farsighted architects who reject the computer and choose to work in the old way, using others to put their designs into the machines, are usually older, established in their profession, and trained in the traditional skills. It is increasingly difficult for those who have been taught to design with the computer to choose to work with the old tools, and yet they must learn to do so if they are to fulfill themselves as architects in this time of transition.

The design process of those who practice the new architecture will differ from those who operate within the parameters of the materialist paradigm in another, perhaps more subtle, way. The desire to define and express the mathematical integrity of the form will necessarily lead to a recognition of the primary importance of the plan, and the grounding of plan, elevations, and ornament in related groups of mathematically derived patterns.

The plan is a two-dimensional representation of a three-dimensional volume. It *implies* the volume and is the trace of our movement through space on the plane of the floor. The elevations, sections, and ornament must emerge *organically* from the plan.

In the great architecture of both past and present, the plan dominates the design, but since the discovery of mechanical perspective in the Renaissance, there has been a growing tendency to design in perspective,

A design studio at the University of Pennsylvania in Philadelphia.

The appeal of the computer is insidious in a society such as ours that values technology for its own sake and lauds a science devoted to the study of quantities of uniform elements. In popular culture, this leads inexorably to a preference for sliced white bread.

A good general rule should be, "Beware the use of machines in all the arts." I once studied sculpture under John Hovannes, who was teaching at the Art Students League in New York. He had the most powerful and elaborate pneumatic carving equipment that I have ever seen. But I could see that through the use of these machines, he had lost his feeling for the simplicity of form. The tool made it easy to cut a complex or intricate shape, and the impulse to use it was irresistible.

Compare this photograph, with its bold, exaggerated perspective, dramatic clouds, and deep blue sky, with the picture of the same architectural stunt shown on page 10. A clever photographer has deliberately manipulated the camera to convey a false image of the actual building. (Photograph © 1988, courtesy of the *Baltimore Sun*.)

emphasizing the single viewpoint of an observer over the geometrical organization of the plan. The tendency has been further reinforced by the development of photography. Today we know buildings primarily through the photographic images selected and reproduced in magazines and books. These images, to a greater or lesser extent, are misleading, as are the perspective drawings that are produced to inform the architect or to persuade a client to proceed with the project. They are misleading because a building is a whole. It exists as a geometric fact, defining form in space. It is never experienced from a single or multiple series of isolated locations, but rather as a totality built up in the mind through the continuous impressions received as the observer passes through space. And, of course, the perspective images are misleading in that they reflect the skill of the photographer or artist in selecting the viewpoint, the lighting, the color, even the clouds in the sky, rather than the merit of the building itself.

Although a few architects still possess facility with a pencil and can quickly sketch the proposed appearance of a construction from any location, even that particular exercise is dangerous: not because it will mislead the client, but because it will inevitably mislead the architect as well. This was noted by Le Corbusier, who refused to use his considerable graphic skills to produce anything other than rough sketches of his intentions. He understood that there can be no substitute for the rigor-

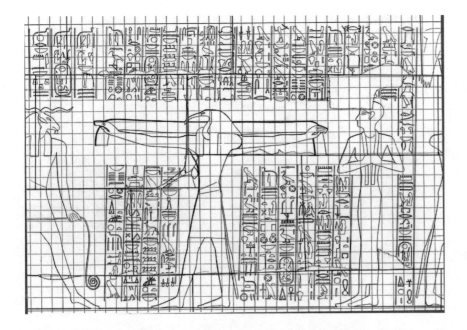

The Egyptian grid shown at left is an analysis by R. A. Schwaller de Lubicz and his assistant Lucy Lamy of the wall in the Temple of Karnak, Egypt, pictured on page 187. (Photograph courtesy of Inner Traditions International, Rochester, Vermont.)

ous, careful visualization of the geometry of a proposed form through study of the plan and elevations.

Behind the construction of the plan and elevations must lie a grasp of pattern. Pattern is the expression of the mathematical principles that are the basis of the design. The most common pattern is the grid of squares used by visual artists and architects all the way back to the Egyptians.[1]

The advantage of working with this kind of grid is that simple whole number ratios and the whole number proportions of orthogonal shapes are readily apparent. But the patterned grids used to underlay designs may be of much greater complexity. Wright, for instance, seems to have relied heavily on the so-called tartan, or interwoven grid.[2] This was iden-tified by Owen Jones as the basis of Islamic ornament.[3] The use of such grids was evidently once widespread. Last year I was able to witness the construction of a sand mandala by a group of Tibetan Buddhist priests. They began by laying out, with compasses and chalk lines, what we would call a tartan grid. The mandala, which represented the plan of the ideal temple and the house of God, was then constructed within the geometry of the grid.

The geometry of the circle and of circular forms can proceed, how-ever, within or without an orthogonal grid. Keith Crichlow, who inves-tigated the ruins of a great monastic complex at Glastonbury, England,

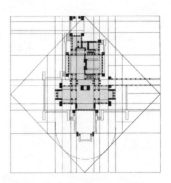

Plan of the Martin house in Buffalo, New York, designed by Frank Lloyd Wright. (From *Frank Lloyd Wright: Principle and Form,* by Paul Laseau and James Tice.)

The first step in the construction of this Tibetan sand mandala was to lay out a tartan grid with lines and circles of chalk. These were selectively erased and others added. The monks did not appear to be working from a predetermined pattern, but, of course, the lineaments of a number of such patterns could have been memorized. The colored sand was then poured from tubes and paper spills. The mandala was quickly constructed and as quickly destroyed to demonstrate the impermanence of all material things. (Photograph courtesy of Inner Traditions International from *Navajo and Tibetan Sacred Wisdom,* by Peter Gold.)

was able to determine that the Vesica Pisces had been the form upon which the design was based. In *The Old Way of Seeing,* Jonathan Hale demonstrates the use of the circle in a number of pre-Modern vernacular buildings.

As always, of course, it is the thought behind the visible form as well as the principles of the creator that in some mysterious way are reflected in the creation. But the tools themselves tend to impose mathematical patterns, and these inevitably influence architects as they endeavor to express in their plans the deepest intuitive truth of which they are aware. The choice and manipulation of the instruments through which the image or the vision may be realized is therefore important.

An architect must bring into conscious reflection the interaction of vision and technical means, from the initial, intuitive dream to the final result. What happens upon his drawing board is the first stage in a long, complex process, and as the design proceeds through its various stages toward actual construction, it becomes increasingly subject to social forces that represent the orientation of the larger society. It is the impact of those forces, and how they may be resolved in a time of transition, that is the subject of the next chapter.

Architect and Society

An architect who would be a creative artist must reject the current, deadly, corporate approach to building the human environment and seek his or her opportunities elsewhere. The corporate architects of today produce elaborate sets of computer plans and specifications that indicate as completely as possible every detail of the work. These constitute a legal document defining the responsibilities of architect, builder, and owner, and the architect who works within this system has come to accept a position between owner and builder. He represents the interest of the owner versus the builder, and in our litigation-prone society architects tend to concentrate their attention on the production of a legal document rather than on the creation of a work of art.

In the corporate world, moreover, as in our larger society, "time is money," and even the production of art is ruled by principles of productive efficiency. But art stands outside of time. Some artists work quickly; some are slow. Corporate architectural practice, however, is

I walked the maze at Chartres Cathedral, following the twistings and turnings, setting aside the wooden chairs that blocked the way. There are no blind alleys: to reach the center it is necessary only to cling tenaciously to the path outlined by the stones in the floor. (Photograph courtesy of Wikimedia Commons, GNUFDL license.)

under constant time pressure to complete the current project and move on to the next. Certainly one should not dawdle and there are legitimate constraints of time, but the creative process must not and cannot be scheduled. And in the interest of productive efficiency, even the process of architectural design itself is now fragmented functionally. An individual architect is often confined to his or her special area of expertise and unaware of the progression of the design from sketch to construction plans, even within the office.

The existing system is hopelessly warped, and if architects are to fulfill their dreams, they must be directly responsible for the construction of the buildings they design and become builders in the ancient sense of the word. The design/build teams, as they are called, have the right idea, but they are still led by those who are tied to the present system of architectural education. Unfortunately, there is more to be unlearned than learned by those who pass through the schools of fine arts as they are now constituted. Those who aspire to the practice of architecture in the sense of its ancient significance will find that a liberal arts curriculum, combined with an apprenticeship to a builder, together with practical, on-the-job experience in the construction trades, and a program of intensive self-education, is a better way to acquire the necessary skills and understanding.

Those of us who went through the architectural schools and tried to pursue a conventional career but were frustrated by the assumptions that underlie our materialistic culture have a different problem. We may understand that materialism is fundamentally hostile to the creation of great art, and wish to create from a different moral and ideological position, but we are trapped within the position to which architecture has devolved in a materialistic society. For most of us, it is too late to begin again. We must function within a more or less conventional practice and do the best we can.

An artist starving in a garret may continue to pursue his art, even to the untimely end of his existence, but architects, to build, must have clients who will mobilize the social forces necessary to bring their designs into material reality. Those who take the other path must search even farther than conventional practitioners in order to find those particular clients who can comprehend the deeper meaning and purpose of the forms and images that take shape upon the drawing boards. This is no longer a near impossible task. The despair that once affected only the most sensitive souls has now affected many, and as a result, ideas regarding the purpose of life and the function of art that were once dismissed with contempt now receive serious consideration. The potential clients are willing to listen; the problem has become *how* to communicate the essential vision.

Design/build companies contract to design and construct a proposed building. Unlike the large corporate firms dominated by builders or engineers, who hire architects as subordinate members of their staff, the people in charge are recognized as architects, whether or not they are licensed or have formal training.

Licensing requirements are designed to compel aspiring architects to pass through the schools. They constitute a formidable, though not insurmountable, barrier, which can be evaded, especially for those architects focusing on the construction of homes and other small buildings.

A principal difficulty is the one-sided devotion of our culture to discursive modes of communication. Painting, sculpture, music, and architecture are nondiscursive: that is, they communicate in ways other than can be expressed in language. We must, therefore, translate our visual concepts into words before they can become widely influential. This is difficult but necessary, and yet for those whose training, aptitudes, and commitments lie in other directions, and in the case of the most profound symbolic concepts, it may not be possible at all. It will certainly take time, dedication, and persistence, and in the interim, until the new vision is more widely accepted, what should an architect do? Without the support of informed clients, how can an architect build to a higher standard that is not recognized as such by the world at large?

Those who pursue the other path should keep in mind that "big" is not automatically better; in fact, it is usually ugly. More often, "small is beautiful," a dictum of E. F. Schumacher, and the title of one of his best-known books.[4] We need to begin with small things, not only because the corporate clients of our time are largely inaccessible to those of us who reject the present system, but also because the sheer size and scale of many of the buildings that we now erect are inappropriate to "the human use of human beings."

Let us then begin with small buildings—houses, offices, and stores, even additions and remodeling. These are ignored as unprofitable by the large commercial firms and thereby provide an opening through which a dedicated architect can bring into being buildings that will enrich rather than degrade the earth.

And after all, is this not what we really seek? Architectural fame and pictures of our buildings in magazines may have once conferred a kind of validation, but that currency has become so debased that it is meaningless. Most of us entered the profession because we wanted to create beautiful things, not just for ourselves, but for our fellow men as well. In a society that does not value beauty except as it affects the bottom line, such a goal is difficult but not impossible to achieve.

One of the most moving passages in the Sermon on the Mount is when the Christ declares:

> *Ask, and it shall be given you;*
> *Seek, and you shall find;*
> *Knock, and it shall be opened unto you:*
> *For every one that asketh receiveth;*
> *And he that seeketh findeth;*
> *And to him that knocketh it shall be opened.*[5]

From my personal experience I can testify to the simple, literal truth of the teaching. There is a force in the universe that resonates to our individual awareness and wishes us to grow toward a deeper comprehension of itself. It may be what we call God; it may be expressed through some lesser form of higher, non-corporeal being; it may be that there is some mysterious organization of reality that operates to ensure that our deepest needs are met. It may even be that we ourselves at some consciously unknown level of being interact with the cosmos to advance our comprehension.

I say that it is in the anthropocosmic nature of the universe, the nature of the divine spiritual reality, that if we seek in a spirit of disinterested love, a way will be found whereby that which we require will be made available to us. To those who are faithful to the vision of a new architecture that has been vouchsafed them, a way will open whereby they will be able to realize their vision and fulfill their lives.

The New Architecture

The attempt to explain the cosmos as a gigantic machine and our existence as an accident wrought a radical change in our conception of the nature of reality. It resulted in a decisive break with the religious and mystical systems of the past, and shattered the belief in the existence of purpose in art and life. The architectural expression of this dominant materialist paradigm of our time culminated in the scientific architecture of the twentieth century. Similarly, the coming of a new paradigm that would recognize the transcendental significance of spirit will effect another dramatic change in the character of the buildings that we, as a society, choose to erect.

I have argued that if architects are to build successfully, both now and in the coming new age, they must deny the materialist paradigm. They must recognize that not only are they the heirs of a once great architectural tradition, but they are also the heirs of a profound spiritual tradition, the "other tradition," that extends back to the origins of human society. I believe that those who accept the other tradition, together with the mystical vision and the anthropocosmic insight, will find it possible to fuse the spiritual and material elements of existence into a new paradigm, a new synthesis. Out of this synthesis will come an architecture founded

The glass pyramid designed by I. M. Pei for the entrance to the Louvre may represent the end of one tradition and the beginning of another: the end of Modernism and the beginning of a new architectural tradition founded upon a fusion of the archetypal needs of the human psyche with the esoteric discipline of sacred mathematics. Pei describes his search for the right shape as an intuitive process of comparing alternatives, while the Great Pyramid at Giza was obviously designed in total cognizance of the complex of mathematical principles incorporated into the structure. I foresee an architecture of the future that will combine the technical brilliance of Pei's achievement with a "scientific" awareness of the significance of the sacred geometric principles that lie behind the ancient form.

upon a different understanding of the nature of the psyche, the order of the cosmos, and our place within the ultimate mystery of existence.

Is it possible to envision the material form of a new architecture? Can we foresee how the buildings of the future will differ from those of the present? Prophecy is always difficult, since the hopes and desires of the prophet are inextricably bound up with the nature of his vision. Nevertheless, if a major shift in the assumptions underlying our society should occur as foreseen, it is possible to predict some features of the new architecture.

Certainly, the buildings of the future will be more than the biotechnically adequate shelters our architects are asked to build. The new architecture will speak to the primal, archetypal demands of the unconscious mind. The images of cave and clearing, of womb and sky, have always been with us. They are a part of the fabric of our being. When they are recognized and accepted, not just intellectually but through a process of intuitive knowing, architects will work in an awareness of our common psychological response to the elements of shelter and space. The archetypal images of our collective experience will then be a part of the fabric of our dwellings and the pattern of our lives.

An architecture based upon timeless principles will necessarily be simple and unpretentious. Architects who understand technology, not as an end, but as a means to an end, will not design grotesque monuments to the technical achievements of the twentieth century such as the Bilbao Museum and the Sydney Opera House. Nor will their work resemble alien artifacts set down in a meadow, like the Farnsworth house and the Ville Savoy. They will belong to the earth.

Designed in awareness of the existence of transcendental moral principles, the major buildings of the future, unlike those of the present, will not be glorified pieces of sculpture or the egotistical expression of individual architects. They will represent the artistic combination and recombination of typical elements by different men and women working within a common tradition. These typical elements will include the large areas of glass made available through contemporary technology that open interior spaces to the sun, to the garden, to the pool. They will include roofs that are responsive to climate and not always arbitrarily flat: Where summers are hot and precipitation high, for instance, roofs will be pitched, with deep overhangs. They will include the use of stone, brick, and wood for texture and as a means of expressing the nature of the materials that come directly from the earth. They will include a considered orientation to the sun and wind, rain and snow, the slope of the ground, the patterns of the larger landscape, and the spin of Earth around the sun.

This architecture will necessarily be local and indigenous as it responds to the combination of factors that vary from region to region. We do not need Grecian temples, Renaissance palazzos, or Gothic churches set down in American streets and fields. The time for these is long past. We should now draw our inspiration from those vernacular buildings of our recent past that were adapted to the land and derived from the natural forms we find around us.

A new symbolic architecture can then reach into the unconscious and mythic layers of being and lead us into a state of higher spiritual awareness. We as a people and as a culture can once more understand the significance of a building as an analogue of creation itself, and the act of building as an act of worship. And if it is accepted that all of life is sacred, and the earth itself divine, it will be impossible to abuse our world as we have so recklessly and thoughtlessly done.

As we renew our faith in a meaningful existence and reaffirm our

The circular zodiac on the ceiling of the Temple of Hathor at Dendera in Egypt was constructed in the time of Augustus Caesar and Jesus Christ. At that time, the rising sun at the vernal equinox was leaving the astrological region of Aries the Ram to enter that of Pisces the Fish. (Photograph courtesy of Inner Traditions International, Rochester, Vermont.)

belief in an ordered cosmos, our architects will surely acknowledge the importance of the sacred geometry that lies behind our sensorial experience of the material world. Geometry and number will then be understood not just as ways in which we represent quantities, but as symbolic expressions of a higher reality as well. The exploration of this higher reality will be recognized as the ultimate, primal concern of the human mind and, as we proceed to grasp the principles that lie behind the appearance of things, the neglected laws of proportion and harmony will be revived. The transcendental, spiritual significance of our material existence will then be expressed in the new, common vocabulary of architectural form.

As our Earth wobbles upon its axis, the sun is now leaving the sign of Pisces and beginning to rise at the spring equinox in the constellation of Aquarius. We conclude a twelfth part of the 26,000-year precessional cycle. We are in a time of astrological transition, and are moving into a new age, under a new zodiacal sign. In the past these times of transition have been associated with major changes in the way that societies function and in the way we think about religion, politics, and art. Our time is therefore a time in which the materialism of the present will be curbed by a greater comprehension of the endless complexities of the interaction of spirit and matter. In our time and the time to come, architects will once more take up their traditional role and build the temples of the Aquarian Age.

And for those of us who will not live to enter this promised land, there remains the opportunity to accomplish lesser tasks with skill and dedication. If, within the constraints of our culture, we who have seen this vision are able to build only a simple house, we can build to the limits of the insight we have achieved. That house will then not merely provide for the comfort of those who dwell within its walls; it will magically reflect the order of the universe and thus be beautiful and true.

NOTES

Chapter 2. The Scientific Architecture of the Twentieth Century

1. Tom Wolfe, *From Bauhaus to Our House* (New York: McGraw-Hill, 1981).
2. Robert Venturi, *Complexity and Contradiction in Architecture* (New York: Museum of Modern Art Press, 1966).
3. Robert Venturi, Denise Scott Brown, and Steven Izenour, *Learning from Las Vegas,* revised ed. (Cambridge, Mass.: M.I.T. Press, 1997), 105, 108–110.
4. Le Corbusier, *The Radiant City* (New York: Orion Press, 1933), 207. French edition: *La Ville Radieuse* (Paris: Vincent, Fréal et Cie, 1933).
5. Ibid., 206.
6. HRH the Prince of Wales, *A Vision of Britain: A Personal View of Architecture* (London: Doubleday, 1989).
7. Lewis Mumford, lecture, University of Pennsylvania, 1954.
8. Alexander Tzonis, *Le Corbusier: The Poetics of Machine and Metaphor* (New York: Universe Publishing, 2001), 135.
9. Elaine S. Hochman, *Architects of Fortune: Mies van der Rohe and the Third Reich* (New York: International Publishing, 1990).
10. Mark Stevens, "Form Follows Fascism," *New York Times,* January 31, 2005, Opinion Section, p. 31.
11. Le Corbusier, *The Radiant City.*
12. Ibid., 143.

Chapter 3. Making the Modern Architect

1. A. T. Mann, *Sacred Architecture* (Rockport, Me.: Element Press, 1993), 7.
2. Ibid., 10.
3. Jonathan Hale, *The Old Way of Seeing* (New York: Houghton Mifflin Co., 1994), 126–127.
4. Siegfried Giedion, *Space, Time and Architecture: The Growth of a New Tradition* (Boston: Cambridge Press, 1941, reissued 1997), xxxiii.
5. Karsten Harries, *The Ethical Function of Architecture* (Cambridge, Mass: M.I.T. Press, 1997), 109–110.
6. Jonathan Hale, *The Old Way of Seeing.*
7. Colin Wilson, *The Outsider* (New York: G. P. Putnam, 1982).

Chapter 4. The Materialist Paradigm

1. Bertrand Russell, *The Autobiography of Bertrand Russell: 1872–1914* (Boston: Little, Brown and Co., 1967), 220–221.
2. Bertrand Russell, as quoted in John Anthony West, *The Case for Astrology* (New York: Viking, 1991), 446–447; as quoted in E. A. Burtt, *The Metaphysical Foundations of Modern Science* (London: Kegan Paul, Trench, Trübner & Co., 1932), 9.
3. Frank Lloyd Wright, *When Democracy Builds* (Chicago: University of Chicago Press, 1945).

Chapter 5. The Return of the Spirit

1. H. P. Blavatsky, *The Secret Doctrine,* vol. 1 (Wheaton, Ill.: Theosophical Press, 1888; Quest Ed., 1993), 477.
2. Stewart C. Easton, *Rudolf Steiner: Herald of a New Epoch* (Hudson, N.Y.: Anthroposophic Press, 1980), 75–76.
3. Ibid.
4. A term coined by John Anthony West.
5. Michael A. Cremo and Richard L. Thompson, *Forbidden Archeology: The Hidden History of the Human Race* (Badger, Calif.: Torchlight, 1996).
6. Aldous Huxley, *The Perennial Philosophy* (New York: Harper and Row, 1944; colophon ed., 1970), viii.

Chapter 6. Intuition and the Creative Mind

1. Sigmund Freud, *The Psychopathology of Everyday Life.* Editor and translator, James Strachy (New York: W. W. Norton and Co., 1965), 185–186.
2. Eugen Herrigel, *Zen in the Art of Archery* (New York: Vintage Books, 1989), 58–59.

3. Kathleen Raine, "Blake, Yeats and Pythagoras," in *Homage to Pythagoras: Rediscovering Sacred Science,* ed. Christopher Bamford (Hudson, N.Y.: Lindisfarne Press, 1982), 276–280.

4. Hans Mersman, ed. *Letters of Wolfgang Amadeus Mozart* (New York: Dover, 1972), editor's preface, vii–viii.

5. Jonathan Hale, *The Old Way of Seeing.*

6. C. G. Jung, *The Archetypes and the Collective Unconscious,* Bollingen Series XX (Princeton, N.J.: Princeton University Press, 1990), 5.

7. Ibid.

Chapter 7. Archetypes of Shelter

1. Erich Maria Remarque, *All Quiet on the Western Front* (New York: Ballantine Books, 1982), 55.

2. Franz Schulze, *Mies van der Rohe: A Critical Biography* (Chicago: University of Chicago Press, 1985), 252–259.

3. Sydney LeBlanc, *The Architectural Traveler: A Guide to 250 Key 20th-Century American Buildings* (New York: W. W. Norton, 2000), 88.

4. Ibid., 281–282.

5. The term "Usonian" was coined by Wright to identify those buildings that expressed his idea of Emersonian democracy. The concept is best explained in his book *When Democracy Builds* (Chicago: University of Chicago Press, 1945).

Chapter 8. Archetypes of Design

1. R. A. Schwaller de Lubicz, *The Temple of Man,* translated by Deborah Lawlor and Robert Lawlor (Rochester, Vt.: Inner Traditions, 1998).

2. Ada Louise Huxtable, "The New Architecture," *The New York Review of Books,* vol. 42, no. 6 (April 6, 1995), 19.

Chapter 9. The Resolution of Form

1. John Anthony West, *Serpent in the Sky: The High Wisdom of Ancient Egypt* (Wheaton, Ill.: Theosophical Publishing House, 1993), 30.

2. Essay by Alan Colquhuon in *Meaning in Architecture,* by Charles Jencks and George Baird (New York: George Braziller, 1969), 267.

3. Robert Venturi, Denise Scott Brown, and Steven Izenour, *Learning from Las Vegas.*

4. Alan Colquhuon, *Meaning in Architecture,* 274.

5. K. Michael Hays, ed. *Architecture Theory Since 1968* (Cambridge, Mass.: M.I.T. Press, 2000), 780.

6. Paul Goldberger, "Artistic License," *The New Yorker,* June 2, 2003, pp. 99–101.

7. R. A. Schwaller de Lubicz, *The Temple of Man,* 335.

8. Piazzi Smith, *The Great Pyramid: Its Secrets and Mysteries Revealed,* 4th ed. (New York: Crown Publishers, 1978), plate VI.

9. Andrea Palladio, 1518–1580, the leading Italian architect of the late Renaissance and author of the influential *Quattro Libri dell' Architettura,* or *The Four Books of Architecture,* translated by Robert Travernor and Richard Schofield (New York: Dover Publications, 1965).

10. Le Corbusier, *The Modulor,* translated by Peter de Francis and Anna Bostock (Cambridge Mass., M.I.T. Press, 1968).

Chapter 10. Geometry and Number

1. Rene Schwaller de Lubicz (1887–1961) is well known for his many works that express the profound spiritual and cosmological insights of ancient Egypt, including the belief that the ancient Egyptians possessed a dynamic understanding of the laws of harmony and proportion. Schwaller's many books on the subject include *Esotericism and Symbol, The Temple in Man, Symbol and the Symbolic, The Egyptian Miracle,* and *The Temple of Man.*

2. R. A. Schwaller de Lubicz, *The Temple of Man* (Rochester, Vt.: Inner Traditions, 1998).

3. John Anthony West, *Serpent in the Sky: The High Wisdom of Ancient Egypt.*

4. Robert Lawlor, *Sacred Geometry: Philosophy and Practice* (New York: Thames and Hudson Ltd.; Crossroads, 1982).

5. Stewart C. Easton, *Rudolf Steiner,* 20.

6. Robert Lawlor, *Sacred Geometry,* 10.

7. St. Bernard of Clairvaux, *On Consideration.* Quoted by Robert Lawlor in *Sacred Geometry: Philosophy and Practice,* 6.

8. The Grand Lodge of Ancient, Free and Accepted Masons of Maryland. *Maryland Manual of Ancient Craft Masonry* (Baltimore, 1935), 37.

9. Robert Lawlor, *Sacred Geometry.*

10. Ibid., 34.

11. Keith Critchlow, *Glastonbury: A Study in Patterns* (London: RILKO, as illustrated by Robert Lawlor), 35.

12. Jonathan Hale, *The Old Way of Seeing,* 51.

13. Quoted in Robert Lawlor, *Sacred Geometry,* 53.

14. Robert Lawlor, *Sacred Geometry,* 20.

15. Ibid., 97 (referring to Keith Critchlow, *Time Stands Still*).

16. Ibid., 98–102.

17. Ibid., 81.

Chapter 11. Architect and Cosmos

1. R. A. Schwaller de Lubicz, *The Temple of Man*, vol. 1, 88–102.
2. John Anthony West, *Serpent in the Sky*, 30.
3. R. A. Schwaller de Lubicz, *The Temple of Man*, 335.
4. Robert Lawlor. *Sacred Geometry*, 92.
5. *Webster's New World Dictionary of the American Language* (G. & C. Merriam Co., 1971), 508.
6. Jonathan Hale, *The Old Way of Seeing*.
7. Andrew J. Lawson, *Cave Art* (Princes Risborough, U.K.: Shire Publications, 1991), 23–25.
8. Ibid., 58. Also C. G. Jung, ed., *Man and His Symbols* (London: Aldus Books, 1964), 235.
9. Robert Lawlor, *Voices of the First Day: Awakening in the Aboriginal Dreamtime* (Rochester, Vt.: Inner Traditions, 1991), 320.
10. C. G. Jung, *Man and His Symbols*.
11. Robert Lawlor, *Sacred Geometry*, 92.
12. R. A. Schwaller de Lubicz, *The Temple of Man*, vol. 2, 796–797. Illustration, vol. 2, plate 60.
13. John James, *The Master Masons of Chartres* (Leura: Australia, West Grinstead Publishing, 1990).
14. R. A. Schwaller de Lubicz, *The Temple of Man*, vol. 1, 81.
15. Ibid., 83.
16. Ibid., 84.
17. *Webster's New World Dictionary of the American Language*, 438.
18. Kathleen Raine, "Blake, Yeats and Pythagoras," 274–280.
19. R. A. Schwaller de Lubicz, *The Temple of Man*.
20. Rudolph Wittkower, *The Architecture of Humanism*, 4th ed. (London: Academy Editions, 1973), 108–109.

Chapter 12. A Time of Transition

1. R. A. Schwaller de Lubicz, *The Temple of Man*, vol. 2, plate 61.
2. Paul Laseau and James Tice, *Frank Lloyd Wright: Between Principle and Form* (New York: Van Nostrand Reinhold, 1992), 64.
3. Owen Jones, *The Grammar of Ornament: A Unique Collection of More Than 2,350 Classic Patterns,* first published in 1856 (New York: D. K. Publishing, 2001).
4. E. F. Schumacher, *Small Is Beautiful* (New York: HarperCollins, 1975).
5. Matthew 7:7–8.

BIBLIOGRAPHY

Alexander, Christopher. *The Nature of Order*. Berkeley, Calif.: Center for Environmental Structure, 2002.

Bamford, Christopher, ed. *Homage to Pythagoras: Rediscovering Sacred Science*. Hudson, N.Y.: Lindisfarne Press, 1994.

Blake, Peter. *The Master Builders: Le Corbusier/Mies van der Rohe/Frank Lloyd Wright*. (Reissued with additional chapters and illustrations). New York: W. W. Norton & Co., 1996.

Blavatsky, H. P. *Isis Unveiled*. 1877. Reprint: Pasadena, Calif.: Theosophical University Press, 1988.

———. *The Secret Doctrine*. 1888. Reprint: Wheaton, Ill.: Theosophical Publishing House, 1993.

Calatrava, Santiago. *Conversations with Students: The MIT Lectures*. New York: Princeton Architectural Press, 2002.

Capra, Fritjof. *The Turning Point: Science, Society, and the Rising Culture*. New York: Bantam Books, 1983.

———. *The Tao of Physics: An Exploration of the Parallels Between Modern Physics and Eastern Mysticism*. Boston: Shambhala Publications, 1991.

Cerver, Francisco Asencio. *Houses of the World*. Barcelona: Arco Editorial, 2000.

Charpentier, Louis. *The Mysteries of Chartres Cathedral*. Translated by Ronald Frazer in collaboration with Janette Jackson. Orpington, Kent: R.I.L.K.O. Books, 1972.

Cook, Theodore Andrea. *The Curves of Life*. New York: Dover, 1979.

Critchlow, Keith. *Order in Space: A Design Source Book*. New York: Thames and Hudson, 1987.

De Sola-Morales, Ignasi, Christian Cirici, and Ferdinand Ramos. *Mies van der Rohe Barcelona Pavilion*. Translated by Graham Thomson. Barcelona: Gustave Gilli, 1993.

Doczi, Gyorgy. *The Power of Limits: Proportional Harmonies in Nature, Art and Architecture*. Boston: Shambhala, 1981.

Easton, Stuart C. *Rudolf Steiner: Herald of a New Epoch*. Hudson, N.Y.: Anthroposophic Press, 1980.

Freud, Sigmund. *The Psychopathology of Everyday Life*. Translated and edited by James Strachey. New York: W. W. Norton & Company, 1989.

Gay, Peter. *The Enlightenment: An Interpretation*. New York: W. W. Norton & Company, 1977.

Giedion, Siegfried. *Space, Time, and Architecture*. Boston: Cambridge Press, 1974.

Ghyka, Matila. *The Geometry of Art and Life*. New York: Dover, 1977.

Hale, Jonathan. *The Old Way of Seeing*. New York: Houghton Mifflin Co., 1994.

Harries, Karsten. *The Ethical Function of Architecture*. Cambridge, Mass.: M.I.T. Press, 1997.

Hays, Michael K., ed. *Architecture Theory Since 1968*. Cambridge, Mass.: M.I.T. Press, 2000.

Herrigel, Eugen. *Zen in the Art of Archery*. Translated by R. F. C. Hull. Introduction by D. T. Suzuki. New York: Pantheon Books, 1999.

Hochman, Elaine S. *Architects of Fortune*. New York: Random House Value Publishing, 1993.

H. R. H. the Prince of Wales. *A Vision of Britain: A Personal View of Architecture*. London: Doubleday, 1989.

Huntley, H. E. *The Divine Proportion: A Study in Mathematical Beauty*. New York: Dover, 1970.

Huxley, Aldous. *The Perennial Philosophy*. New York: Harper Colophon, 1970.

James, John. *The Master Masons of Chartres*. Leura, Australia: West Grinstead Publishing, 1990.

———. *The Traveler's Key to Medieval France*. New York: Knopf, 1986.

Jencks, Charles, and George Baird, eds. *Meaning in Architecture*. New York: George Braziller, Inc. 1989.

Jones, Owen. *The Grammar of Ornament*. Reprint, New York: D. K. Publishing, 2001.

Jung, C. G. *The Archetypes and the Collective Unconscious*. Translated by R. F. C. Hull. New York: Princeton/Bollingen, 1990.

Jung, C. G., M. L. von Franz, Joseph L. Henderson, Jolande Jacobi, and Aniela Jaffe. *Man and His Symbols*. New York: Doubleday & Company, 1979.

Kaufmann, Edgar, ed. *An American Architecture: Frank Lloyd Wright*. New York: Horizon Press, 1955.

Lawlor, Robert. *Sacred Geometry: Philosophy and Practice*. London: Thames and Hudson Ltd.; New York: Crossroads Publishing Company, 1982.

Laseau, Paul, and James Tice. *Frank Lloyd Wright: Between Principle and Form*. New York: Van Nostrand Reinhold, 1992.

Lawson, Andrew J. *Cave Art*. Princes Risborough, U.K.: Shire Publications, 1991.

Leach, Neil, ed. *Rethinking Architecture: A Reader in Cultural Theory*. New York: Routledge, 1997.

Le Blanc, Sydney. *The Architecture Traveler: A Guide to 250 Key Twentieth-Century American Buildings*. New York: Norton, 2000.

Le Corbusier, [Charles-Edouard Jenneret]. *The City of Tomorrow and Its Planning*. Translated and with an introduction by Frederick Etchells. New York: Dover, 1987.

———. *The Modulor*. Cambridge, Mass.: M.I.T. Press, 1971.

———. *Towards a New Architecture*. New York: Dover, 1986.

———. *The Radiant City*. London: Grossman Publishers and Faber and Faber, 1967.

Lundy, Miranda. *Sacred Geometry*. New York: Walker & Company, 2001.

Mann, A. T. *Sacred Architecture*. Rockport, Mass.: Element Inc., 1993.

Milton, Richard. *Shattering the Myths of Darwinism*. Rochester, Vt.: Inner Traditions, 1997.

Milton, Richard. *Alternative Science*. Rochester, Vt.: Inner Traditions, 1996.

Rand, Ayn. *The Fountainhead*. New York: Penguin Books, 1993.

Schneider, Michael S. *A Beginner's Guide to Constructing the Universe: The Mathematical Archetypes of Nature, Art and Science*. New York: Harper, 1995.

Schwaller de Lubicz, R. A. *The Temple in Man: Sacred Architecture and the Perfect Man*. Rochester, Vt.: Inner Traditions, 1977.

———. *Sacred Science*. Rochester, Vt.: Inner Traditions, 1988.

———. *The Temple of Man*. Translated by Robert and Deborah Lawlor. Rochester, Vt.: Inner Traditions, 1998.

Schulze, Franz. *Mies van der Rohe: A Critical Biography*. Chicago: University of Chicago Press, 1985.

Seaman, David, ed. *Dwelling, Seeing, and Designing: Toward a Phenomenological Ecology*. New York: Albany, State University of New York Press, 1993.

Spaeth, David. *Mies Van der Rohe*. Preface by Kenneth Frampton. New York: Rizzoli, 1985.

Stevenson, Ian. *Twenty Cases Suggestive of Reincarnation: Second Edition Revised and Enlarged by Ian Stevenson*. Charlottesville: University of Virginia Press, 1974 (paperback, fifth printing, 1999).

Tzonis, Alexander. *Le Corbusier: The Poetics of Machine and Metaphor*. New York: Universe Publishing, 2001.

Underhill, Evelyn. *The Mystic As Creative Artist*. Photographic copy from *The Quest*, July 1913. Ramona, Calif.: Mountain Wind Press, 1977.

Venturi, Robert. *Complexity and Contradiction in Architecture*. New York: Museum of Modern Art, 1985.

Venturi, Robert, Denise Scott Brown, and Steven Izenour. *Learning from Las Vegas: The Forgotten Symbolism of Architectural Form*. Revised ed., Cambridge, Mass.: M.I.T. Press, 1997.

West, John Anthony. *Serpent in the Sky: The High Wisdom of Ancient Egypt*. Wheaton, Ill.: Theosophical Publishing House, 1993.

———. *The Traveler's Key to Ancient Egypt*. Wheaton, Ill.: Theosophical Publishing House, 1993.

Wilson, Colin. *The Occult: A History*. New York: Barnes and Noble, 1995.

———. *The Outsider*. New York: G. P. Putnam's Sons, 1982.

Wittkower, Rudolph. *Architectural Principles in the Age of Humanism*. New York: St. Martin's Press, 1988.

Wolfe, Tom. *From Bauhaus to Our House*. New York: Farrar Straus Giroux, 1981.

Wright, Frank Lloyd. *The Natural House*. New York: Bramhall House, 1954.

———. *When Democracy Builds*. Chicago: University of Chicago Press, 1945.

INDEX

biotechnical determinism. *See* architecture, theories of

Blake, William, 78, *illus. 48*, 191

Blavatsky, Helena Petrovna, 63, 69, *illus. 63*

Blenheim Palace, 111. *See also* water

Bonaparte, Napoleon, 60, 150

Breuer, Marcel, 5, 129–30, *illus. 130*

Brotherhood of Solomon. *See* Knights Templar

Buddha sculpture, *illus. 190. See also* mathematical truth

Burke and Hume, 134, 146, *mq 134*

Calatrava, Santiago, 139

Campbell, Joseph, 184

canon, 143–46

cave, 29, 87–93, *illus. 87, 89*
  archetypal image of shelter, 87
  earth as the mother, 88
  at Lascaux, 183
  padded cave, 90
  at Ronchamps. *See* Le Corbusier
  sacred cave, 88–89
  in Usonian homes. *See* Wright, Frank Lloyd

Chartres Cathedral
  crossing, *illus. 3*
  first visit, impact of, 1–3
  maze, 201, *illus. 201*
  nave, crossing and choir, *illus. 90*
  south aisle, *illus. 121*
  south portal, *illus. 119*
  south rose window, *illus. 70*
  south tower, *illus. 119*
  south transept and nave wall, *illus. xvi*

Chase House, *illus. 96*

Christianity and The Church, 51–53
  and the Enlightenment, 51
  and the other tradition, 60–61
  See also Church, The

Church, The
  and the bible, 52–53
  biotechnical determinimalism, 136–37, 139
  Church of Progress, 65
  and the enlightenment, 51–52
  intelligibility of, 140
  and the other tradition, 60–62

churches, Modern, 29–32, *illus. 30, 31, 32, 93*

circle, 154–55, *illus. 155*

clearing, 94–97, *illus. 94, 95. See also* Wright, Frank Lloyd, fusion of cave and clearing

compasses, 155, *illus. 155*

computer, 196–97
  as a danger, *mq. 196*
  insidious appeal, 197
  in the schools, 197, *illus. 197*

consciousness, stream of, 74

corporate architecture
  art as business, 46–47
  practice/procedure, 201–2
  typical office, *illus. 45*

cosmic mind, 69

cosmos
  harmony of, 143–44
  new model, 50–51
  origin of, 177–78

Costa, Lucio, 38, 44

Critchlow, Keith, 156, *illus. 156, 199–200*

crypt. *See* cave

Dasien-in Temple, 109, 114, *illus. 109. See also* water

Darwin, Charles, 51, 68

Da Vinci, Leonardo, 186, *illus. 177*

design/build, 202

double square, 156–57, *illus. 157*

drawing, 193–96, 198

duality, 117–22, *illus. 119(3), 120, 121*
  yin-yang diagram, 117, *illus. 117*

Durer, Albrecht, 186

ego in design, 11, 76, 189–90

Einstein, Albert, 66–67

engineer, 37, 42

Enlightenment, 3, 51–52, 134. *See also* Church, The

environment
  destruction of, 13–16, *illus. 13–15*
  quality of, 21–23

Ephrata Cloister, 141–42, *illus. 142*

esoteric meaning of geometry and number, 143–44

Ethical Function of Architecture,The, 48.

factories, *illus. 25*
  and machines, 5
  occasional beauty of, 24–5
  schools as factories, 28